Inside the Pentagon Papers

Modern War Studies

Inside the Pentagon Papers

Edited by
John Prados and Margaret Pratt Porter

University Press of Kansas

Published by the
University Press of
Kansas (Lawrence,
Kansas 66049),
which was organized
by the Kansas Board
of Regents and is
operated and funded
by Emporia State
University, Fort Hays
State University,
Kansas State
University, Pittsburg
State University, the
University of
Kansas, and Wichita
State University

© 2004
by the University Press of Kansas

Library of Congress Cataloging-in-Publication Data

Inside the Pentagon papers / edited by John Prados and Margaret
Pratt Porter.

    p. cm.—(Modern war studies)

  Includes bibliographical references and index.

  ISBN 0-7006-1325-0 (alk. paper)

  1. United States—Foreign relations—Vietnam—Congresses.
2. Vietnam—Foreign relations—United States—Congresses.
3. Pentagon Papers—Congresses. 4. Vietnam—Politics and
government—1945–1975—Congresses. 5. Vietnamese Conflict,
1961–1975—Congresses. I. Prados, John. II. Porter, Margaret Pratt.
III. Series.

  E183.8.V51575   2004

  959.704'3373—dc22   2004001961

British Library Cataloguing-in-Publication Data is available.

Printed in the United States of America

10   9   8   7   6   5   4   3   2   1

The paper used in this publication meets the minimum
requirements of the American National Standard for
Permanence of Paper for Printed Library Materials
Z39.48-1984.

For all Vietnam veterans

A cantankerous press, an obstinate press, a ubiquitous press must be suffered by those in authority in order to preserve the even greater values of freedom of expression and the right of the people to know.
— Judge Murray Gurfein

Contents

Acknowledgments

To Vietnam Veterans of America (VVA), which had the vision to see that a symposium at the National Press Club in June 2001 to commemorate the thirtieth anniversary of the Pentagon Papers was part of its continuing mission to help find the truth, learn from, and heal from America's longest war.

To George C. Duggins and Thomas H. Corey, VVA's former and current presidents, for their support of the symposium, the Web site for the symposium, http://www.vva.org/pentagon/pentagon.html, and this book.

To the VVA Public Affairs Committee and the Finance Committee for their backing of this project. To VVA's national board of directors, the Vietnam Veterans Assistance Fund, and VVA's staff for their support of and assistance with the conference

To the journalists, lawyers, scholars, historians, authors, and Vietnam veterans who participated in the Pentagon Papers symposium: George C. Duggins, James Doyle, Daniel Ellsberg, Marc Leepson, Michael J. Gaffney, James C. Goodale, Don Oberdorfer, William R. Glendon, Hedrick Smith, Sanford Ungar, David Rudenstine, Richard Weidman, Senator Mike Gravel, Colonel Herbert Schandler, Howard Margolis, William F. Crandell, Anthony Russo Jr., Thomas Powers, Marcus Raskin, and Morton H. Halperin for their time, their candor, and their insight.

To Hadiza Alio, Pam Turner, Ellen Pinzur, Joseph Sternburg, and Michael J. Gaffney, VVA's General Counsel, for their care, time, and invaluable contributions to this book.

To the National Security Archive for use of certain transcripts of the White House tape recordings of President Richard M. Nixon, and the evidentiary analysis of the Pentagon Papers legal briefs. Additional legal briefs and other materials are available in the online briefing book on the Pentagon Papers at the National Security Archive website, http://www.gwu.edu/~nsarchiv/.

To Dr. Edward Meadows of George Washington University for some of the transcriptions of the Nixon Oval Office telephone calls.

To Michael Keating, Carol Engle, Pam Turner, and Xande Anderer for their innumerable contributions to this project and their dedication to Vietnam veterans.

To Georgia Pratt, Michael Duberstein, Janet Alheit, Paula Oser, and Dwight Porter for their contributions during the research for this book.

To Mike Briggs and Melinda Wirkus for their yeoman efforts on behalf of this project.

And to James, Alexandra, Christopher, and Elizabeth Porter for their enduring support.

Introduction

On June 13, 1971, the *New York Times* front page carried the first installment of a major series on the Vietnam War, one based upon a massive, top-secret study compiled by the Pentagon. Under the headline VIETNAM ARCHIVE: PENTAGON STUDY TRACES THREE DECADES OF GROWING U.S. INVOLVEMENT, the *Times* reported on the innermost thoughts of administrations from Harry S Truman's to Lyndon Johnson's during crucial moments of the war from its inception. A related background story noted that the newspaper had acquired a copy of the Pentagon study and promised a series of forthcoming articles that would detail its contents. The *New York Times* story represented the first public revelation of what became known as the "Pentagon Papers," an inside account of U.S. government choices on the Vietnam War that raised eyebrows throughout America, indeed throughout the world.

It is important today to recapture something of the atmosphere of that moment. The Vietnam War was still in full swing. A new round of intense fighting had begun in the demilitarized zone that separated North and South Vietnam, and just two months before American-backed South Vietnamese forces had pulled out of Laos after failing to break the back of the key North Vietnamese supply route to the South. The president of that day, Richard Nixon, nevertheless insisted the invasion had been a success and had demonstrated the success of his strategy of Vietnamization. Not to be diverted, the Nixon administration had resorted to bombing raids in northern Laos using huge B-52 jet aircraft, all sorts of activities supporting Cambodians who were fighting communist insurgents, and continued military efforts in South Vietnam. The administration was claiming that "understandings" unilaterally declared by the Johnson administration before suspending its bombing campaign against North Vietnam in 1968 gave Nixon's commanders justification for renewed attacks on the North.

Manipulation of information, constant and widespread, remained central to the government's conduct of the Vietnam War, with the bombing "understandings" only one example. In another egregious case, for years the government had claimed there were no Americans involved in the war in Laos, where the CIA was running a massive covert paramilitary program and the United States steadily furnishing aid to the Laotian armed forces. Richard Nixon actually made a televised public declaration denying U.S. involvement in Laos. American reporters had stumbled into bases for the CIA's secret army of thousands of Hmong tribesmen and had written about them even as the administration continued its denials. Congress had held hearings on the Laotian programs and gotten material onto the record, but when Nixon administration officials released an approved version of the proceedings, data on the U.S. involvement had been concealed by being deemed classified. Similarly misleading maneuvers were undertaken to conceal information on the exact roles Americans played in prisoner interrogations in South Vietnam, the Cambodian invasion, the Laotian incursion, the secret bombing of Cambodia carried out in 1969–1970, and many other instances. American citizens were increasingly forced to question what their government said in its official pronouncements.

The most controversial conflict in U.S. history since the Civil War, the republic had struggled for years to respond to the challenge of Vietnam. By 1968 the consensus had taken hold that the nation had to get out of Vietnam, yet here, three years later, the war ground on. The Nixon administration was gradually pulling its ground forces out of South Vietnam but increasingly relying upon airpower. Driven by their fears for the republic, and by increasingly vocal protests from the public, legislative leaders reacted with horror as the Nixon administration escalated the war, invading Cambodia in 1970 and now Laos. They voted to repeal the original claimed authority for the Vietnam War, the Gulf of Tonkin Resolution, which Lyndon B. Johnson had gotten in 1964. Then they began offering bills, amendments, riders to legislation, all with the aim of restricting in some fashion Nixon's freedom of action in Southeast Asia. Even after Laos, however, Richard Nixon insisted he would continue the war to free American prisoners and would keep U.S. advisers in Vietnam for as long as they were needed by the U.S.-supported Saigon government.

The Laotian invasion had sparked massive demonstrations on both the East and West Coasts, including a huge march on Washington, a strong protest by Vietnam veterans who threw their medals back at the Capitol, and an effort at civil disobedience by protesters intent on preventing the Nixon administration from conducting business as usual. The latter action, called May Day by protesters, had been met with elite army troops occupying the nation's capital, and by large-scale unlawful detentions of thousands of demonstrators by police and security forces. A few days later, the American ambassador to South Vietnam blandly told an interviewer he foresaw the need for American advisers and combat aircraft for at least several more years.

Into this climate the Pentagon Papers dropped like a huge stink bomb. Suddenly the hidden intentions of American policymakers, at least through 1968, and their own understandings of the real situation in the Vietnam War, stood revealed. Suddenly there was something with which Americans could compare what they had been told about the war. That was the essential purpose of the person who leaked the Pentagon Papers. Daniel Ellsberg had worked in the Office of the Secretary of Defense during the Johnson years, had spent two years in Vietnam as a civilian analyst, numbered among the authors of the Pentagon Papers, and had since gone on to the RAND Corporation, a private think tank that worked closely with the U.S. military. Ellsberg felt mortified at the way the American public had been misled on Vietnam and thought that somehow prosecution of the war would become impossible if its shaky real underpinnings were revealed to public scrutiny. The blinding light of truth would end the war. It was Ellsberg who stood behind the articles that appeared in the *New York Times* on June 13, 1971.

This book is about the Pentagon Papers. It is for both the past and the present, for the issues that remain three decades after the massive leak the Pentagon Papers represented, but also about the legal and moral issues posed, timeless dilemmas that may be even more important today than when this episode sparked renewed self-examination during the Vietnam period. Government continues to tell citizens as little as possible, to exaggerate where it thinks it desirable, and to employ euphemisms rather than speak plainly. Starting with the intent of preserving secrecy for good operational reasons, too often the result is the imposition of secrecy for political motives. As they did at the beginning of the Vietnam experience, Americans took the government at its word after September 11, 2001. Only gradually, especially in the wake of the second Iraqi War and occupation, have Americans begun to be plagued by doubts about what they have been told. As with Vietnam, the current war on terrorism has a secret backstory far different from the one retailed so earnestly, even glibly, by administration spokespersons. We make no claims for what that reality may be, rather we want to study Vietnam and specifically the Pentagon Papers and what flowed from that episode, to illuminate questions of responsibility both public and private.

The Pentagon Papers were created as a top-secret project within the Department of Defense, and that is a story for later on in this book, but they came to the attention of the American people by virtue of the very frustrations and intense controversies just outlined. The vehicle for doing that was a leak. For a multitude of reasons, not least because the primary sources of leaks are government officials themselves, leakers almost never acknowledge their actions. In this case, the source of the Pentagon Papers leak acknowledged his role days after the papers' first appearance in the press. Daniel Ellsberg within four years had been brought to the stark place where he saw revealing them as a measure that might help end the Vietnam War. The fact of the leak, and the right of the

American people to learn of the contents of the Pentagon Papers, would be the main focus of the legal actions by the U.S. government against the media that are a subject here. This book will discuss court cases that flowed from these actions, as well as the process by which media outlets and a U.S. senator brought the Pentagon Papers to Americans. But without the leak there would have been no court cases. It is necessary to set the stage by briefly outlining why and how Dr. Ellsberg, a former marine officer, came to leak the Pentagon Papers.

A well-known defense analyst, Ellsberg had worked on nuclear weapons strategy and counterinsurgency theory. He had been in and out of the RAND Corporation, a think tank largely funded at the time by the U.S. Air Force, and had worked for the Office of the Secretary of Defense. There, the assistant secretary for international security affairs, John T. McNaughton, had brought Dr. Ellsberg on board in August 1964, the same day that U.S. warships in the Gulf of Tonkin claimed to have been attacked a second time by the North Vietnamese; that claim was used as the basis for a bombing raid on the North. Though the naval commander on the scene followed up his original report with cables expressing doubts, so that the reality of the attack stood in question from the first moments, Washington confidently asserted its charges against Hanoi and went ahead with the attack. (Today this second Gulf of Tonkin incident, on August 4, 1964, is believed not to have occurred.) Ellsberg was struck by the discrepancies between the U.S. government's private knowledge and its public statements. Repeatedly observing similar episodes, he came to believe that Washington was conducting the Vietnam War by systematically deceiving the American people.

In the summer of 1965, as the Johnson administration committed the nation to full-scale war, sending troops to fight on the ground in South Vietnam, Ellsberg did his part by volunteering for a mission that was intended to monitor the progress of the war right in the field, for which he transferred to State Department employment roles and worked under Edward G. Lansdale, a retired air force officer and CIA operative with long connections in South Vietnam. For two years Ellsberg put his doubts aside and worked to improve the efficiency of the war effort in Vietnam. Different misgivings grew during this period, as Ellsberg saw the United States unable to adopt proper tactics for the war it was fighting, and unwilling to draw appropriate political conclusions regarding the forces in South Vietnamese society that made Saigon an ineffective ally. Nevertheless Dr. Ellsberg worked hard, argued forcefully, and ended up as the special assistant to the deputy U.S. ambassador in charge of all pacification programs. Toward the end of that time, Ellsberg contracted hepatitis and had to return to the United States.

A defining moment came in October 1966, when Ellsberg hitched a ride on a plane bringing defense secretary Robert S. McNamara back from one of his periodic inspection visits to South Vietnam. During the long plane ride home, McNamara called Ellsberg over to adjudicate an argument he was having with Robert Komer, then White House pacification chief, where McNamara took the line that the war situation was worse than it had ever been. Ellsberg then saw McNamara emerge from the plane when it landed at Andrews Air Force Base to tell reporters that Vietnam trends were much improved and he was greatly encouraged. Witnessing this episode rekindled Ellsberg's fears of government lying.

Daniel Ellsberg's Vietnam tour ended just after Secretary McNamara had ordered the creation of the Pentagon Papers study. He returned to Washington to complete the process of leaving government service and used the visit to carry his message of troubles in Vietnam to anyone who would listen. Dr. Ellsberg spent an hour with Robert McNamara, who he discovered was trying to rein in the ineffective bombing campaign over North Vietnam, and had an appointment with presidential national security adviser Walt W. Rostow, who proved completely impervious to any assertion that the Vietnam situation was other than good (and getting better). Ellsberg's views had little impact as he warned of unalterable stalemate in Vietnam and impending deterioration of the U.S. position, but he carried the word to Pentagon science advisers, groups of media executives, even to then-Senator Robert F. Kennedy.

Ellsberg's ultimate destination was the RAND Corporation, again, but there would be another detour through Washington. Dan knew several of the senior officials coordinating the Pentagon Papers effort. As a long-service defense analyst with considerable Vietnam experience, Ellsberg was a natural choice to work on the study and he figured among the early hires. Seconded from RAND to the Office of the Secretary of Defense, Dan Ellsberg spent months reviewing the record of the CIA's intelligence estimates on Vietnam, as well as studying the decisions made by President John Kennedy. A draft for this portion of the study would be Ellsberg's contribution to the Pentagon Papers. Still consulting for RAND at the Pentagon early in 1968 when North Vietnam and the National Liberation Front unleashed their countrywide Tet Offensive, Ellsberg saw the top-secret recommendations to send more American troops to Vietnam that flowed from senior commanders. The RAND analyst was less shocked at the offensive than by the demands it triggered. Generals told Congress that nuclear weapons would be used in South Vietnam if required to save one American base under siege. The Joint Chiefs of Staff used the occasion to ask for massive reinforcements, 206,000 troops, the exact number they had requested (but had been turned down by President Johnson) in early 1967, in effect pressing their case for U.S. national mobilization. The reinforcement scheme foundered after word of it leaked to the newspapers. By his own account this taught Dan Ellsberg that presidents' ability to escalate the war had depended upon secrecy and the ability to avoid disclosures of their strategy.

The Tet Offensive that engulfed South Vietnam early in 1968 turned Dan Ellsberg very strongly against the Vietnam War. He became a frequent participant at conferences on Vietnam, including ones sponsored by the antiwar movement, and completed his evolution into a vocal opponent of U.S. involvement. Unlike other historians or Vietnam analysts, however, Ellsberg knew of the existence of the Pentagon Papers, which showed from the government's own secret files how its decisions had been made on faulty grounds from the very earliest stages of the war. Government secrecy, in Ellsberg's view, had functioned to perpetuate and escalate a policy that was damaging larger U.S. interests (he himself would later characterize this even more starkly as genocidal).

Americans thought they were voting for peace in Vietnam in the 1968 election that brought to power Richard M. Nixon. By then negotiations on a settlement and U.S. withdrawal from South Vietnam had begun. As part of the Nixon presidential transition, newly minted National Security Adviser Henry A. Kissinger decided to conduct a policy review on the Vietnam War and engaged the RAND Corporation to write an options paper and an associated study that could identify the differences among U.S. agencies on progress (or the lack thereof) in Vietnam. Among Dr. Ellsberg's final tasks for the U.S. government was to compile the set of questions used in this study and do the initial draft of the options paper. Ellsberg later helped assemble the agency responses to the questionnaire. Kissinger aide Winston Lord wrote most of the summary report that analyzed the material, in collaboration with Ellsberg and Morton H. Halperin, another Kissinger aide, as well as a former McNamara Pentagon official. In the course of this work, Ellsberg learned that the Nixon administration policy paper had been revised to drop the option for an American withdrawal from South Vietnam. The option for an attempt to win the war had been kept. When the Nixon administration's secret bombing of Cambodia was revealed, followed by its invasion of that country in 1970 and then of Laos in 1971, it seemed as if the win-the-war strategy was the one in play. Dan Ellsberg went into public dissent in October 1969 when he and five other senior analysts at RAND sent an open letter opposing the Vietnam War that was published in the *Washington Post.*

Dan Ellsberg's path to leaking the Pentagon Papers began then. In the first part of 1969, he read the full text of the massive Pentagon Papers, a set of which was held in storage at RAND. Around the time of the letter incident, Ellsberg determined to somehow use the McNamara study of the war to influence the course of events. Dr. Ellsberg's initial idea was to get the document to Congress and use it as the focus for intense investigative hearings that could expose the real history of the war. That required having a copy of the documents he could show around to enlist supporters. Ellsberg went to a friend and former RAND colleague, Anthony Russo, who was in full agreement with any measures that could help stop the Vietnam War. Russo, if anything more militant than Ellsberg, arranged for the use of a photocopying machine and helped Ellsberg make actual copies of the Pentagon Papers. With more help from Ellsberg's children, eventually reproductions of forty-three of the forty-seven volumes of the Pentagon Papers were made.

Dan Ellsberg's next move was to begin soliciting allies. During a November 1969 visit to Washington, he saw the powerful chairman of the Senate Foreign Relations Committee, J. William Fulbright, who was known to be angry at the way his legislative unit had been deliberately misled by the Johnson administration at the time of the Gulf of Tonkin incidents in 1964. Fulbright wanted to help but thought the way to go would be to get the Nixon administration to provide the Pentagon study through official channels. He therefore wrote to Defense Secretary Melvin R. Laird requesting the documents on November 8, 1969. Laird replied just before Christmas that the Pentagon would furnish the Congress with information about U.S. policies in Vietnam, but not with the Pentagon Papers, which he asserted had been constructed from contributions provided on the basis of promises of confidentiality. Senator Fulbright renewed his demand for the documents in late January 1970, and Laird waited more than six months before rejecting it that summer. In April 1971, just prior to the massive demonstrations that protested the Laotian invasion, Fulbright sent a third request for release of the Pentagon Papers. In the meantime the Senate Foreign Relations Committee had Dr. Ellsberg come before them as a witness at least two times.

None of this informed the American people as Ellsberg wished to do. At the hearings, without documents, the participants could only speak generally of U.S. policies. Fulbright made no open use of the Pentagon study, several thousand pages of which by now resided in the committee's vault. In 1970 again, Ellsberg also approached California congressman Ron Dellums, who brought staff aide Michael Duberstein along to a lunch where Ellsberg did not seem so certain of his course. Toward the end of that year and into the next winter, however, Dr. Ellsberg was in contact with South Dakota senator George S. McGovern (who would be the eventual Democratic Party candidate for president in 1972) in a fresh effort to get out the documents, but McGovern did not bite. The senator later told others he saw Ellsberg as a Vietnam hawk with a bad conscience. Ellsberg remembers his exchange with McGovern as being very positive, but that they never discussed the reasons when the senator backed away a week later from the initial commitment he made to filibuster with the Pentagon Papers.

Dan Ellsberg came to the fourth estate by this indirection. After failing with Congress, he began to reach out to writers and journalists. He provided some materials from the Pentagon Papers to Marcus Raskin, Richard Barnett, and Ralph Stavins of the Institute for Policy Studies (IPS). They were at work on a project that became the book *Washington Plans an Aggressive War,* which showed U.S. policy in Vietnam as lurching into war through blind resort to coercive diplomacy. Neither the IPS analysts nor anyone else received any of the four volumes of the Pentagon Papers that dealt with U.S. attempts to open negotiations with Hanoi. In March 1971 Ellsberg gave most of the Pentagon Papers text to reporter Neil Sheehan of the *New York Times.* That act set in motion the leak that we consider here.

This study of the Pentagon Papers would have been impossible without the efforts of many people, but most important the members of the Vietnam Veterans of America (VVA), a congressionally chartered veterans service organization whose members are primarily Vietnam vets, for whom the appearance of the Pentagon Papers had both social and political consequences. VVA took up the challenge of holding a conference to reflect on the Pentagon Papers three decades on. VVA decided to explore the creation of the Pentagon Papers, the press handling of what became a huge editorial project, the court cases that followed initial publication by the *New York Times,* and the impact of the Pentagon Papers in American history. VVA organizers found participants in all these aspects of the events of the time and asked them to participate in the planned conference, which was eventually held at the National Press Club in Washington, D.C., on June 5, 2001. Through this effort VVA created a fresh pool of primary source material gathered directly from persons involved at the time.

A number of questions about the Pentagon Papers remain even after the passage of three decades, and there are also several important areas for reflection upon the experience. Perhaps because the Nixon administration focused quite quickly upon the leak, and the courts ruled on the legal issues of First Amendment rights and freedom of the press, even at this late date we lack a coherent account of exactly where the Pentagon Papers came from and how they were created. How reporters dealt with the Pentagon Papers has been commented upon mostly from the points of view of editors or owners of newspapers (Ben Bradlee and Katharine Graham for the *Washington Post* and Harrison Salisbury for the *New York Times*), but less so from the perspective of working-level journalists laboring on a major story of this dimension or frantically covering the legal maneuvers that followed the leak. The First Amendment issues are so vital that commentaries from participating lawyers and legal scholars need to be part of the record. Reflections on the consequences of the appearance of the Pentagon Papers, for the Vietnam War, for the antiwar movement, for freedom of information, and for American history writ large, form another dimension of the overall enterprise. At its conference VVA held panel discussions on each of these issues.

The editors sought additional materials to answer other questions that remain about these events in 1971. How, precisely, did Richard Nixon decide to suppress the media reports of the Pentagon Papers — an action unprecedented in American history — and how did he go about trying to achieve that goal? The direct, primary source here is President Nixon's telephone calls with his senior White House staffers when publication of the Pentagon Papers started. This book, for the first time, presents transcripts of the relevant telephone conversations between Nixon and National Security Adviser Henry Kissinger, Chief of Staff H. R. Haldeman, domestic counselor John Ehrlichman, Deputy National Security Adviser Alexander M. Haig, political operative Charles Colson, Attorney General John Mitchell, Secretary of State William P. Rogers, and others. The transcripts make crystal clear how the Nixon administration intended to reach its goals. These presidential conversations of 1971 are perhaps extreme for the genus (of presidents complaining about leaks), but they are nevertheless characteristic. As recently as the end of 2001, President George W. Bush, angered by leaks on his own watch, tried to restrict the flow of all executive branch intelligence and military information to Congress for reasons similar to those expressed here by Richard Nixon.

During the heat of the court proceedings on the injunctions with which the Nixon administration prohibited the American press from publishing the Pentagon Papers, the government made claims as to the damage to U.S. national security that would be made by any disclosure of the secret government study, which was composed of a narrative portion with related documents attached as exhibits. Today the same kinds of claims about effects on U.S. security are made every day by government agencies responding to requests for release of records under the Freedom of Information Act (FOIA). This is a vital and continuing aspect of the operation of the FOIA system in the United States. The Pentagon Papers are the biggest and most detailed example that exist to this day of exactly how the U.S. government constructs arguments about damage to national security in the cases of records sought under FOIA. In view of that fact, we deemed it appropriate to analyze the exact claims of national security made by the U.S. government in the Pentagon Papers case.

It is a revealing fact that in past and present decisions on releasing materials to the American public, publication in the Pentagon Papers has been used by government officials as a reason to release, but the Pentagon Papers themselves *remain secret to this day*. This is despite the existence in the public record of the Senator Mike Gravel edition of the Pentagon Papers (which consists of virtually the entire text of the forty-three volumes that formed part of the 1971 leak), as well as a Nixon administration-authorized version of the same documents that was printed by the House Armed Services Committee. An early 1990s FOIA request for the Pentagon Papers also, we are informed, was "lost" somewhere in the judge advocate general's office of the Department of Defense. At this writing, *three years* since one of the editors applied anew under the relevant provisions of FOIA, and more than *three decades* since the actual documents were already in the public domain, the U.S. government continues to hold the originals of the Pentagon Papers in its top-secret vaults. This is true even though the Vietnam War is over, the South Vietnamese government we supported no longer exists, the records themselves are of obvious historical value, and the applicable government regulations on declassification (a presidential executive order issued by Bill Clinton and modified by George W. Bush) specifies that government documents should be released after twenty-five years. The four volumes that Ellsberg withheld in 1971, the ones that concerned diplomatic negotiations that were deemed too sensitive at the time, were released in expurgated form in the 1980s to Morton H. Halperin and to George Herring, and finally in their full text under our FOIA request in May 2002. But the previously leaked material is still secret.

However arbitrary the U.S. government's treatment of the formerly secret (but in fact well-known) Pentagon Papers may appear, every American should understand that this represents the norm, not any aberration, in the operation of the declassification system. Examples of the excessive secrecy encouraged by the system range from the merely arbitrary to the completely absurd. To cite one more, from an issue area of great importance today, the CIA, in its weekly situation summary on international terrorism for the week before Christmas 1974, included a joke item that reported with a straight face how a terrorist coalition dedicated to the memory of Ebenezer Scrooge planned to take action against the aerial delivery system (i.e., sleigh) of the government of the North Pole operated by Santa Claus. In declassifying a "sanitized" version of this weekly document in September 1999, the CIA cut out the Santa Claus item on national security grounds.[1] We know of the existence of the Santa Claus joke, however, because in October 1997, the agency had already declassified the same document and left that passage in it.

The entire problem has only been magnified by the consequences of the events of September 11, 2001. Officials in doubt are now enjoined to keep records secret rather than release them, where the opposite predisposition had applied before, and the government is recalling documents previously declassified on the supposition that the records could somehow aid terrorists. For example, in navy records, documents on tankers sunk in the North Atlantic by German submarines during World War II have been reclassified on the grounds they have relevance to current U.S. national security.

Continuing growth and deepening of patterns of government secrecy is coupled with strong temptation on the part of government to preserve that secrecy by the abridgment of individual and constitutional rights, exactly as the Nixon administration attempted in the Pentagon Papers case. The attempt to impose prior restraint on the press and prevent the appearance in the media of material drawn from the Pentagon Papers, had it succeeded, would have given government the ability to avoid disclosure in any subsequent situation in which its actions were in question, were embarrassing, or where calling them into question was simply judged politically inconvenient by some executive. This is why the story of the Pentagon Papers, and what followed when Daniel Ellsberg leaked them, are of key importance for Americans today.

The government claims in the 1971 court cases were based on specific passages of the text of the documents involved, just as are assertions of privilege in FOIA cases today. The legal brief by the solicitor general of the United States, Erwin N. Griswold, was itself secret at the time and remained so for many years afterward. In the late 1970s *New York Times* columnist Anthony Lewis sought the secret brief and eventually obtained it in a separate FOIA request. Lewis provided a copy of the brief at our request, and editor John Prados undertook a detailed evidentiary analysis. Lawyers at the time of the 1971 court case had filed responses to the government brief but lacked the time, knowledge, and government records to craft anything more than a general argument, which led to assertions later that the government was protecting real secrets in the Pentagon Papers case. The evidentiary analysis here finds the exact portions of the study cited by the Griswold brief, notes the claims made about those texts, and then presents arguments on the appropriateness of the national security claim on each item. Because the evidentiary analysis is keyed to the specific items in the Griswold brief, that document itself appears here (for the first time in public print) to furnish the necessary context. This represents an unprecedented example of the freedom of information system in practice.

In view of the crucial First Amendment, freedom of information, prior restraint, and press issues involved in the Pentagon Papers case, we have asked Michael Gaffney, a partner at the Washington, D.C., law firm of Gaffney & Schember and general counsel to VVA, for a separate essay on this subject.

Except for the material used in our presentation on the evidence in the Pentagon Papers case, and for our showing of the actual list of the forty-seven volumes of the government study, we make *no* effort here to reproduce the contents of the Pentagon Papers or any portions thereof. Our focus remains on the backstory of the Pentagon Papers and the resulting court cases, and on issues that flow *from* this episode of the Vietnam War and its continuing importance for America today.

CHAPTER ONE

Creating the Pentagon Papers

As the story is told, it was November 1966 when Secretary of Defense Robert S. McNamara went to Cambridge, Massachusetts. There he was to appear as a guest lecturer for the new Kennedy Institute of Politics, including in a defense policy seminar taught by Professor Henry A. Kissinger. Arriving in the city, McNamara encountered a throng of strident antiwar protesters denouncing the policies of his president, Lyndon Baines Johnson, who had led America into full-scale warfare in Vietnam. McNamara had a hard time with the protesters. He was cornered by the crowd and forced to rush into Quincy House to escape the throng. Later, he faced tough questions at his lecture and thought to recover that evening at dinner with a number of the Harvard faculty.

Perhaps the dinner proved more reflective than relaxing, or perhaps McNamara had had his idea before coming to Harvard that day, or possibly he was responding to the dinner table conversation, which kept coming back to how the United States had gotten into Vietnam. McNamara recalls the occasion: "The conversation proved frank but friendly. For the first time, I believe, I voiced my feeling that, because the war was not going as hoped, future scholars would surely wish to study why."[1] In any case Ernest R. May, one of the faculty and another of the guests that night, remembers the secretary of defense talking of an investigation into the Skybolt program, a Kennedy administration missile development effort.[2] Possibly something like that could be done about Vietnam. Unknown to McNamara's companions at dinner that night, venerable Harvard dons like Don K. Price, or indeed to Daniel Ellsberg, who had witnessed McNamara's remarkable expression of optimism upon returning from a visit to South Vietnam a month earlier, Secretary McNamara's memoranda to President Johnson had already begun expressing serious doubts regarding the course of the American war in Southeast Asia. Senior presidential adviser W. Averell Harriman, according to McNamara, had a record of his expressing doubts about Vietnam before the end of 1965, the year when the big U.S. troop commitment was first made.[3]

McNamara's host at the Cambridge dinner was Professor Richard E. Neustadt, a man who already had some experience of secret studies for government. A well-known expert on American politics, Neustadt had made a career out of establishing the notion that presidents rule not so much by fiat as by convincing people to do things that seem to be in their own interest, the "president in sneakers" in Neustadt's memorable imagery. The book *Presidential Power,* in which Neustadt laid out his arguments at length, had already gone through several editions (and would go through a number of others), enough to bring him to the attention of denizens of the White House.

It was Neustadt who had done the Skybolt report for John F. Kennedy, Johnson's predecessor and the man who had hired McNamara for secretary of defense. President Kennedy had gotten into a royal mess with the government of Great Britain over the Skybolt. To rein in an independent British nuclear force, Kennedy had offered to sell London a new air-launched missile system that existed only on the drawing board. The missile was never built and Kennedy eventually had to admit to his British friends that it would not be. Beyond his acute embarrassment, and his red face at the Bermuda Conference where Kennedy had to own up to the truth and try to induce London to accept an alternative, President Kennedy had wanted to learn something from the affair. He had commissioned Professor Neustadt to write an inside account of the Skybolt fiasco based on the U.S. government's own secret records of the program and the meetings at which assorted officials focused merely on budgets and technical matters and compromised the missile out of existence. Thus, Richard Neustadt knew something of internal histories of controversial subjects, and the Vietnam War had to be the most controversial of all.

Meanwhile, President Johnson continued to do his best to rally public support for the Vietnam War, even as he escalated the conflict. The McNamara visit to Harvard had been part of that very campaign. So was another campus appearance McNamara made at Amherst College in February 1967. Again, the secretary of defense faced antiwar protesters and searching questions. After the Amherst appearance, McNamara spoke to his military assistant, air force colonel Robert Pursley, about the need for an "encyclopedia" of Vietnam. The secretary of defense apparently meant by that a collection of documents from the Pentagon and other agencies. He discussed such a collection with his assistant secretary for international security affairs, John T. McNaughton, who shared McNamara's doubts about the war. McNaughton agreed to proceed with the project. McNamara has said and written that he had historians in mind in collecting this document set and that he feared important materials would be misplaced or not preserved for future reference. The secretary of defense's second military assistant, army lieutenant colonel Robert G. Gard, who would become the staff action officer on the project, recalls being told that the set would be for the use of McNamara and his then-deputy secretary, Cyrus R. Vance.[4]

Colonel Gard's telephone had a red button that connected directly to McNamara. The first he heard of the Pentagon Papers was one day in the spring of 1967 — he cannot place the exact date — when that button lit up. At the other end of the line was the secretary of defense.

"Bob," McNamara said, "I want a thorough study done of the background of the Vietnam War."

Gard initiated the project with a series of three or four memoranda he submitted through Senior Military Assistant, Air Force Colonel Robert E. Pursley. In the first one, Gard remembers, he told McNamara that if this was to be a serious project, they were going to have to provide the analysts with access to high-level documents, even to the caliber of the material in McNamara's walk-in safe. McNamara approved without comment or asking to speak to his aide. Then Colonel Gard proposed to go see the assistant secretary for international security affairs about a staff. McNamara approved that, too. Soon they had also agreed that a "skunkworks" for the project would be quietly located in a conference room down the hall, past Gard's office.

The Pentagon Papers seems to have begun with a telephone call to Richard Neustadt at Harvard, asking if he would be interested in heading a project on how the United States had gotten itself into the Vietnam War. The caller was John T. McNaughton. It was spring of 1967. In his account of the *New York Times* and the Pentagon Papers, Harrison E. Salisbury dates this in May.[5] Salisbury clearly writes that McNaughton spoke of a "study," not a documentary collection. It was supposed to be a comprehensive interagency study like the Skybolt report Neustadt had done for John Kennedy. Though McNamara may have wanted something different at that stage, all agree he wanted the work done immediately, while the subject was on people's minds and before details were lost in the mists of time.

The concept changed repeatedly. Ten days or so after their initial conversation, Neustadt got another call from McNaughton saying they could not do an interagency study; it would have to be primarily an internal Pentagon affair. John McNaughton would be lost to the study — and his contributions to American government lost as well — as the result of tragedy. Returning from vacation in July 1967, McNaughton and his entire family perished in a plane crash. McNamara had nominated John McNaughton to be the new secretary of the navy, but that would never be. Paul R. Ignatius took over the navy instead. Paul Warnke would become the new assistant secretary of defense for international security affairs. In that capacity Warnke would be the senior official responsible for the Pentagon Papers.

According to Morton H. Halperin, McNaughton's deputy who stayed on under Warnke and rode herd on the project, the Pentagon restrictions, as well as the specific top-secret classification the Pentagon Papers were given, started as a device to keep knowledge of the study away from President Johnson's national security adviser, Walt W. Rostow. White House cooperation could not be had without Rostow's collaboration, while Rostow's optimism on the war stood in marked contrast to the increasing doubts at the Department of Defense (DoD). Pentagon officials feared that if Rostow knew of the project, he would intercede with the president to cancel the study, whose conclusions might well jar LBJ. Rostow later said that he was vaguely aware of a project under way at the Pentagon but had no detailed knowledge of the Pentagon Papers. Military assistant Gard recalls that he did approach the White House for documents and that the Pentagon task force did receive some White House materials. A reading of the finished Pentagon Papers, though, shows few White House or National Security Council materials.

At some point, Richard Neustadt withdrew from the project. Halperin needed a new manager. Colonel Gard brought in a former Senate staffer and another Harvard man (like both Halperin and Gard, who had Harvard Ph.D.'s), Leslie H. Gelb. The manager was a professional analyst who had been at the Pentagon for just a few weeks before he was made project director. Gelb stayed with the study through to its conclusion.

According to McNamara, it was Gelb, either orally or in writing, who first said, "Let's add a study of what the documents say" to the collection of the documents themselves. McNamara approved.[6] According to Gelb, the project started "after Robert McNamara . . . asked for classified answers to about one hundred of what I would call 'dirty questions.' They were the kinds of questions that would be asked at a heated press conference: Are our data on pacification accurate? Are we lying about the number killed in action? Can we win this war? Are the services lying to the civilian leaders? Are the civilian leaders lying to the American people? . . . There were about eight or so questions that were directly historical: Could Ho Chi Minh have been an Asian Tito? Did the U.S. violate the Geneva Accords of 1954?"[7] Some accounts maintain the questions were developed directly between McNamara and McNaughton and given to Gelb in handwritten form. Colonel Gard does not recall seeing any list of questions.

Richard Neustadt was far from the only Harvard influence upon what became the Pentagon Papers. Both Halperin and Gelb had been faculty assistants to Henry A. Kissinger at Harvard, and Kissinger consulted on the structure of the secret Pentagon study. There was talk of Kissinger actually doing part of the work, but he did not ultimately participate. Kissinger was, however, active in diplomatic initiatives in the summer and fall of 1967 that would be subjects of the Pentagon study. He is also said to have read portions of the report. Kissinger's recent account of the Johnson years of Vietnam, in a new version of his memoirs, is completely silent on the degree of his involvement in the creation of the Pentagon Papers.[8] Robert Gard and Daniel Ellsberg had both studied under Thomas Schelling at Harvard. A number of other Pentagon Papers analysts would be Harvard alumni also.

Harvard historian Ernest R. May was brought in as well. May was called in by Paul Warnke and Les Gelb and asked to come on board. They believed Dr. May could do one of the component studies and finish that summer, in time to be back in Cambridge for the fall semester at Harvard. May agreed and worked on the materials available at the Pentagon about a long (thirty-seven-day) bombing pause that had taken place at the end of 1965 and into 1966, in tandem with peace feelers from the Johnson administration to Hanoi. May managed to write what he recalls as "half a chapter" on the bombing pause before deciding that the story just could not be told without a lot more White House source documents. He said as much to Gelb and left the project at that point.[9]

Dr. May's effort responded to one of Gelb's one hundred "dirty questions." These had been boiled down to a program for sixteen separate studies. The scheme has been dated to June 7, 1967. The idea was for a staff of six full-time professionals, half military officers, half civilians, to complete the work within three months. The list of studies quickly increased to twenty and ultimately to thirty-seven. Morton Halperin met with Gelb, and together they decided McNamara's expressed desire for an encyclopedic approach would be satisfied by covering as much ground as possible, including the air and ground wars, pacification, relations with the Saigon government, military aid, the advisory effort, and diplomacy. As Pentagon Papers analyst Richard H. Ullman later put it, "The purpose of the study was not to get at the larger questions of right and wrong . . . but to present an account of how it had come about that in the middle of 1967 . . . half a million Americans found themselves in South Vietnam fighting a land and air war against an intransigent Asian enemy."[10]

The expansion of the set of studies was basically in response to the desire for comprehensiveness. Leslie Gelb kept a list of the set of subjects to be covered. Sometimes he dropped an item from the list, more often adding one. He decided arbitrarily to end the series with March 31, 1968, the date of President Johnson's speech withdrawing from the presidential election of that year. The Johnson speech marked a turning point in U.S. Vietnam policy in response to the Tet Offensive. To Gelb, it seemed a reasonable stopping point. At least three extensions were given for the project, but even so there was no time to complete an index of the studies and materials, which had been one element of John McNaughton's original oral instructions to Gelb.

Lieutenant Colonel Robert Gard served as liaison between the secretary of defense, Assistant Secretary Warnke, Manager Halperin, and Study Director

Gelb. The study director himself tried to see McNamara many times to amplify his guidance, but the defense secretary never had the time. Instead messages were conveyed through Colonel Gard. Gelb heard that what he was doing was "just fine," to press on and complete the work, and that McNamara wished to keep his distance so that he could not be said to have influenced the result.

The Vietnam Study Task Force was officially created on June 17, 1967. The original program of studies expanded serendipitously, with one added as late as the spring of 1968, plus fifteen collections of supporting documents, for a total of forty-three volumes, amounting to four thousand pages of narrative material and three thousand pages of documents. Four additional volumes on the diplomacy of the Vietnam War were kept separate from the rest of the report. The final touches were not put on the report until January 1969.

In the end, the Pentagon Papers analysts did not depend solely on DoD documents. Colonel Gard took the mass of Vietnam documents from McNamara's walk-in safe and moved them to file cabinets along the wall of the conference room where the Vietnam Task Force would congregate. McNamara's holdings included much CIA and State Department material as well. They also had access to everything in John McNaughton's Pentagon files. The defense secretary did not speak to Secretary of State Dean Rusk. "When Dean asked me later why I had not told him or the president about the project, I felt chagrined," McNamara would recall. "I should have."[11] Instead Colonel Robert Pursley called State's executive secretary Benjamin J. Reed to make arrangements to supply diplomatic material. This included both State's historical records and materials held by Assistant Secretary William P. Bundy. Gard subsequently handled the occasional contacts with Reed that furthered the Pentagon Papers. Deputy Secretary Nicolas deB. Katzenbach may also have been aware of the project. McNamara is not known to have arranged with CIA director Richard M. Helms for a supply of intelligence material, and Gard recalls no big shipments of CIA material arriving at the Pentagon, but the Pentagon Papers contain numerous CIA documents nonetheless. Gelb notes that he arranged with the CIA for materials to be furnished upon request. The study director also reports having access to an extensive collection of White House National Security Council (NSC) staff memos and a full set of studies and decisions, but only occasional access to NSC meeting minutes, and none at all to the cover memoranda or notes of national security advisers to the presidents. In all Gelb estimates that his analysts were able to use about 90 percent of classified Vietnam documents and 95 percent of the most important memoranda by the principals.[12]

Task force members were specifically ordered *not* to seek interviews with participants in the events they were examining. The lack of personal contact with principals in the Vietnam decisions, while costing valuable historical sources, helped keep the Pentagon Papers off the radar scope at the White House, particularly in Walt Rostow's office. McNamara's reasoning for task force consumption, according to Leslie Gelb, was that he "did not want the collecting and weighing of the documents to be influenced by anyone."[13] Elsewhere Gelb described the result as "not so much a documentary history, as a history based solely on documents — checked and re-checked with ant-like diligence."[14] Two years later, soon after the Pentagon Papers became public, Gelb would write in a similar vein: "We had a much broader sweep of the record of the written word than is ever available for official government histories or for any individual writing his memoirs, but we did not feel we were writing the definitive history."[15]

The Vietnam Study Task Force on the third floor of E-Ring of the Pentagon was right down the hall from Secretary McNamara's own office. McNamara could have dropped by anytime, but there is little evidence that he did so. An account of the march that antiwar protesters made on the Pentagon in October 1967 has McNamara watching the demonstration from the windows in that conference room. Some of the task force staff, Daniel Ellsberg most prominently, were there also. This is the only evidence of direct contact between McNamara and the Vietnam Study Task Force that we have so far. Evidently McNamara was serious about not becoming involved. The secretary issued no orders, was not interviewed, and made no inquiries. Colonel Gard placed the volumes of the study on his desk as they were completed, and these came back with McNamara's initials but no other evidence the secretary had actually read them.

The Gelb group moved out of the conference room in February 1968 when Clark M. Clifford replaced McNamara as secretary of defense. Clifford placed no obstacle in the way of the project, and the last study was added to Gelb's plate on Clifford's watch, an analysis of the change in U.S. strategy in Vietnam that followed the Tet Offensive early that year. Secretary Clifford preferred to talk to people and read almost nothing; there is no evidence he read any of the Pentagon Papers.

As Leslie Gelb's study mushroomed, so did his staff. Six professionals finally turned out to be thirty-six analysts, some military, many drawn from the ranks of the defense intellectual community, which the testimonials following this introduction will make clear. Exactly half the authors were serving military officers. Half of the rest were civilian employees of the federal government. The final nine were professional scholars. As Gelb put it at the height of the Pentagon Papers controversy, "We were not a flock of doves working our vengeance on the Vietnam War. . . . I would say about one-fourth [of the authors] were basically supporters of administration policy, a handful were highly critical of the U.S. commitment, and the bulk did not question the commitment so much as the means for meeting the commitment. No one was ever asked his views before being signed on."[16]

Whenever Leslie Gelb developed new personnel needs, he would go to Colonel Robert Gard and state the requirement, and the two would discuss people for possible recruitment. Gelb and Gard talked perhaps twice a day on any and all administrative matters connected to the initiative. Gard handled the paperwork connected with the personnel searches. Once hired, new analysts would be briefed by Gard on the Pentagon Papers project.

A few weeks into the project, Les Gelb, an analyst himself, came by to beg Bob Gard for help on management. Gelb wanted a good military officer by his side. Gard suggested Army Colonel Paul F. Gorman, a West Point classmate. Gorman was soon Gelb's chief of staff. A battalion commander in Vietnam, Gorman had been McNaughton's resident counterinsurgency expert. Gorman later retired as a full general and commander of the U.S. Latin American regional military command during the Reagan administration's Central American wars.

When the study manager needed someone to do the key year of 1964, Colonel Gorman recruited an air force lieutenant colonel who had previously worked for him, William R. Simons, then on detached service at RAND. Simons worked diligently on a series of studies that covered that year. He recalls having had access to papers from McNamara's safe, a good set of the cable traffic, State Department material from William P. Bundy, but precious little from the Joint Chiefs of Staff and no National Security Council documents. On the highly controversial events of the Tonkin Gulf affair, Simons never had access to the National Security Agency intercepts of North Vietnamese communications that were central to the events of the day. As an example of the way the structure of the Pentagon Papers changed, Simons recalls he originally crafted three different studies to cover 1964 but they later became one single volume.[17]

One man who was *not* recruited as a Pentagon Papers analyst was then-Colonel Alexander M. Haig Jr. At one point in the summer of 1967, Gelb went to Gard and said he needed a military officer with recent combat experience as a battalion commander in Vietnam. Haig had been a battalion leader, had distinguished himself in a firefight northeast of Saigon a few months earlier, and was under orders to head one of the cadet regiments at West Point starting in the fall. Project managers thought he could do a study and finish in time for the West Point assignment. Haig did not think so much of the idea and contrived to have army staff reject his assignment to the Vietnam Task Force. Once Colonel Gard learned that, he made no request for Haig's services.[18]

Even today we do not know everyone who worked on the project. Those who are known should be noted, however. Richard H. Ullman, already mentioned, had been Halperin's colleague at Harvard and took a leave from Princeton to work briefly for Rostow on the National Security Council staff in 1967, before moving over to the Pentagon to do one of the studies. Ullman stayed on under Halperin to work on nuclear arms control, which became one of his main concerns. In the 1990s Ullman originated the term "shock and awe," which acquired such prominence in the Iraq War of 2003. Another author, Richard Holbrooke, a State Department officer with Vietnam experience, was taking time off from the White House staff that dealt with pacification matters. Holbrooke would go on to participate in the Paris peace negotiations on the delegation led by Averell Harriman. That introduction to techniques in countering adversary intransigence stood Holbrooke in good stead when he negotiated peace in Bosnia for the Clinton administration in the mid-1990s.

Typically an author would come on to the Vietnam Task Force, read into the available material, and produce his piece of the study about three months later. This put a premium on analysts who could take temporary assignments, making think tanks natural and fertile recruiting grounds. Both Washington's Institute for Defense Analysis and Santa Monica's RAND Corporation would be primary sources for the people who compiled the Pentagon Papers. In tandem with Gelb, Gus Schubert, a vice president at RAND, coordinated the hires from his shop. Daniel Ellsberg was only one of the RAND people. Another was Melvin Gurtov, crafter of the volume on the Eisenhower administration and Dien Bien Phu, who would also become a cosigner with Ellsberg of a 1969 letter in which a number of RAND employees collectively protested the Vietnam War, creating a controversy of their own at the California think tank. Other RAND recruits included Colonel William R. Simons, as already noted; Hans Heymann, who would go on to work as a Soviet analyst at the CIA and wrote the Pentagon Papers sections for early 1965; and Richard Moorstein, who had just recently moved from the Pentagon to RAND. William M. Kaufman, who had helped McNamara in his annual production of comprehensive reports for Congress and would write a biography of the secretary, was a former RAND analyst. The Institute for Defense Analysis provided Howard N. Margolis and others.

The Pentagon itself was an important source for staffing. Among its people on Gelb's task force would be a White House fellow assigned to the department, Richard E. Balhizer; a member of Halperin's staff, Major Charles M. Cooke Jr.; a special assistant to McNamara on Southeast Asian matters, Martin Bailey; and an aide to Secretary Clifford, who had also led a battalion in Vietnam, Colonel Herbert Y. Schandler. Cooke and Schandler were both army officers. That service also detailed another of its Washington staff, Colonel Robert L. Schweitzer, to the Pentagon study. It has been estimated that roughly two-thirds of the Pentagon Papers analysts had had Vietnam experience.[19]

As the analysts came on board, Les Gelb would pass along the basic marching orders. He wanted the authors to take the documents and interpret them, presenting a narrative that would not only connect the materials but also aid in understanding them. As the study director would later recall: "These instructions were followed in varying degrees by the authors. In those cases where the author or authors finished their study without closely following instructions, I had no recourse but to accept the study. Most of the authors, like myself, were moonlighters, continuing to work on their regular current policy assignments, even as they worked on the Vietnam Task Force. I could rarely extend their tours with the Task Force."[20] What Gelb did was write a summary for each study to help inject a note of uniformity.

For the most part, work on the Pentagon Papers proceeded smoothly. William Simons remembers there were typically about a dozen people at work in the third floor Pentagon office. Simons arrived in August 1967. At the time his colleagues included Richard Holbrooke, Daniel Ellsberg, Melvin Gurtov, Air Force Major Daniel Clelland, Hans Heymann, and several others whose names are lost to this history. Only Holbrooke and Ellsberg had desks up against the windows. They seemed to spend a lot of time on the telephone or reading the papers compiled by the rest of the crew. Others buried themselves in the source materials. Simons got the impression that the window analysts were a sort of "murder board" supposed to critique the studies done by the others.

Robert Gard recalls just one management problem on the studies and that concerns Daniel Ellsberg. Gelb entered Gard's office one day to say he had a concern that Ellsberg was reading everything but not doing any writing, indicating that Simons's impression of Ellsberg's assignment had to be mistaken. Indeed Ellsberg had taken on the task of doing the portion of the study concerning the early Kennedy administration. Ellsberg was scheduled to return to the RAND Corporation shortly, and Gelb wanted his Vietnam Task Force Study finished. Colonel Gard later had Ellsberg in his office and, as he recounted in an interview, fixed him with a steely gaze, shook his finger in Ellsberg's face, and remonstrated with him. Dr. Ellsberg explained he had been trying to find patterns in the material with all his reading. Ellsberg promised to finish the study, even if he needed to write it after returning to RAND. Both Ellsberg and his replacement on the Vietnam Task Force, Howard Margolis, comment on the episode in their presentations later in this chapter. Incidentally, the study upon which they worked would be considered in retrospect among the best by project director Gelb. So would Melvin Gurtov's contribution on the United States and the Geneva Conference of 1954.

Director Gelb's evaluation of which were the best monographs (or those completed last, with the most complete documentation) in the Pentagon Papers should be noted. In addition to the above, Gelb cites the following volumes: *U.S. Involvement in the Franco-Viet Minh War, 1950–1954; Origins of the Insurgency; Military Pressures against North Vietnam, February 1964–January 1965; Marine*

Combat Units Go to Da Nang, March 1965; Phase I in the Buildup of U.S. Forces, March–July 1965; U.S. Ground Strategy and Force Deployments, 1965–1968; Air War in the North, 1965–1968; Reemphasis on Pacification, 1965–1967; and *U.S.-GVN Relations, 1964–1967.* The volume on pacification was completed early during the task force project but in Gelb's view remained among the best.[21]

A somewhat different problem arose from the way documents arrived and were used by the analysts. The huge array of source material and the variances among agencies in what they furnished, when, and how, resulted in cases where documents important to a study were discovered only after that paper had been finished. Occasionally analysts at work on a later study that covered some of the same historical period found new data that were different or shed different light on earlier Pentagon Papers studies. This led to certain contradictions within the Pentagon Papers themselves. Project director Gelb intended to reach back into the early studies once all the work was completed to rectify such contradictions, but like the idea for an index, there was just never enough time.

The absence of White House cooperation with the study had the important consequence that the analysts lacked the record of presidents' private ruminations or security advisers' notes made at meetings of the National Security Council. This led journalists like Hedrick Smith to characterize the Pentagon Papers as a "middle echelon and official view of the war."[22] Once the papers became public, they were defended against some of these same charges. For example, Richard Ullman argued that his own previous studies in diplomatic history showed that records of British prime ministers and other top leaders had not contributed that much extra to the materials available from government agencies.[23] In truth, most White House decisions and many policy deliberations *were* reflected in the agency records available to Pentagon Papers analysts.

For its time, the Pentagon Papers were an authoritative account of U.S. policy in the Vietnam War. Leslie H. Gelb went on to write an influential book, together with Richard K. Betts, on how the United States makes national security policy, which posited that bureaucracies tend to provide presidents with options that are unattainable and unacceptable surrounding an option that is essentially more of the same (the "A," "B," and "C" options as they usually appeared in policy papers).[24] The insights represented in that study, which appeared only at the end of the 1970s, were drawn directly from the Pentagon Papers. They are prefigured in Gelb's writing only months after the leak of the secret government study. "Memos to the President invariably contained three options," Gelb wrote, "two patently unacceptable extremes of humiliating defeat and total war, and Option B. If you are ever out of town when a decision is made, you can rest assured that Option B won again." The consensus option would be full of contradictions, and those "were disastrous for our Vietnam policy." Beyond false options, the predominance of tactical considerations over fundamental ones, the repeated failure to question assumptions, and the drive to "fine-tune" policies to the point where they became grotesque, were marks of the process revealed by the Pentagon Papers studies and identified publicly by Leslie Gelb shortly after the Big Leak.[25] Daniel Ellsberg drew different but related conclusions, arguing that the policy process led to a "Stalemate Machine."[26]

Passage of time and the progressive release of formerly secret White House records and tape recordings of presidential conversations add a considerable dimension to the account given in the Pentagon Papers. This is clear from the practice of historians and political scientists reexamining the Vietnam War in subsequent years, for whom the Pentagon Papers have diminished as a source for citations.

This chapter includes a series of contributions from some of the analysts who worked on the project. Melvin Gurtov supplies a short written reminiscence. Herbert Schandler, Daniel Ellsberg, and Howard N. Margolis participate in a discussion of what it was like to work on the project. Even a brief examination of the list of volumes in the Pentagon Papers shows that the project produced a huge compendium of authoritative commentary on one of the most important issues of the day. The recollections of the analysts demonstrate that all involved were aware of the significance of their work.

Working on the Pentagon Papers: Mel Gurtov

It was the spring of 1967, and I had been at the RAND Corporation less than a year, fresh from language study on Taiwan. I received a call from the Pentagon (it may have been from Mort Halperin) asking if I would agree to be detached from RAND in order to participate in a Vietnam history project within the office of the secretary of defense, Robert S. McNamara. The objective was to inform the secretary of the origins and evolution of U.S. involvement in Indochina. Since I had published a book on U.S. involvement during the postwar years of French colonialism — in fact, it was my master's thesis at Columbia — the invitation was to work on that period, using whatever classified materials I wished.

RAND was quite willing to detach me, and I was happy to accept the invitation. Virtually nothing was said to me about how the idea for such a study originated or how deeply it was intended to probe the U.S. policymaking process. I interpreted McNamara's authorization of the project to mean it would be taken seriously, and might just influence his thinking about the war, since by then I think it was fairly widely believed that his steadfast support of LBJ's policies was wavering. But what McNamara might take from the study, how widely it would be distributed, and what other senior officials would do with it were impossible for me to assess.

By then my own thinking on the war had changed dramatically from my student days, when I was convinced Vietnam was worth fighting for to contain communism. As soon as I arrived at RAND, I was put to work on its "Viet Cong Motivation and Morale Project," whose objective was to assess (largely for psychological warfare purposes) the strength of commitment and vulnerabilities of captured North Vietnamese and Vietcong soldiers. Exposure to this large set of confidential interviews and other documents put the war in a new light for me: a battle for Vietnamese national identity and social justice, rather than another contest between East and West for strategic and ideological advantage. Thus, by the time I went to Washington to work on the papers project, I was convinced that U.S. involvement — *intervention,* to be precise — was futile, wrongheaded, and destructive. Participating in the project was for me an opportunity to help push McNamara, and perhaps others similarly torn between loyalty to administration policy and common sense, toward our side.

I was led to expect that my participation would take about a month and that the entire study would be wrapped up in about three months. I stayed three months, and the study took many months longer, its various sections passing through many hands. My responsibility was to focus on the history roughly from the end of World War II and the French return to Indochina, to the Geneva Conference of 1954 that partitioned Vietnam. Les Gelb and Mort Halperin developed a series of questions that guided my research. As the work began, only about a half-dozen people worked together in the secretary's outer offices; but by the time I left, several others had been brought in, the scope of the study expanded, and what was once contemplated to be a concise account of U.S. policy became, in the manner of most government studies, a massive collection of commentary and documents.

Working on the immediate postwar period was not as sensitive, obviously, as working on the 1960s. I had access to a large collection of cable traffic, intelligence estimates, and other materials classified through top secret, as well as the usual array of academic studies. CIA materials were readily available to me. The one area I did not have access to was presidential archives, though I did request access. In the case of research on the 1950s, this restriction meant I would be unable to explore perhaps the only issue that is still not entirely resolved: whether or not John Foster Dulles in the spring of 1954 offered the French atomic bombs, as the French foreign minister would later claim, to sustain the French military position at Dien Bien Phu in northwestern Vietnam. Dealing with atomic weapons was clearly off-limits, nor was I cleared for research at that level of classification.

The research environment was pleasant enough. As a very young scholar new to Washington, it was fascinating to be a Pentagon regular, going to work there every day, getting to know the layout and individuals that make it such an extraordinary place, and exchanging views with colleagues on the project whenever interesting documents appeared. Those were also days of protest; we had only to look out the window to see antiwar demonstrators, with whom several of us openly sympathized. Inside, however, there were no great arguments about the justifiability of the war. We had differences of view — though I would say that on balance, critical views of U.S. policy were in the majority — but the atmosphere was generally serious and academic. Research, writing, and considerable rewriting dominated our time.

Yet the study, as I witnessed it, did have its politics in subtle ways. On one hand, I cannot recall any overt political pressure that sought to move my research in a particular direction. But my research was not the final word. I had been under the impression, perhaps naively, that my study of the early history would, with no more than the usual editing, become the opening segment of the project's final document. In fact, my contribution was only a first cut; when the Pentagon Papers were eventually published, I could discern some of my work, but could also see much that had changed as the study's director, Les Gelb, added questions and refocused answers. Moreover, the bent of some of what I had written had also been changed. For example, there was the nagging question of Ho Chi Minh's credentials as the Vietnamese resistance began. Was he a hard-nosed communist or primarily a nationalist? My research convinced me that though Ho was of course a committed socialist, he was nobody's tool and was above all motivated by Vietnamese nationalism in the age-old battle against foreign imperialists. That was never the official American view, and I tend to think the Pentagon project's leaders shaded depictions of Ho toward the "responsible center" so as not to offend higher-level people who might read the study.

By itself, my part of the study was not that important in the debate over the meaning of the papers. But unexpectedly, it *did* play a small part in another context: the government's attempt to convict Dan Ellsberg and Tony Russo of treasonous conduct in their Los Angeles trial. I testified on their behalf, mainly to underscore the point that their release of secret documents could hardly have endangered national security inasmuch as all of the important information was already in the public domain. The secret materials merely lent further credence to what had already been said in the press and in academic studies. In fact, the same conclusion applied to every other section of the study. Secrecy and "national security" merely segregated Vietnam policymaking from democratic processes and protected its authors from serious scrutiny.

In my mind — and I said so publicly once the *New York Times* began printing the Pentagon Papers — the crux of those documents was what they revealed about the duplicity of U.S. leaders, who consistently lied to the American people, the

Congress, and the press about many aspects of the war in the Kennedy and Johnson years. Presidents and their national security advisers knew the war was being lost, knew their Vietnamese opponents had popular support while their allies in Saigon did not, and knew that military firepower was no substitute for political legitimacy. But they told the American people the opposite. The antiwar movement, at its best moments, demonstrated the role an "aroused citizenry" can play in speaking truth to power. Here is where the Pentagon Papers contributed: Its real message, the one to which I would like to feel I contributed something, is that government leaders often become captives of their ideological inclinations. The average attentive citizen has more than enough information to raise doubts about and if necessary resist official policy, foreign no less than domestic.

But did the papers make a difference prior to their release? I can only infer from McNamara's *In Retrospect* that they did make something of an impact, in combination with other information that he later had time to consider. The lessons he drew in his recollections are powerful ones, and while his "conversion" remains incomplete, he should be credited with at least acknowledging two critical points: first, that the United States has no "God-given right" to try to determine other people's revolutions; second, that the United States made a number of serious misjudgments of its capabilities and its adversaries' intentions, the reasons for which have been disregarded down to the present. That's saying a lot.

Still, my guess is that had the papers remained under government seal, their impact would have been extremely limited. Under wraps, their meaning could easily have been manipulated by those who felt most threatened by their exposure. When I learned what Dan Ellsberg had done, I quickly realized that his was not only an act of great courage, but also a necessary step to ensure that the papers — which is to say, the record of government deceitfulness — would become part of the national debate. Without that step, I feel certain we would have nothing to celebrate today.

———————————

Howard Margolis: I'll tell an anecdote about Daniel Ellsberg. We were driving across the country on a tourist trip out in the West, when we heard over the radio about the Pentagon Papers being leaked. The next day, or so, hearing that it was Dan Ellsberg who did it, I mentioned to my wife, you know, I followed Ellsberg to the same college by a year or two. Later on I followed him to OSD (Office of Secretary of Defense) by a year or two. And then, later on, I followed him to MIT — remember the MIT episode — then I followed him to the Pentagon Papers. I said to my wife, I hope the son of a bitch isn't leading me to jail, now. Dan has assured me since that that's where he thought he was going, so, it was a great relief.

On the Pentagon Papers, I don't remember whether it was Les Gelb or Mort Halperin who asked me to participate in it. This is thirty years ago. Somebody asked me, and I agreed to do it. For me, this was an in-and-out thing. I believe it lasted just about three months. I came in, and Les Gelb asked me if I would finish up an account that Dan had written on Kennedy's decisions in 1961. But when I went to look at Dan's decisions — I [have] learned from Dan that there was some rather momentous screwup — all I found was an extensive treatment of the intelligence situation from a previous year, which does appear in the Pentagon Papers in the volume they had of Eisenhower's decisions. And then, just four or five pages, a beginning of an account of the Kennedy decisions. Like any writer, I just wanted to do it my way, and it was only four or five pages, so I told Gelb this was a whole job to be done, I would just write that piece. Dan has just told me he wrote four hundred pages, and he still has it, so, I'm going to get to read it. In a sense, my piece is just accidental.

One of the questions I was asked to talk about was to what extent was control exercised? My recollection is no control whatsoever was exercised. I don't know if the others remember, but my recollection was we were in some basement warren of the Pentagon. We'd go down there in these dark halls with no windows and write — of those of you who are writers, you probably have a common experience, you can do it about four hours a day, and then you have to do something else — I wrote my piece over a period of the three months.

After I got through writing my piece for the day, or as much as I felt comfortable doing for the day, I would snoop around and read other people's pieces. I had two overwhelming impressions: one from the morning when I was writing my own piece; one from the afternoon when I'd snoop around and read other people's pieces. On my piece — and this may reflect just a predisposition to like President Kennedy and dislike the war. The way it seemed to me — Hedrick Smith, who, I believe, wrote the *Times* version of it may have a somewhat different view — my impression was of somebody exercising extremely good judgment in an extremely difficult position. And I think this is much stronger if you read my account in the Pentagon Papers — I think the summary in the *Times* was written under vastly greater time pressure. The times were very difficult for a president who wanted to behave cautiously about getting us involved in a war in Southeast Asia. Here you had a very young president, elected by a hair-thin margin — the closest thing to the election we were going through in [2000] — at a time when the cold war was at its absolute height of intensity, at a time we were being bloodied one time after another by having to give up in Laos, which apparently the Eisenhower administration had not favored, but Kennedy decided there was no hope in Laos, we were going to hope for neutral government. By the fiasco in Cuba, the Bay of

Pigs. By enormous blustering by Khrushchev, including a lot of barking about how he was going to sign a peace treaty with East Berlin and then the West would have no rights. It was a very difficult time for an American president to avoid being bold. The argument that was made over and over again was, where are you going to draw the line? What happened over the course of that, not quite a full year, was time after time, rumors would come up about how we had to make an absolute commitment to Vietnam, or put our troops into combat, which, in a way, was even stronger than making a verbal commitment. What happens over and over again is these recommendations come up to the White House where they sink out of sight. A few days later, a new recommendation comes up, which is, sometimes, even bolder in its rhetoric but leaves out the troops and never involves making an absolute commitment. So, it seemed to me striking, the extent to which Kennedy was prudent to avoid making the kind of commitment that Johnson, everybody, I think, thinks, tragically, did make, under conditions vastly more favorable: rather than having just been elected by a very narrow margin, had been elected by enormous margin — rather than having been elected on showing the United States was going to be bold and build up its defenses and such, having been elected as the peace candidate — not before the Cuban missile crisis and when there was a Berlin crisis looming and all these other things, but after those things. We had the [nuclear] test ban treaty and various other things. It struck me one of the lessons of it was, who is president really makes a difference. I certainly would not claim that had Kennedy lived, we would not have gotten involved in American troops fighting that war, but certainly the basis was laid to leave the president's options open. So, I think that is one striking lesson of the thing.

Let me say a word or two about what I read in the afternoon when I came to look at other people's pieces of paper, because there you had another cycle, this one entirely dismal, and that is recurring themes of this government Republic [South Vietnam] is not a government that deserves the loyalty of its people. This is not a government that could actually win. We should help them. We have an obligation to help them. We have a great power interest in helping them. So, we have reasons to want to help them. There was no sense of "it is morally distressing for us to help." Perhaps that should have been there, but that wasn't there. There was a sense that we should help them, but we can't help them if they won't help themselves. Therefore, throughout, there is a recurring theme of, OK, we'll crank up our aid another notch, but they'll promise to reform. It goes through the cycle over and over where that's what we are going to do. Six months or a year later, it becomes apparent that nothing is happening, and then we go through the same travail again. Obviously, at some point, we face the decision of this just isn't going to work at all. Certainly, you know, the record seems to suggest that we made that decision at least ten years too late.

I hate to give a talk and not say something politically incorrect. And here, obviously, the most incorrect thing is to say a kind word or two for lying by government officials.

As [Ellsberg] suggested — I think here Dan and I are probably in essential agreement — lying by government officials is in a day's work. It's not an American thing or a late-twentieth-century thing. I'm sure if we could go back to ancient Greek times, we would find the officials are very careful about what they say in public. If you can get away with lying without actually lying, of course, you prefer that. It's more comfortable, and it can't get caught and such. But if you get really stuck, what can a poor fellow do?

It is in the nature of things that government officials engage in deception. The healthiest thing, though, is not to wring your hands about it and talk moralistically about how that shouldn't happen, but just be aware that that's part of the game. I think the healthiest thing about the leakage of the Pentagon Papers — for which I'm grateful to Dan for doing and to the press for making sure it got out — is that somebody, by reading those papers, can see that going on. Not in the sense of having moral outrage at this or that administration, but in the sense of understanding that that's what's going on. These fellows were not only lying to people in the press or people in the public, they were lying to each other throughout.

I remember there was a fellow who was head of the Institute for Defense Analysis [IDA], which is where I was working at the time I did those three months, Al Flacks, who had been secretary of the air force.

I remember he once, I don't know what the occasion was, took me aside and said, let me tell you one thing, never write anything down on paper that you are not prepared to see in the *Washington Post* tomorrow morning. It is a terrific inhibition on anyone who has to make decisions that are subject to the approval of other people to be very careful about that aspect.

Flacks's predecessor, as president of IDA, was Maxwell Taylor, who was a reasonable candidate to be called a great man. He was really an outstanding fellow. He was President Kennedy's special military adviser at the time, in 1961, and headed the mission to Vietnam to provide the president with a plan in the fall of that year after Diem asked more intensely for bigger scale help.

One of the things that happened during this was we were told we would just use the documents from the secretary's files. I suspect, because McNamara didn't want everybody in town knowing this was going on. If we are all free to go out and call our friends in the State Department and ask for files, everybody would know about this, and there was a good chance it would be squelched — another example of secrecy in government.

To get this done, we were limited to the documents we faced. I remember, and here's a bit of manipulation by even as innocent a fellow as me, obviously, when I came back from my stint across the Pentagon, I was in the building, and there was General Maxwell Taylor, a floor above me, who was a key person in this whole game. I could have walked into his office and said, "General, what do you think about this?" I did not. However much I admired Maxwell Taylor, I did not want to either be bound by Maxwell Taylor's interpretation of the Taylor mission or be in the awkward position of telling my boss he was wrong on something that was a big part of his life.

I remember, afterwards, when it came out, he said, "Gee, why didn't you come in and see me? I would have been glad to talk to you. I could have given you some information." Of course, I used the cover story of we were told we were just limited to the files. He did, however, confirm, and there was really no doubt about the key point of the thing, when I specifically mentioned this issue of wanting troops, of people continually pushing Kennedy to want troops, then, in a mysterious fashion, a revised recommendation coming in without troops. He was characteristically blunt, and he was blunt on that. He said, you are right. We wanted troops, Kennedy didn't, and that's why, you know, you had to go around, you did.

Daniel Ellsberg: It's very interesting, my old friend, Howard Margolis, I really had a bone to pick with, for thirty years now. Howard wrote the volume on 1961, which I had written a draft of. The volume in the Pentagon Papers has almost no overlap with my draft. I understood he was rewriting my account. So, I've always really felt, well, yours is very good, Howard. It is very good. It's no problem. But jeez, I thought as good of stuff in my draft, and why is it not there? You know, none of it. I felt rather rejected. And Howard tells me he never saw that draft. I have it at home, so, he's going to get his own copy. I'm sure he'll be interested in it. At least I feel better about that.

So, the question of why I was in the study, or, why I accepted the invitation to be in the study. I am not a historian. There were a few certified historians in this study, Mel Gurtov, for example. Most of them were not. They had the criteria, as Gelb had said, in print, of people, some of whom had been in Vietnam. Most of them were military. I won't go through all the criteria, but I fit the criteria, and a lot of them came from RAND.

I had been in Vietnam for two years. I had even served in a clerk role in ISA (International Security Affairs) in 1964. So, I had had a window on the high-level decision making. Not so many people combined that, or, really ever did, except Herb Schandler, for example.

I had an extreme interest in seeing studies like this done. What I wanted to see, exactly, and what I had proposed earlier, even in a memo that I hoped got to McNamara, but I didn't have any indication that it had. I wrote from Vietnam a memo to McNamara and asked my friend Alain Enthoven, then an assistant secretary of defense for systems analysis. I knew he had access to McNamara's office. I said, if you will, place this memo on his desk. I knew he could do that. But I never heard back whether this had happened or not. Most of the time these things get filed.

My proposal was — writing with hepatitis in Vietnam in the spring of 1967 after two years there, I was lying on my back writing a number of memos — the time has come for a Richard Neustadt–type study, which, I had talked to Neustadt about when he was writing his study on Skybolt and on the Skybolt so-called crisis of our decision making.

At that time, it was top secret. It was based on interviews at high levels with presidential access, so, he got frankness — that was very extraordinary, even in England — and documents, a fuller range of documents, because, Kennedy had wondered, how did we get into this mess with the British?

How did this happen to me, the president? How did my government function this way, that I was hit by John T. McNaughton with enormous complaints that I didn't see coming? Neustadt did the interviews. I talked to him about it quite a bit in 1963. It seemed like the perfect thing to do about Vietnam.

Let's understand not only what has happened, but what is happening. And not only for the future, but if we want to understand how to get out of this thing, and so forth, this is a case, while the people are still in there, that must be done. Now, as I say, I have no evidence that was ever seen by McNamara. Perfectly natural approach, I think, Neustadt or May were asked if they would head it. But in the end, they didn't.

They would have been good. To show how serious I was about this, I said, I would love to participate in such a study. I would even be willing to head it, if necessary. Now, as my wife or anybody knows, this is an amazing proposal. I can't organize; I'm not very organized. I couldn't have done nearly, remotely, the job that Mort Halperin, or Les Gelb, or Paul Gorman, or any of these people. I didn't have that time. But I was really saying, I'll even give myself to that task, if just to get this done. Well, I certainly wasn't asked to head it.

My condition of coming in, which Les Gelb has never remembered, and I remember it vividly, but no need for him to, was, I said, I don't want to write a study. I want to analyze the different studies. You are going to have studies of each year, each process, and so forth. What I'm good at, and what I want to do, is compare. I had done this before in the government, with Western studies and various other studies. I'm good at seeing where the patterns are.

I'm an analyst, I'm not a historian. I want to read the whole study and put in something on patterns that are revealed. Gelb said, no one gets to read this study if they haven't worked on it. He said, you'll have to write a volume. I didn't want to write a volume. I had no interest in writing a volume or doing original historical research. He said, that's a condition; you've got to do it.

My understanding was I could read the study, later, the whole study, if I put in this time doing it. Les has never remembered then, or later, that he made such a promise. But I acted on it. I insisted, through Harry Rowen and others, that I get at this, and it is a fact, of course, that I was given access to the whole study.

That's what I wanted, ultimately. That's why I had it all in my safe. Les may not have connected that to anything earlier; it may not have been connected, except in my mind. But I did end up with the whole study so that I could look at patterns, including my own volume and then [Howard Margolis's]. We had two versions of that.

The reason I picked 1961 to work on was, in the year 1967, when I came back from Vietnam with hepatitis, I didn't feel I would have learned much from the 1964, 1965 time when I had been in the Pentagon. I assumed that I would have seen all those documents already. The documents that are in the Pentagon Papers, published, I had seen already.

There wasn't much, because it was mainly McNamara's files and John McNaughton's files. Well, I had seen those at that time as his special assistant. There were several things missing from this study, very clearly, for a good history of the period. Howard has alluded to one: the requirement there be no interviews, a big, big limitation. Documents alone don't tell the story. They do not tell motivations. Lies are written down on top-secret documents as much as they are said to the public. You cannot go alone by documents.

On the other hand, interviews without documents, I've seen, from reading people's memoirs for a long time, don't tell the story either. They are self-serving. Memory fails, God knows, I know that — worse every month, you might say. And they lie. But a combination of documents and interviews is what you need to do it. We didn't have the interviews.

Second, we didn't have much from the CIA. They were very careful about what they gave to this study, and I'm sure they were very happy in the end that they had been so careful when the stuff came out. They really only gave us the estimates that make them look relatively good, not as good as they say, but relatively good, which led some people to think the whole thing was a plot, putting this out to make the CIA look good. It is true that the estimates looked pretty good, and I'll come back to that point. Intelligence and Research in State looked much better than the CIA.

The civilian intelligence analysts did look pretty good in their predictions of what the cause and the prospects would be. You didn't have the CIA covert operations. They didn't give that. So, that's a big thing missing from Vietnam, as it would be from any such history.

Third, you did not have special intelligence. I had had all these clearances for communications intelligence, for other kinds of intelligence. Many of the people had. But the study we did was only at the top-secret level. It was not at the code-word level higher. That's why I knew I would not be revealing codes. I did read every word of the study several times.

But I didn't have to read it. I could not plausibly be accused of putting out code-word information, putting out communications intelligence, breaking codes, or anything, because it was only top secret. Top secret in the Pentagon where I worked was like toilet paper. That was not true at RAND. It was treated very sensitively at RAND. But in the Pentagon, everything we read was top secret, practically.

The other is a secrecy system. Which, if I were presenting this for the first time to an audience, there are some people in this audience whose blood would run cold at what I'm about to say, because they know that I'm a person within the system who is actually talking about it.

But I'm really only quoting what I read in James Bamford's books about the National Security Agency; a current one is *Body of Secrets*. He really has gotten an awful lot of stuff from interviews, I presume, or whatever. The point of which is, the top-secret system and secret and confidential can almost be regarded as a cover system of secrecy to distract people from the real secrecy system. It is an information management system which allows you to dole out secrets to this reporter or that reporter as you wish. But what's in the code-word system when, and Bamford gives some of the code words that I remember, Umbra, other words, that would be Ruff, various things. That would be additional on top, it wouldn't be top-secret sensitive, it would be top-secret Umbra Ruff, dah, dah, dah.

As I say, Bamford puts all this out. This stuff doesn't get in the *Washington Post*. Secrets in Washington can be very well kept for a very long time. Everybody in that system knows that. The notion that it all appears in the *New York Times* is a lie. It is a secret. Some of that is stuff that most of us here in this room, even I would say deserves to be secret. It's the real secret, for a while, for some period. You know, it shouldn't get out. And we don't want our codes [out].

Colonel Herbert Schandler: I wrote the last portion of the Pentagon Papers, which covered the Tet Offensive of 1968, the request for, I think it was 206,000 troops by General Westmoreland, the evolution of that request and its finality, and Lyndon Johnson's speech of the thirty-first of March 1968, withdrawing from the presidency.

I was never a member of the DoD Pentagon Papers Study Group. I didn't want to be a member of the DoD Study Group. I was recruited for the study group, and a large number of my friends served on the group, military officers who had been to graduate school with me, who had taught at West Point with me. I had frequent contact with many of them who were seeking documents from the army staff. I helped them in their search for documents.

I was assigned, at that time, to the Vietnam desk of the Strategic Plans and Policy Directorate of the Deputy Chief of Staff of Military Operations, Department of the Army. I enjoyed this particular position. I was uniquely qualified to fill it, I think. I had just finished my first Vietnam tour, 1965–1966. I had spent seven months in combat as the Executive Officer, Second Battalion, Second Infantry, First Infantry Division. We had significant regimental-size battles in November and December of 1965.

Shortly thereafter, my battalion commander, who was a wonderful soldier, was transferred, and I sought transfer myself, seven months out in the field. Escaping bullets was enough for me. I was transferred to J-33, the revolutionary development branch of MACV J-3.

In that capacity, among other things, there were three of us, two army and an air force officer who were charged with developing a concept to coordinate the American military and civilian effort in Vietnam in order to coordinate and increase the effectiveness of our whole effort. We briefed Ambassador Lodge and the mission counsel on our program, and it was approved. My last act in Vietnam in 1966 was to brief McNamara, Katzenbach, and Komer on this concept.

Shortly after I left Vietnam, the CORDS concept (Civil Operations and Revolutionary Development Support) was implemented under the direction of Ambassador Komer. Being on the army staff when I came back from Vietnam put me in a perfect position to explain what was happening on this reorganization in Vietnam to the chief of staff of the army. I'd come into the Pentagon at 7:30 in the morning, and somebody would grab me and say, the chief of staff wants to see you. I'd say, somebody get me a copy of the *New York Times* so I can see what he wants to talk about this morning.

After a year of doing this on the army staff, I was transferred to be assistant for Southeast Asian Affairs on the Policy Planning Staff of the Office of the Assistant Secretary of Defense for International Security Affairs. The deputy assistant secretary was Mort Halperin, and the head of the Policy Planning Staff was Les Gelb. The Pentagon Papers Study Group had been disbanded by this point, and the study, I supposed, had been concluded. I really didn't know very much about it, except my friends who were on the group had been returned to their duties.

The Tet Offensive began on the thirtieth and thirty-first of January 1968. A new secretary of defense, Clark Clifford, was sworn in on the first of March 1968. It was an exciting time. Halperin and Gelb were charged by the new secretary of defense and his assistant secretary, Paul Warnke, for an A-to-Z review of our Vietnam policy. Clark Clifford, in my opinion, was one government official who did not lie and who quickly discovered that the Joint Chiefs of Staff had no plan for ending the war; that this request for 206,000 men really had no strategy behind it. It was going to pile up their dead bodies faster than our dead bodies, and that was, sort of, the Joint Chiefs of Staff strategy.

So, we went through this review, and we weren't really too surprised when Neil Sheehan had this article in the newspaper about the 206,000 request, because, by that time, it was really a dead issue in the Pentagon. The president was not going to do that. Clark Clifford, as his secretary of defense, was not going to do that. This review, under Clifford's direction, ended with the president's speech of March 31, in which he withdrew. Clifford had a great deal to do with that.

Those of us — I was an action officer way down the line — who had something to do with that took great pleasure that a ceiling had been put on American forces in Vietnam, and that our strategy, the president's strategy, not the Joint Chiefs of Staff strategy, had been implemented, and there would be no more escalation. From that point on, thirty-first of March 1968, to the fourth of April, the North Vietnamese agreed to begin negotiations in Paris. From that time on, I was a member of an interagency group developing U.S. negotiating positions, basically with the State Department.

In November 1968, Dr. Gelb indicated to me that what has come to be known as the Pentagon Papers had not been completed. He felt they should be completed, and they should be completed prior to the change in administrations, which would occur subsequent to the election of Richard Nixon, in November of 1968.

So, I was charged with spending November and December writing the last volume concerning the Tet Offensive of 1968 and the request for 206,000 men, and the A-to-Z reassessment that had been conducted by Les Gelb, Mort Halperin, and those of us who were action officers under them. Since I had access to most of the papers that had been developed for the secretary of defense during that episode, I was clearly qualified to write this last volume of the Pentagon Papers. This I accomplished.

Since it was a documentary history, I had the documents. I had access to the DoD documents. I put them together. I turned in my volume, the last volume of the Pentagon Papers, to Dr. Gelb at the end of December, prior to the inauguration of Richard Nixon and the change in administration. So, the Pentagon Papers officially was ended at that particular point.

As a footnote, the Pentagon and the Office of the Assistant Secretary of International Security Affairs were quite different places after 1968. The appointed officials, of course, Dr. Halperin and Dr. Gelb, left. But those who remained, both military and civilian, and I was one of those who had served in the previous administration, didn't seem to be really trusted by the new administration. We really weren't consulted on most issues.

For a brief period of time, the only copy of the forty-seven volumes of what is called the Pentagon Papers was locked in a file cabinet in my office. Some [have] said nobody read the whole thing. Well, I spent a lot of time during that period reading the whole thing, because I had custody of the only copy of it that existed.

Finally, at a level much higher than mine, a decision was made to reproduce that one copy into nineteen separate copies and to distribute them to appropriate places: one copy to the LBJ Library, one copy to Clark Clifford's files, two copies to the RAND Corporation — I suppose, that's where Dan Ellsberg got a hold of his copy. Because of Mr. Ellsberg and his activities, and because of my initial custody of the papers, I did have a rather stressful day being quizzed by the Federal Bureau of Investigation.

Although I was not on Dr. Gelb's Pentagon Study Task Force, my association with the Pentagon Papers was close and continuing. My wife kept cautioning me when they were published that I shouldn't go around saying my good friend Dan Ellsberg has unclassified some of my finest work, that I would be tapped, my phone would be tapped, and I would be investigated. I didn't believe her at the time, but I think that's probably what happened.

Again, my association with the Pentagon Papers did not end there. I really didn't think much about it, but after my second tour in Vietnam where I commanded an infantry battalion, this is when the Pentagon Papers came out in 1971. I was then serving in the Office of Chief of Staff of the Army, General Westmoreland. That year, Professor Ernie May of Harvard did a critique of the Pentagon Papers as history for the American Historical Association. He decided it was very bad history, there weren't any interviews. They didn't take into [consideration] newspaper accounts. They didn't put into context what was happening in other parts of the world. They didn't say which memoranda that had been published in the Pentagon Papers were important and which weren't important. Some had been written by people and had never been read by the higher authority. Ernie May said, and I've memorized this, there was one volume, however, that was far more sophisticated in the author's use of the documents than the others.

That was my volume. That resulted in my Ph.D. dissertation, *Lyndon Johnson and Vietnam: The Unmaking of a President.* So I'm very grateful to Dan Ellsberg, my friend, who released some of my finest work.

Ellsberg: What was not in the Pentagon Papers that were in 1964, 1965 that I didn't know at the time, and I hadn't seen in the Pentagon, came out first with Larry Berman's book, *Planning a Tragedy*.

Then later, on the critique of the McNamara position by McGeorge Bundy from the White House, in the Pentagon Papers, we had very little access to White House papers. So, that was a major limitation in terms of understanding. In this study, which was first an appendix to Larry Berman's book, it was McGeorge Bundy July 1 of 1965, critiquing McNamara. "Dear Bob, your latest proposal seems to me rash to the point of folly."

Now, that is not bureaucratic language. I don't know if we could point to those words, anything corresponding to them, anywhere in those seven thousand pages. That's not how diplomats write or talk to each other. He then proceeded to a point-by-point refutation, or criticism, saying, you know, of the policy, which we were about to implement, which I would have said, I still say, if I had seen that at the time, I can hardly believe that I would have volunteered to go to Vietnam the next month.

I never saw anything like it when I was working as the special assistant with this high access. Later, over the years, and really, this comes out year by year, I've discovered what I knew not at all, at the time, that far from a situation where we'd get five hundred thousand troops; who could have realized that there was possibly an alternative to this approach. We were all cold warriors. This is McNamara's line, by the way, we were all cold warriors. We couldn't conceive of any alternative to what we were doing.

The documents now that have come out and interviews since the Pentagon Papers, not one of which is in the Pentagon Papers, because we didn't have access to it at the top-secret level, and the OSD [Office of the Secretary of Defense] level, were statements as detailed, critiques of our policy, as you could want at this point. And detailed accounts of how the president could and should get out of there. Those came, not only from George Ball who is for this the house dove, and whose documents did come out later. But if you want to protest, go ahead.

Schandler: No, no. I want to give the other side. There was an alternative to what was being proposed.

Ellsberg: Well, the JCS [Joint Chiefs of Staff] approach.

Schandler: That was the JCS alternative. I want to talk to that. I'll tell you how we got the five hundred thousand troops.

Ellsberg: But that is in the papers. The hawk alternative, the one that I didn't quite see at the time, but as I'm rereading it now, I'm seeing. What I was looking at there, and what Johnson was rejecting from his chief military advisers, over and over again, was insane. He was in an administration with an insane group of people.

Now, I don't think they were insane, and I don't think they were dumb. [How is it that] people representing an agency, a service in a particular position in a political climate, smart, intelligent people, and that is true of most of the Joint Chiefs, if not all, can recommend an insane policy?

Schandler: I will tell you why.

Ellsberg: That insane policy was not super-secret. It was right in the government. The president had always to deal with the fact that they might hand that top-secret stuff over to Goldwater in the Senate, or, that could very well leak. The stuff that was really super-secret were the dove proposals. It must not be known that the president was being presented with cogent, detailed analyses that the current policy could not succeed and the Joint Chiefs policy could not succeed, and the only real alternative was to get out.

Those policies were coming from people of the stature, all cold warriors, like myself, at the time. But these were charter cold warriors, Bill Bundy, Clark Clifford, who almost could be said to be the inventors of the cold war in some sense. Hubert Humphrey, who wanted to ban the Communist Party, the vice president of the United States, was writing papers drafted for him by Tom Hughes and some by the head of INR [the Bureau of Intelligence and Research at the State Department was actually headed by Hughes during this period] on how to get out, why he should get out, and what to do.

As I said, this, from McGeorge Bundy, various others, Richard Russell, chief cold warrior in the Senate, chief hawk, was giving the president the strongest advice in telling him how to do it, how to get out. [Senator] Fulbright, not just McGovern and Church, who are much junior to these people, Fulbright, Russell, and the Senate majority leader, Mike Mansfield, could not have been better. They cannot be faulted for withholding their views from the president.

But not one of them told even their colleagues in the Senate or elsewhere. These people didn't know of the other [track]; I'm telling you as somebody who worked on the Pentagon Papers, not one of those memos is to be found in the Pentagon Papers, and not because it was censored, but because nothing was held more closely.

People like McNamara. People like Kennedy. They perceived that the public had this infirmity. That if the information got out that our limited war approach in Vietnam was hopeless, and that was on every piece of paper you could find that were Pentagon Papers, if that wasn't kept secret, the public would have the following attitude, win or get out. The president regarded how to win. Well, there really wasn't a way to win. But the Joint Chiefs believed there was. They had ties with Congress, ties to Republicans, and so forth.

The president regarded that, correctly in my view, as a disastrous course for the nation, and if it led to nuclear war, possibly for humanity. That was disastrous for him as a Democrat, he believed, even though Humphrey and others said, "stalemate will be even more disastrous." So, if you can't either win or get out, then stalemate it is, and pretend to the public that you are being told it was adequate, although that was a lie.

Schandler: There were two alternatives to a limited war. One was the Joint Chiefs of Staff and one was the political situation at the time. One, Lyndon Johnson was not going to be the next Democratic president that lost a country to communism. The Democrats had been through that argument at losing and that accusation of losing China to communism. John Kennedy might have been able to do that, but Lyndon Johnson would not lose another country to communism while he was president. He wanted a limited war for limited results in a limited geographic area. On the other hand, the Joint Chiefs of Staff had learned several lessons; the military had learned several lessons from the Korean War. The one thing they had learned was they didn't like limited war, and so we don't fight limited wars. When we have a war, we go in and blast them, with overwhelming power, killing them. The president wasn't going to do that.

Every time the Joint Chiefs of Staff came in with a recommendation to do that, the president was pushed by them. He wouldn't do it. It got to be a joke in the Pentagon among us action officers, because every six months the president would call the Joint Chiefs of Staff in and say, how can we make faster progress in Vietnam? The Joint Chiefs of Staff would study that for a month and come back, and they'd say, well, in order to make faster progress in Vietnam, you have to bomb Hanoi, invade Laos and Cambodia, and mobilize the reserves. And the president would say, I'm not going to do that.

But within the current political limitations, how can we make faster progress? And they would say, OK, give the army more, give the navy more, give the marines more, give the air force more. And the president would say, well, how much more can I give you without mobilizing the reserves, which he would not do, to put the country on a war footing and destroy the Great Society programs that he was interested in. The Joint Chiefs of Staff would study this, and the services would study it, and they'd say, well, we can get twenty-five thousand more. The president would say, good, come in for twenty-five thousand. They would come in for twenty-five thousand, and he would say, approved. I've given the field commander everything he ever asked for.

Then six months later, he would tell the Joint Chiefs of Staff, how can we make faster progress in Vietnam? They'd say, mine Haiphong, bomb Hanoi, invade Laos and Cambodia, and mobilize the reserves. And he said, I'm not going to do that. They said, well, give the army, the navy, the air force, the marines a little bit more. How many can I give you? Thirty thousand more. And he'd say, good, ask for thirty thousand. I've given the field commander everything he ever asked for.

And that's how we got up to five hundred thousand without a viable strategy, because the Joint Chiefs of Staff adopted a strategy in Vietnam which could not win without mining Haiphong, bombing Hanoi, invading Laos and Cambodia, and mobilizing reserves, which the president was never going to approve. So, the Joint Chiefs of Staff went ahead, decided that they would develop a strategy, follow a strategy, which they needed those authorities to win with, which the president would never give them, hoping that some day the president might see it their way.

There was never any agreed strategy. This is what Mr. Clifford found out. What were we going to do with the 206,000 men requested? Well, we are going to mine Haiphong, bomb Hanoi, invade Laos and Cambodia, and mobilize the reserves. And he was not going to do that. They had no plan to win without those authorities, and they were never going to get those authorities. So, Lyndon Johnson was resisting pressure from the far right, from the Joint Chiefs of Staff. He was looking at the political situation. And he was also resisting pressure from the far left to get out. He couldn't just get out.

Ellsberg: We are not in any disagreement on any of that.

Schandler: Good. OK. But there were two forces, both from the left and from the right.

Margolis: I spent three months on this stuff and haven't thought about it, particularly, in the past thirty years, in contrast to some of my colleagues for whom this is a significant part of their lives. This last exchange, I think, reinforces the point I made about it makes a difference who was president, because, for reasons I said, Kennedy's situation was more difficult in his time, and he avoided making that kind of commitment.

Second, if I may speak a little disrespectfully of the Joint Chiefs, the sort of people who are making that argument when the Russians went into Afghanistan, they said, they won't be restrained, you'll see they clean that up in six months. But the Russians tried the Joint Chiefs strategy. It didn't work.

Schandler: Of course. And Nixon tried it, and it didn't work.

John Prados: Dr. Ellsberg made a comment a little bit earlier about a particular piece of paper that he had seen from McGeorge Bundy that had very striking language in it. What was it that it had?

Ellsberg: Rash to the point of folly. Not only proposed, but followed.

Prados: Rash to the point of folly. And this ties in with where the Pentagon Papers came from and where they were going to. You heard that in order to not raise the hackles of other agencies in Washington, the analysts who worked on the papers were told to confine themselves to the files of the secretary of defense. That meant they didn't have access to the White House files.

Now, if you look at the White House records from 1961 to 1966, which is when Mac Bundy served two presidents in the White House, Kennedy and Johnson. He had a very characteristic way of memo writing, and this kind of flashy language was in a lot of his memos. He said about George Ball, Mr. President, you want to listen hard to this guy and then turn him down flat. He said of the French in Vietnam, you know, when Johnson asked him for an opinion, we'll never lose the way they did, because we don't have the burdens and the baggage that they did, and on and on and on.

He made comments about the British when Johnson was trying to get more flags. He was trying to get foreign troops into the U.S. program. He made a comment about the British national security adviser, his opposite number in England, a guy named Burke Trend, about how LBJ might want to, basically, slap him across the face to get a British brigade into Vietnam.

So, it was very characteristic of Bundy's writing style. Oh, and then there is the Fork in the Road memo about the bombing of North Vietnam. When we decide to start bombing the North, he actually poses for Johnson, the question of, let's withdraw from Vietnam, or let's do something really big like go bomb the North, which leads to my question, and that is this, we are depending here on the secretary of defense documents which exclude stuff like this kind of White House material that might have given a whole different view to the analysts of the Pentagon Papers. But given that that is true, how come the Pentagon Papers contain all of these negotiating documents, which presumably wouldn't have been DoD stuff either?

Ellsberg: We got a lot of State Department material and a certain amount of White House, but not much. That wasn't so unusual. Some from the CIA. The concern was not other agencies. Bill Bundy, in particular, was very cooperative and gave his whole files from the assistant secretary of state, having been in ISA himself, of course, before he went to State. My understanding, and I don't know this in detail, but my understanding was always that the reason it had to be kept so quiet was fear of Walt Rostow in the White House, that he would not want a documentary record of this decision. He was the hawk, along with Johnson. Walt Rostow would close the project down.

My understanding is that that's why the documents were put in the RAND Corporation by Paul Gorman, Leslie Gelb, and Mort Halperin in the Washington office, initially, and to keep them out of the top-secret system. That was a requirement testified to a great deal. Very strange, of course it was very embarrassing to Harry Rowen, the president of RAND, when it came out, but it was not that unusual.

There was a fair amount of stuff that was not logged into the top-secret system. That made it look like a guilty conscience of some kind. But of course, they were kept in top-secret safes. They were handled by couriers. They were handled exactly like top-secret, but they weren't logged in. My understanding then and now, subject to correction by these people, is the major reason for that was fear that Walt Rostow would learn about this study after being out of the office, track it down, and destroy it.

Pat Eddington: When I resigned from the CIA in 1996 over the Gulf War Syndrome controversy, my role model was the late CIA analyst Sam Adams.

During that 1967, 1968 period is when the whole order of battle controversy was just brewing within the intelligence community. I'm wondering, how much of that were you all aware of as you were compiling these documents? How did it influence you?

Ellsberg: I was fully cognizant of it.

Schandler: I wasn't cognizant of it at all, and it didn't enter into the reporting. What we were interested in was strategy that the president and the Joint Chiefs of Staff and the secretary of defense were following. And we had a new secretary of defense who was trying to come to terms with that and couldn't, and risked, he said, his relationship with the president to tell him. He said, what was the worst thing a defense lawyer can tell his client? And that is, plead guilty. Get it out. Quit. You can't win.

Ellsberg: An old associate, George Allen, who was one of the top people in CIA on this estimating, kept me quite informed on that, as did the systems analysis people who were working on it. This is 1967, remember I came back with hepatitis in June. A major reason, by the way, I think, like Gelb, I can tell you about, it had a lot to do with my having hepatitis in the fall of 1967, why my piece had to be rewritten, I'll just mention. He wanted me to edit it myself. He wanted it done in Washington, the editing. With my hepatitis, I was working; I had an arrangement with the infirmary in the Pentagon where I worked two hours in the morning. I crawled, if any of you have had hepatitis, energy drained like a bathtub, you know, just pulling the plug, I suddenly went down like this. I pulled myself over to the infirmary in the Pentagon, slept for two hours, came back refreshed, had two more hours work, and then crawled out of there. So, I had enough of that after a couple of months. Then after I finished the draft, Gelb says, it must be finished in Washington, probably because he didn't trust me to do the editing back in California, in dreamland, you know, and so forth.

I said, I can't stay here any more, I have to go back to California. So, he said, I'll have somebody else do it. OK. And [Howard Margolis] never saw the draft, unfortunately.

But the answer to your question is, in 1967, then, when I was doing this, I was talking to the people involved in that controversy. I don't remember hearing the name, Sam Adams, but when I heard it later, you couldn't have had a better role model. He was an absolutely superb analyst, an honest, conscientious, brave person for which he was hounded out of the government, of course, and of the agency. He testified at the trial, by the way. Having said later that he didn't like me, didn't like what I had done, and didn't approve of it in any way. Didn't like me as a person, as he said in his memoir. I didn't know that, because I didn't have contact with him, but [he]wanted to testify to tell the truth in this trial, which cost him his career, essentially.

Now, one point on that, this order of battle testimony. It is the subject of the CBS documentary for which Westmoreland later sued for libel. The theme with the CBS documentary was that Westmoreland had deliberately withheld from the president the best intelligence available to him on the size of the Vietcong and DRV [Democratic Republic of Vietnam] forces, their North Vietnamese Army forces, but especially the guerrilla forces, the cadres. He had simply eliminated them from the order of battle, underestimating the total forces we were facing, enormously, in fact, that they were twice as large when these village guerrillas, village militia, and so forth were included as they used to be and should be.

Should you put the guerrillas in the infrastructure, in it or not, because if you did, you would give the lie to Westmoreland's public statements that the attrition strategy was succeeding.

It would show that, in fact, the overall structure, the Vietcong, despite all of our bombing, despite all of our efforts, despite four hundred thousand men going on five hundred thousand men, we were facing more enemy year by year than before. And therefore, you could make no claim of progress. My current understanding, which, I would have guessed at the time, is that Westmoreland was doing that, lying to the Congress, lying to the public, and so forth. Or, foolishness on the orders [or] by desire of the President, who did not want to go in an election year and say the Vietcong are bigger than they were last year. So, it was a political directive to Westmoreland, but I didn't know that so much at the time.

Prados: If you had been aware of the order of battle dispute at the time you were working on the Pentagon Papers, would that have made a difference in your analysis?

Schandler: It would have had absolutely no effect on the strategy the United States was following at the time under Clark Clifford, the secretary of defense. That was in 1968, and even in 1967, I think it had absolutely no effect upon the strategy. We didn't look at those orders of battle. And Westmoreland wasn't going to change his strategy, and he was never going to get the authority to carry it out.

Ellsberg: Well, let me put out a little piece of journalistic history here. In March 1968, after the Tet Offensive, [I was] facing what I thought was going to be the possibility the president might go. On the A-to-Z issue, where I think I was the only consultant from outside the Pentagon who was involved in that, my memory is that we were not at all [aware] that the president would not [approve] that request. And thus, you know, in retrospect, he didn't, for a lot of reasons, but it wasn't clear that he would not. I thought that would be disastrous. But facing what I thought was a terribly reckless, rash policy against the United States, for the first time in my career, I had never considered leaking, never considered it. I knew other people did it, unauthorized disclosures, outside the government. I had been in that system for a number of years. I really looked down on people who had done that. You shouldn't play the game that way. You shouldn't do it. And I had never even thought of doing it.

In March of 1968 I decided one way to oppose that escalation and its political context in which Johnson was making the decision was several leaks. The first thing I leaked was Sam Adams. By this time, I did know his name, knew CIA order of battle. Neil Sheehan wrote that story. I think Hedrick Smith also worked on such stories, revealing the CIA had just doubled the size of the Vietcong in their estimates — [a] rather dramatic story, which, by the way, did have a bearing on where these people that we had just killed in such enormous numbers in the Tet Offensive had come from. Somebody else, I think it was Arthur Goldberg, asked the CIA or the JCS after Tet. He said, gee, you are claiming a victory here. You've killed forty thousand people. What's your estimate of how many wounded for every killed person? He said, well, we figure, two to one, three to one. We think, for them, because their hospitals, you know, whatever, it was four to one or something.

So, that adds up to killed and wounded and missing, you know, like 180,000, whatever it was. Why do they have anything left? The reason they had anything left was many of those killed had been in the village infrastructure in the guerrillas which had been withheld from the order of battle earlier. So, Sam Adams had the new estimate and I put it out.

George Duggins (Vietnam Veterans of America): After the leaking of the Pentagon Papers, did any of you have a conversation with Secretary McNamara, and if you did, how did that conversation go?

Schandler: My conversations with him have been more recent, like 1998 and 1999. We went to Hanoi, and McNamara was very interested in finding out why the war went the way it did. This is part of the rationale for his developing the Pentagon Papers as well. He wanted to see how the American decisions were made. He then went to North Vietnam to talk to the participants in those decisions to see how their decisions were made, to get their point of view.

So he could find out where we went wrong, where they went wrong, where were the missed opportunities to find peace without going through these two to three million people killed and how these issues could be applied in the future. Again, he started with the Kennedy administration, which is when he came into power, and he asked the North Vietnamese, why did you become our enemy in 1961 when I came into power? They said, oh, we didn't become your enemy in 1961. They said, we became your enemy in 1956, maybe even 1954.

They said, you know, we were at Dien Bien Phu, we were out in the jungle fighting; we weren't sophisticated diplomatically. Our Chinese and Russian friends came to us and said, we are having a meeting in Geneva in three weeks and you will attend, and this is what you will agree to. You get half of Vietnam now; you get half of Vietnam in two years. We said does that mean the French get out? They said, yes, the French will get out. We went to Geneva. We were, sort of, nonplussed by the American reaction there.

We signed the document that said we got half of Vietnam, and the French left. Then we asked the British, and we asked the French, and we asked the Canadians, and we asked the International Control Commission, now, who is in charge of these elections? We couldn't find anybody much interested. Then we looked across the border, and there were the Americans replacing the French with another puppet government. So, we could not abandon our brothers in the South; the war was on.

That's one of the lessons that McNamara learned. Bob Sorley just wrote about how we won the war in 1968. The North Vietnamese never knew that. We didn't win the war in 1968. There was no one to win it for. There was no South Vietnamese government that could defend itself and defend its people.

The war was never won. In the minds of the North Vietnamese it was never lost. Every change in American strategy indicated to them the triumph of their strategy; we had to change in order to meet it.

Ellsberg: Many Vietnamese I know would have given a different answer to this question of when we became, effectively, their enemy. They would go back to the period when Ho Chi Minh's approaches that we live by the Atlantic Charter and the American Revolution and so forth and support their self-determination and their freedom from colonial rule were simply ignored. They were ignored because, for geopolitical reasons, we didn't want to antagonize the French or the British.

So, we were, effectively, their enemy. By 1953, well before Dien Bien Phu, we were paying 80 percent of the cost of the war. My friend Trang Ngoc Chau, who had been a battalion commander in the Vietminh fighting the French and then worked for Diem, told me something recently. He said, the communists claim to be leaders against the Trotskyites, well, the Trotskyites were rather important, the VNQDD [an anticommunist nationalist party], various other leaderships were [also]. [The Vietminh] could [ask for] support from the Soviets.

Later, the claim came from the communists, for the communists were in China. But even before that, Chau said, we heard in the Vietminh that people said in the beginning, against the French alone, we don't need support from Russia. Against the French and the United States, we need support from Russia. We can't do without it.

The communists could offer something in particular, which was, eventually, when we'll need it, we'll have some friends from major allies to counteract the Americans.

Margolis: I remember, sometime in the late sixties, I just happened to go into the National Archives. On display, in a room with our Declaration of Independence, were various old historic documents, one of which turned out to be a letter from Ho Chi Minh to the peace conference of Versailles, where he asked for support for independent Vietnam.

So, this was not something we would expect him to readily give up. On the other hand, I remember, some conversations with people from the State Department at the time of the negotiations and being taken aback at what I was told were our very reasonable minimal demands.

Our very reasonable minimal demands sounded to me like a call for absolute surrender of North Vietnam. So, what is surprising is McNamara would, at this late date, still be surprised.

John Judge: I wanted to know if any of the work you did in the study, or subsequent documents that you've seen, throw light on the controversy about the intentions of JFK to pull out of Vietnam. In the [commentary volume of the] Gravel edition of the Pentagon Papers, Peter Dale Scott worked to reconstruct, from public comments, National Security Action Memoranda 263. [Pierre] Salinger [JFK's press secretary] has said that he doesn't know why it's a controversy, because he was told to announce it at a press conference. My mother worked in the Pentagon. Her job was as a manpower analyst. She had to project the draft call figures for the Joint Chiefs, based on projections they gave her, including combat projections. She had to be right within one hundred people either way for annual, national calls five years in advance.

After she retired, she told me [that] in April of 1963, for the first time, she was told to change projections on White House orders for the beginnings of a full withdrawal from Vietnam. I asked her when did they reverse that or go to an escalation, and she told me in late November 1963, the Monday following the Kennedy assassination, she was handed papers by the Joint Chiefs for a massive escalation.

She took them back up to the Joint Chiefs and said these can't be right. They told her that the war would last ten years, that fifty-seven thousand Americans would die, and she should put that into her figures.

Ellsberg: The plan for withdrawing from Vietnam, in which the Joint Chiefs concurred, with whatever reluctance, and Maxwell Taylor certainly concurred, was premised on success of some kind. It really never said, we'll get out no matter what, win or lose. A plan that could get the assent of Maxwell Taylor did not say, clearly, we'll get out win or lose.

John McNaughton told me he had been told by Robert McNamara that McNamara had an oral understanding with Kennedy that they would get out by 1965, win or lose. He has never talked at all about his conversations that go beyond documents with either Kennedy or Johnson.

I have my disagreements with [McNamara], but I believe he has an enormous amount of information still in his head, more than any other living person in this country, that he has not yet told us.

It was taken for granted that our planning was based on, if the Chinese come in, we use nuclear weapons, nuclear war. So, we have two possibilities, conventional war with China or nuclear war with China, even worse, whether or not it escalated to the Russians.

I saw things differently, later, when I had a better sense of history. I didn't think the stakes were trivial. They did. But to think they were worth the risk of nuclear war with China, that is what I was referring to when I said insane. I now believe the pressure for mobilization, which was not needed for an attrition strategy in South Vietnam, meant when you mobilize, then we are at war.

They wanted this in 1964, 1965 on. When we are at war, the American public will demand that we do it our way to win this war. They will demand it be won. Johnson knew that if that happened, as George Ball always says, when you mount the tiger, you can't be sure when you'll get off; therefore, we shouldn't mount the tiger. [LBJ] had mounted the tiger. The tiger he had mounted was not just the Vietnam War, it was the Joint Chiefs. That tiger would get away from him if he did what they wanted, which was to bomb near China, mine Haiphong, do all this stuff. I now entertain the hypothesis, there were some people out there who didn't [oppose] nuclear war with China, which only had a few nuclear weapons. Not Russia, nobody wanted nuclear war with Russia. But nuclear war with China might have looked all right to some people, very one way, roll back, get rid of those Chinese, those Chinks, those dirty commies.

I think the documents should be looked at from that point of view. There's certainly Joint Chiefs who collectively said, we are prepared to risk nuclear war with China. Now that I call insane. But some of them may have felt that would be a good thing.

James Hershberg: On the China business, Chen Jian, a scholar at [the University of Virginia] and I are working on a piece about secret signaling going on between Beijing and Washington in the spring of 1965 in which both sides were explicitly trying to learn from the experience of 1950 and not repeat it. Basically, the Chinese were signaling the Americans, China will not initiate war. China is prepared for war. If war comes, we will not be limited in our response. Best of all, this time, believe us. Because, of course, in 1950 [in the Korean War], they had also sent a warning, and Acheson, MacArthur, Truman, all decided it was a bluff. So, there was a delicate, two-way communication.

Who wrote the diplomatic volumes of the paper? Can you clarify? We are now beginning to get the communist side of these [Marigold, Sunflower, Kiwi, etc.] episodes, and I'd be very interested to find out who wrote them.

Was there consideration given to bringing Henry Kissinger onto the team, given that he was, at the time, consulting for both Harriman at State and for McNamara? He was a Harvard historian.

Ellsberg: Gelb had worked with Kissinger at Harvard. Henry Kissinger had been urged to join the study and looked into it, but chose not to join the study.

On the diplomatic volumes, I don't know, except, inferentially in this way: I was at the American Historical Association when Ernie May made his critique of the Pentagon Papers. I knew he was the only person as a RAND consultant, aside from me, who was studying these, who was given access. He was given access after I was.

Harry Rowen also had access as the president [of RAND], but he didn't exercise that very much. I heard [him] saying how awful this history was, you know, and so forth. I turned to Les Gelb, next to me at the panel, and I said, Les, did he work on any of the volumes, the negotiation volumes, particularly? And Les said, "I stand mute," I think is what he said, I have no comment.

So, I got up, and I said, "[May], I'm asking you, did you work on the Pentagon Papers?" And he gave some answer, like, yes and no, or something like that. But it was kind of irritating to me, because he had given no indication that he had anything to do with this horribly designed and executed study.

Murray Marder: At the time I was diplomatic reporter for the *Washington Post*. Chal Roberts of the *Washington Post* and I used to meet periodically with John McNaughton during the Vietnam period. At one lunch John came in very dispirited and said he had something he'd like to bounce off us. Could either of us think of anything that could be proposed to the North Vietnamese to convince them the United States really wanted to get out of Vietnam?

I said, yes, I can think of something. He said, what? I said, get out. He said, but specifically? I said, well, just off the top of my head, I said, if you've ever seen the massive ammunition dumps at [U.S. bases], the North Vietnamese could never believe the United States would walk away and leave a massive amount of materiel there, but they don't know that we've done that all over Europe in World War II. I said, why not propose that? He said, what, specifically? I said, propose that the United States will offer [these] to be put in the control of the secretary general of the United Nations as evidence of good faith and see if that has any effect. John said, well, that's not a bad idea, I think I'll try that.

I heard later that he did raise that. He raised it, and the Joint Chiefs of Staff laughed at him.

Ellsberg: I was in Vietnam from 1965 to 1967. I left him in mid-1965. That sounds to me like something that happened later. I don't remember it being represented in the Pentagon Papers. But there is nothing unusual about that.

The documents of the Pentagon Papers are so misleading about the views of my boss John McNaughton, so unrepresentative of his actual personal views, which he never put down on paper, and I loved McNaughton. I had no social relation with him. He didn't believe in dining with his staff, ever. I spent twelve hours a day in and out of his office and I really liked him. It would have been very hard for me to think of putting out the Pentagon Papers — I would hope that I would have, despite that, but I can't be sure — if he'd been alive. He died in mid-1967. It was not only embarrassing to him, but I would have said unfair to him. It would have been very hard. My loyalty to him would have made that quite hard. I didn't feel the same personal relationship with McNamara or some of the others, only with John McNaughton.

Where it misrepresented him is right in line with your anecdote. As early as the time I worked for him in 1964, John McNaughton thought we should be out of Vietnam, last year, ten years ago, next month, anytime, out. I'll give you one thing that arose. After he removed me from the job of special assistant, I suggested the job of long-range planning, meaning six months ahead.

I said, look, this is 1965, there is still a long-range planning group on the Berlin crisis. The Berlin crisis is essentially over by 1962. So, three years later, we have a six-month-ahead strategy and so forth on Berlin. We don't have it on Vietnam.

He said, Dan, you don't understand, I don't want to be in Vietnam in six months. I want out, out, out. Look for that attitude by any official in the documents for the Pentagon Papers, there is a very severe limitation, and the limitation is on the existence of officials who understood that the president's policy was disastrous. That the Joint Chiefs, as John McNaughton did understand, was also disastrous. And that we should be out. And John McNaughton was a cold warrior.

Schandler: Well, just one thing, John McNaughton is quoted in the Pentagon Papers in 1967 as saying to the secretary of defense, we must get together and decide on the philosophy of this war. I don't understand what he meant by that, because there were two philosophies. There was the Joint Staff philosophy and there was the president's philosophy.

Ellsberg: I'll tell you what he meant. Mort Halperin was working for him at that point. Mort Halperin then wrote under John a much bigger document.

Halperin, in May of 1967, about the time you are talking, had just come aboard and was given the job by McNaughton, with very little guidelines, except by McNaughton, to draft McNamara's memo to the president, May 19.

Prados: That May 19, 1967, memo, which was written by Halperin, is fundamental in the turning of the American course in the first appeal for the two hundred thousand troops, but it is also one of the documents that the government claimed in the Pentagon Papers case were classified materials that had to be protected.

CHAPTER TWO

Publishing the Papers

Daniel Ellsberg had made some efforts to get the Nixon administration to learn from the Pentagon Papers in parallel to his efforts with assorted congressmen. With National Security Adviser Henry A. Kissinger at the very outset, when the RAND analyst was in New York to help with the transition team's Vietnam options paper, Ellsberg tried to warn Kissinger against becoming prisoner to the hubris encouraged by access to classified information. In two visits during 1970, after he had come out openly against the Vietnam War, Ellsberg had tried to speak truth to Kissinger's power. On the second occasion, that August, Ellsberg asked if Kissinger knew of the Pentagon Papers and begged him to read them. According to Ellsberg, asked if he had read the studies, Kissinger replied, "No, should I?" Faced with Ellsberg's persistence, Kissinger had shot back, "But do we really have anything to learn from this study?" Then Kissinger had objected, "After all, we make decisions very differently now."[1]

The substance of this exchange has been in the public domain since late 1973, when journalist Jann Wenner published a two-part interview with Ellsberg in the magazine *Rolling Stone*. All three volumes of Kissinger's memoirs, plus a partly personal study of diplomacy, plus a reprise of his memoirs specifically on Vietnam, have all appeared since Ellsberg's account of Kissinger's attitude became known. Kissinger never denied the attributions. He also did not admit, then or later, that his knowledge of the Pentagon Papers was more extensive than suggested by his denials of interest to Ellsberg.

From Kissinger's own point of view, the snubbing of Ellsberg and the Pentagon Papers proved unfortunate. The exchanges left Ellsberg frustrated and even more determined to use the material to strike a blow against the war. Had Kissinger responded positively, at a minimum he would have gained more time in which to work his combinations on war policy. As it was, the exchanges can only have put Ellsberg on notice he would need to act by himself. All of which brings us back to the time of the invasion of Laos, with which we began this book. As American troops were already in action, clearing the territory out to the Laotian border for the South Vietnamese to begin their phase of the operation, Kissinger appeared at a conference that Ellsberg attended. The U.S. government was embargoing news about the invasion preparations and, in fact, denying that anything was going on. Ellsberg asked the provocative question that forced Nixon's national security adviser to concede, even through his silence, that the administration had no estimate of the consequences of its policies in terms of casualties, particularly of Vietnamese. At his own panel of the conference, Ellsberg remarked that he foresaw the administration's probable next move as an invasion of Laos. Within days, the prediction came true. Ellsberg wrote a scathing article in protest, but he was already doing more.

The Institute for Policy Studies was a Washington think tank begun on the premise that progressive politics should have a policy-oriented voice of its own. Very much opposed to the war, three senior analysts at the institute, Marcus Raskin, Richard Barnett, and Ralph Stavins, had been working on a detailed critique of U.S. policy in Southeast Asia since the beginning of 1970. Raskin and Barnett had both been officials in the Kennedy administration, when the Vietnam War turned white-hot, and their book focused on the years from 1961 to 1965. The powers that be were already aware of the book, which would eventually be published as *Washington Plans an Aggressive War.*[2] In fact, Walt Rostow, who had continued to work for former president Lyndon B. Johnson, warned LBJ in a memo as early as November 20, 1970, that the IPS project was on the way. Ellsberg knew also, and he backed up his interest in this project by giving the authors extracts from the Pentagon Papers.

In Washington for yet another conference, the evening of February 28, 1971, Ellsberg had dinner with Raskin, Barnett, and Stavins and told them of his disappointing inability to get anyone in Congress to make the Pentagon Papers the basis for a major public critique of the war. The IPS scholars recommended that Ellsberg take the secret documents and leak them to the *New York Times.* Ellsberg had always thought of going to the media as a fall-back option in his effort to make use of the Pentagon Papers, and this time the advice fell on fertile ground. A couple of days later, at just the point where Senator George McGovern rejected the proposal to reveal the secret government study himself, Ellsberg stayed overnight at the home of Neil Sheehan, a *Times* reporter and friend from Vietnam. Sheehan knew of the existence of the papers, not from Ellsberg, but from the IPS scholars, who had let him read a few choice documents. Before the night was out, the two were talking about putting the Pentagon Papers in the newspapers.

An old hand among reporters of Vietnam, Sheehan had covered the early days of the war, had been back to Vietnam, and labored diligently as a correspondent at the State Department and the Pentagon. He had broken some significant stories, had followed others when more trendy journalists moved on after their initial scoops, and was no stranger to big journalistic projects. Sheehan had sufficient experience to ensure that his suggestions would be listened to and enough knowledge of Vietnam to appreciate what Dan Ellsberg was offering. He first took the idea to the Washington bureau of the *Times,* where he presented it to news editor Robert Phelps. Sheehan also had a suspicion that the newspaper's Washington offices might be bugged, so he conspiratorially asked Phelps to step outside with him and stand by the elevators.

At that point, Neil Sheehan framed the idea simply in terms of the leak. As Harrison Salisbury of the *Times* recounts the story, Sheehan told Phelps he had a chance at getting a major internal Pentagon study of the Vietnam War, but a condition was involved — the paper would have to print the whole thing. Sheehan did not know (or did not say) exactly how long the Pentagon Papers were, but he did tell the bureau chief he expected the study would be "very, very long."[3] Phelps instructed Sheehan to take the suggestion to other *Times* officials, including James R. ("Scotty") Reston and Max Frankel. Columnist Tom Wicker also advised Sheehan to take the proposal to Scotty Reston, who was not just a columnist but a vice president of the Times Corporation. Max Frankel, Sheehan's immediate boss, happened to be out of town. Reston epitomized the journalistic establishment — he counted Henry Kissinger among those he could call on a story — but he had a gumshoe reporter's nose for news. Scotty favored going ahead. Arthur Ochs Sulzberger, the newspaper's publisher, is reported as thinking the appearance of the Pentagon Papers could damage his own views on Vietnam but that publication had to go ahead. By March 13, when, at Washington's annual Gridiron Dinner, Max Frankel quietly told *Times* lawyer James Goodale about the existence of a project having to do with the Pentagon study of the Vietnam War, journalists were already in motion on the effort.

While a certain amount of scurrying continued among *Times* executives, another newspaper caused new heartburn. This was the *Boston Globe,* which ran a story on March 7 mentioning the McNamara study of the Vietnam War and asserting that only three persons had read it. The story specifically mentioned Leslie Gelb, Morton Halperin, and Daniel Ellsberg. This news item upset Ellsberg, who feared he was already under FBI surveillance. The copying of documents out of the RAND vault had somehow become known to the FBI, which had quizzed Ellsberg's former wife after she learned of the photocopying from their children. Now Ellsberg worried the FBI could show up and seize the documents. He therefore resolved to make a third copy (two copies of the material already existed) of the papers and distribute all three in different locations, so they could not be so easily confiscated. It was during this process that Neil Sheehan came to Boston to get the promised documents. In an early indication of how closely the newspaper would hold its work on this project, the reporter and his wife stayed in a Cambridge hotel under assumed names. Sheehan raised some eyebrows at the newspaper when he asked its Boston office for cash for duplication costs ($1,500), and there was probably some chuckling at the subterfuges employed (Sheehan was sent to predesignated telephone booths to await a call that eventually sent him to a third place to collect shopping bags full of documents that he then had to copy and return), but the reporter got his cash and the *Times* got the Pentagon Papers. Ellsberg, meanwhile, would later put his multiple copies of the Pentagon Papers to good use.

On March 22, Neil Sheehan returned to Washington. He brought the Pentagon Papers down from Boston. At home he began to sort through the materials with the help of *Times* editor Jerry Gold, sent from New York. Gradually shipments of the papers went up to New York City, where additional copies were made in Arthur Sulzberger's office. Within a couple of weeks, the reporters could announce they had a huge scoop. By late April, Sheehan was prepared to deliver a detailed presentation.

A meeting of almost two dozen senior officials and editors took place in Scotty Reston's office on April 20. There the *Times* pondered its fundamental decision to publish. Neil Sheehan showed some documents, described the study, answered questions on content and authenticity, and so on. Sheehan concealed Ellsberg's role as leaker by talking about "sources," according to the IPS scholars, rather more credit than deserved since their own material derived from Ellsberg also. The reporter also made clear from the beginning that the study was missing its four diplomatic volumes. There was some question as to approach — whether to publish all at once, in a few installments, in many, and so on. Different plans included twelve, twenty, or other numbers of installments, and participants also differed on how to treat the Pentagon Papers. The consensus viewed them as a history by the government itself. Harrison Salisbury writes: "[Max] Frankel then put the key question to his colleagues — journalistically, did the story warrant defying the government and possible government legal action; did the documents in fact betray a pattern of deception, of consistent and repeated deception by the American government of the American people. . . . There was agreement in the room that this was precisely what the documents showed."[4] In the same vein, asked what he had learned by an editor the evening after the first *Times* story from the Pentagon Papers appeared, Rick Smith would respond, "I've learned that never again will I trust any source in the government."[5]

This entire debate among executives of the *New York Times* on publishing the Pentagon Papers reflects all the classic elements of journalistic dilemma. Here was a case where the newspaper had a source of unimpeachable integrity on a subject of major concern to its readers and, indeed, all Americans. The source and story concerned national security, which the government would be sure to invoke in appeals not to publish. The *Times* also had before it earlier cases of national security leaks where it had gone along with the government only to have *that* course emerge as the error. President Kennedy, after the Bay of Pigs, had told the newspaper's publisher that if it had featured its leak on that CIA operation — which JFK had begged the *Times* not to do — the United States might have been saved from great embarrassment. The *Times* had published the story but as a minor one in the interior of the paper. Its appearance had not dissuaded the Kennedy administration from moving ahead with the Bay of Pigs.

How much current national security would be affected by publication of materials that originated in the period from 1945 to 1968 was a judgment call. So were the questions of whether to handle the scoop by printing one story or a series, or by printing documents only versus reportage based on the documents. Another judgment call resided in the issue of how to fulfill the newspaper's commitment to the source of its information, Daniel Ellsberg, who had placed conditions on the material he provided to the *Times*.[6] In short, from the first moment there could be no doubt the manner of handling the Pentagon Papers involved the central issues of journalistic practice.

Lawyer James C. Goodale rejected the legal arguments against publication and armed the newspaper's executives with arguments they could use against such claims, but he worried that there would be a leak, that too many knew of the project. Editor A. M. Rosenthal had private doubts on the true authenticity of the papers but resolved to press ahead full speed nonetheless. The newspaper's major law firm, meanwhile, New York's Lord, Day & Lord, refused to represent the corporation in this circumstance and ended a long relationship, without turning the *Times* aside from its determination to pursue the Pentagon Papers project. However, the legal doubts of Lord, Day & Lord, which feared prosecution under the Espionage Act (see chapter 6), extended for weeks and involved several meetings with top executives. The misgivings of Arthur Sulzberger, in particular, endured but were not permitted to get in the way of Project X, as the *Times* privately called its Pentagon Papers editorial preparation effort. Nor did the threats from the old law firm, which had represented the *Times* for decades. On the other side, a number of editors and reporters felt so strongly in favor of publication that not to do so would have thrown the *Times* into chaos. No final decision would be made until June 10, 1971.

Desire for secrecy led the *Times* to take rooms on the eleventh and thirteenth floors of the New York Hilton. There, under guard by the paper's own security people, Sheehan began constructing a series of articles based on the documents. Hedrick Smith, another *Times* reporter who had worked with Sheehan on previous assignments, became his main collaborator in this work. Delaying his departure for the Soviet Union, where Smith had been scheduled to take over as Moscow bureau chief, the reporter quickly appreciated what a huge task the Pentagon Papers would be. His recollections appear following this account of the publication.

Supervising the reporters would be editor James L. Greenfield, one of the participants in the key April 20 publication conference. Other reporters who helped with the project included E. W. Kenworthy and Fox Butterfield. Research was done by Linda Amster. Separate biographies of persons who appeared in the documents or Pentagon Papers studies were prepared by Linda Charlton. Later the *Times* also put several more editors and researchers, plus a stable of assistants, to work preparing an abridged version of the Pentagon Papers, built around the newspaper's own summary news articles, for publication as a book.

Sheehan, Smith, and their colleagues labored on the stories the paper would print. By early June 1971 they had completed the first few of a set of overview articles, outlined the rest, and selected illustrative documents from the Pentagon Papers to accompany the news features. Completed copy and accompanying documentation then went to publisher Sulzberger. In company with his senior editors, "Punch" Sulzberger made the final decision to proceed several days ahead of time. Meanwhile a room had been prepared on the ninth floor of the *Times* building for a completely independent (thus secure) typesetting and layout crew to prepare the Pentagon Papers installments for the printing press. Confirming the late, final decision on publication is the fact that this room was set aside only on June 8. For the first day's story the newspaper's regular editors were warned to save space on the front page for the leader and six full pages inside the paper. Executives ordered a print run for the first *Times* issue to feature the papers, the one for Sunday, June 13, 1971, at 1,500,000 copies, perhaps 50,000 more than the newspaper had been averaging for its Sunday issues.

Last-minute possibilities for the *Times* to tip its hand on the big scoop remained. Despite all precautions, Scotty Reston, who had been among the inner circle in deciding what to do with the Pentagon Papers, practically gave away the game the day before publication. Determined to do a column focused on the papers, but away at a vacation home in Virginia for the wedding of his son, Reston phoned in the text for his piece. He used the regular phone transcriptionists and failed to put any restriction on the item that would prevent its being circulated by service to the other periodicals that subscribed to the *Times* service. Reston also mentioned the impending publication to Katharine Graham, a friend and one of his guests, who incidentally happened to be publisher of the *Washington Post*. After the Saturday afternoon reception, Graham phoned *Post* editor Benjamin C. Bradlee and warned him the New York arch competitor had some kind of big scoop coming up the following morning.

When Sunday, June 13, came around, it would not be just Daniel Ellsberg in Cambridge who made sure to get extra copies of the *New York Times*. "Kay" Graham sent into Warrenton for ten copies for herself, family, and friends. Bradlee got extra copies also.

By his account the *Washington Post* editor had heard rumors for weeks of some impending *Times* breakthrough in reporting on Vietnam. Once the Pentagon Papers began appearing in the New York paper, he faced the need to respond to the story. Depending on the competition grated on Bradlee. Obviously he had to get the *Post*'s own story into the paper, but "every other paragraph of the *Post* story had to include some form of the words 'according to the *New York Times*,' blood visible only to us."[7] Naturally the Washington newspaper wanted its own set of Pentagon Papers upon which to base coverage independent of that being provided by the *Times*. Bradlee got another telephone call the afternoon of the *Times* publication, which was from his friend Marcus Raskin of the Institute for Policy Studies. Raskin asked to have breakfast the next morning. On Monday, June 14, when the *Times*' feature on the papers concerned the evolving consensus on pressuring North Vietnam the Johnson administration had come to beginning in early 1964, Raskin offered Bradlee the manuscript for the IPS study "Washington Plans an Aggressive War." Based on the Pentagon Papers, the IPS study whetted Bradlee's appetite but did not have enough meat in it, in terms of documents, for the *Post* to base its own stories. *Post* editorial page chief Philip Geyelin then reported a Boston friend had offered him a couple of hundred pages of material from the papers and the *Post* got them, but the substance of the material appeared in the *Times* the very next day. That was the day the Justice Department went to court and obtained an order that enjoined the *Times* from publication (see chapter 5), but the *Post* remained far behind.

The paper's national editor Ben H. Bagdikian, meanwhile, had written a book on the media during which period he had enjoyed an office at the RAND Corporation. When the Pentagon Papers began to appear, Bagdikian instantly felt a possible source might be Daniel Ellsberg, and he began trying to get in touch. They made contact the evening of June 16, and the next day Bagdikian flew to Boston. He returned with two big cardboard boxes — the material was too much for the empty suitcase he had brought along — filled with photocopies for which he bought a first-class seat on the airplane. Now the *Post* had about 4,400 pages of the Pentagon Papers, not the full study but certainly enough upon which to base independent reporting. Bagdikian hand carried the material to Ben Bradlee's home on N Street in Georgetown. That became a combination newsroom and conference hall for the next day.

The *Washington Post* would have the same difficulties with its lawyers that its New York competitor had had. The *Post*'s firm, Royall, Koegell & Wells, advised that publication might involve the newspaper with the espionage laws and that the government, since it had moved against the *Times,* would certainly seek and obtain a court injunction prohibiting publication. In addition the *Post* corporation was up before the Federal Communications Commission for approval of certain broadcasting licenses, and the company had just offered itself as a publicly traded stock and was therefore vulnerable in the markets. These were huge stakes. They impressed the chairman of the corporate board, not merely the lawyers.

Ben Bradlee strongly favored publication. So did the journalists sorting frantically through the papers. Several of them threatened to quit if the *Post* did not go ahead. Bradlee finally got a second opinion from another lawyer, Edward Bennett Williams, a friend of his and also Kay Graham's.

"I've been in this city for thirty years," his biographer quotes Williams as having said, "And for thirty years I've watched respectable and responsible journalists tell Congress and the executive branch to go fuck themselves. What's Nixon going to do? Put every major editor and publisher in jail? Nixon doesn't have the balls to go after you, Bradlee."[8] In short his advice was to publish.

Publisher Katharine Graham, beset with her own set of divided counselors, was finally confronted when Bradlee called on the phone. She had to balance warnings that the paper could be damaged by publishing with others that it could be destroyed by failing to do so.

"Go ahead," Kay Graham finally said. "Let's go. Let's publish."[9]

By then the *Post* team had already missed the deadline for their first edition and had to scramble for their second. Ben Bagdikian rushed down to the newspaper's offices on L Street with the copy for the first completed article, one by Chalmers Roberts on the U.S. efforts to negate provisions of the 1954 Geneva agreements that required free elections on national reunification be held throughout Vietnam within two years. Even a last-minute effort by lawyers to stop the process with a new concern about collusion with the *Times* ultimately did not halt the move to print.

Don Oberdorfer numbered among the reporters who labored on this madcap but huge project for the *Washington Post*. Aside from Roberts, his colleagues included Murray Marder and editors Howard Simons, Phil Geyelin, and Meg Greenfield. Oberdorfer joined Hedrick Smith to furnish the reporters' perspective on the Pentagon Papers story that follows this introduction. The importance of the story and their pride in having worked on it are evident from their remarks.

The Chalmers Roberts article drawn from 1954 material in the Pentagon Papers was billed as the first of a series. Before the day was out, however, Assistant Attorney General William H. Rehnquist had called editor Bradlee to order the *Washington Post* to cease publication, and late that afternoon, Justice Department lawyers went to court for an order to this effect.

The legal aspects of the Pentagon Papers will be covered elsewhere, but here it should be noted that the determination of reporters and editors to cover this story was manifested not merely at the two newspapers discussed so far. In fact the imposition of a prior restraint on the *Times* and the *Post* led to other periodicals jumping into the fray. The result was a ripple effect, and if anything a form of collective protest by the media against the U.S. government action in attempting to suppress this story, which eventually involved nineteen newspapers.

On June 22 the *Boston Globe* led with a major exposé under the headline SECRET PENTAGON DOCUMENTS BARE JFK'S ROLE IN VIETNAM WAR. The paper had its next feature on the press when the Justice Department stopped it with another restraining order. On June 23 the *Chicago Sun-Times* published the first of four installments it would run based on access to people who had seen the Pentagon Papers plus its own collection of formerly secret documents. The *Sun-Times* did not actually have a set of the Pentagon Papers but consulted with people who did. At least one of the paper's features was quite possibly based on documents about the Diem assassination the Nixon administration was itself interested in leaking in order to smear the Kennedys. On the other hand, another of the Chicago newspaper's stories directly concerned Nixon, dealing with CIA reporting to the White House in 1969.

Thursday, June 24, saw a veritable flood of coverage from around the country. The *Los Angeles Times* carried two stories from the period of the Diem assassination and the coup plotting that had preceded it. The authors, Stuart H. Loory and David Kraslow, were extremely well connected in Washington, and their reporting elsewhere on Johnson administration peace initiatives closely paralleled the (still secret) diplomatic volumes of the Pentagon Papers. In the dozen different dailies of the Knight chain appeared a feature article on another Pentagon Papers topic, Robert McNamara's disillusionment on the war, which had become apparent to the public in 1967, and undoubtedly figured in President Johnson's replacing him with Clark Clifford not long afterward. In addition, the *Chicago Sun-Times* continued its string of reports with one on Lyndon Johnson's visit to South Vietnam in 1961.

The *St. Louis Post-Dispatch* got into the act on June 25 with a story on pacification in Vietnam. The following day the Justice Department shut it down with a restraining order just as a new installment of its coverage was on the presses. Other papers that jumped on the story over the next days included the *Baltimore Sun,* the *Christian Science Monitor,* and the Long Island daily *Newsday.*

Even as the press was lifting the curtain on the Pentagon Papers and the lawyers were fighting out the attempt at censorship in the courts, a U.S. senator tore away the cloak of secrecy altogether. Senator Mike Gravel of Alaska was opposed to the military draft, and the legislation that authorized the selective service system was due to expire at midnight, June 30. Gravel, a Democratic maverick, was determined to mount a filibuster against the draft starting the previous night and to do so by reading from the Pentagon Papers, a set of which he had gotten from Daniel Ellsberg not long after the Nixon administration first succeeded in halting publication in the *New York Times*. Gravel made elaborate preparations for his filibuster as he recounts here, but he did not actually get to make it, being headed off by a Republican parliamentary maneuver.

Gravel then used his chairmanship of the obscure Subcommittee on Buildings and Grounds of the Public Works Committee to call a hearing on the night of June 29 to receive testimony from New York congressman John Dow on how the Vietnam War had soaked up the funds that might have paid for federal buildings. This was simply a device to enable Gravel to read portions of the Pentagon Papers in his opening remarks and through the hearing. He read past midnight, until he could not any longer. Then he handed out the excerpts that he had put in the record.

Mike Gravel did even more than that. He was the sole member of the subcommittee present. As chairman, Senator Gravel used his powers to request "unanimous consent" that the balance of the Pentagon Papers be entered into the public record. There were no Republicans present to object. When other legislators learned what had happened, there were efforts to declare Gravel's hearing illegal, but all these attempts failed.

Afterward Senator Gravel began arranging to publish the full text of the Pentagon Papers, not simply the documents selected by the *New York Times* for the book version of its newspaper series, which would be published in July 1971. There were discussions with Simon & Schuster and with the MIT Press. The New York publisher backed away after the appearance of the *Times* version, which became a very successful paperback and appeared in hardcover also. The MIT Press was scared off by worries that its government research contracts could be cut in retaliation if it published and by vague fears that publication itself could be a criminal act. Such fears did not hold back Boston's Beacon Press, which eventually put out the Pentagon Papers in a "Senator Gravel Edition" of four volumes. Beacon also commissioned a book of essays analyzing the Pentagon Papers, which effectively became a fifth volume and appeared about a year later. When the books first appeared there was some concern in publishing circles that Beacon Press might be prosecuted for revealing secret information, along the lines that the MIT lawyers had worried about. The threat of criminal prosecution turned out to be a hollow one.

The Senator Gravel Edition: The Pentagon Papers: The Defense Department History of United States Decisionmaking on Vietnam[10] contains most but not all of the actual set of studies known as the Pentagon Papers (which amounted to 7,000 pages). The Gravel edition includes 2,900 pages of narrative, 1,000 pages of attached documents, and 200 pages of justifications for the war, which were a collection of public statements by government officials. Unaccountably, a key portion of the narrative, in fact the passage that deals specifically with the Gulf of Tonkin incidents, that should have appeared in volume 3 of the Gravel edition, went entirely missing. Eventually this material would be incorporated into the book of reflections edited by Noam Chomsky and Howard Zinn.[11] *The Pentagon Papers as Published by the New York Times*[12] also contains certain documents that do not appear in the Gravel edition.

Meanwhile the Nixon administration, in the course of its arguments in the Pentagon Papers legal cases, had undertaken to issue a properly declassified version of the material within a reasonable amount of time. That promise led to a third edition of the Pentagon Papers, one handed to Congress by the DoD on September 20, 1971. This edition contains almost all the narrative of the original Pentagon Papers, or at least of the forty-three studies that dealt with military aspects of the war, but it is heavily expurgated.[13] In particular, the government edition's set of supporting documents excludes the bulk of the more recent materials that appear in both the other editions. In contrast its supporting documents for the Eisenhower period, particularly, are much more ample than those included in the Gravel edition. As will be shown in our examination of the secrets in the Pentagon Papers (chapter 5), many of the deletions the Nixon administration made were highly questionable ones.

Finally, the four notorious diplomatic volumes of the Pentagon Papers, which amounted to close to 900 pages in all, were substantially released as a result of FOIA requests and court proceedings between 1975 and 1977. A second version of this material existed at the Lyndon B. Johnson Presidential Library of the National Archives. Historian George C. Herring melded these two versions together and published them in 1983 as *The Secret Diplomacy of the Vietnam War: The Negotiating Volumes of the Pentagon Papers.*[14] About 110 pages of the whole were partially or wholly deleted in the versions that Herring used. The latter were released, and a complete set of the diplomatic volumes of the Pentagon Papers was finally obtained in 2002 as a result of requests by historian John Prados and the National Security Archive. The complete "Negotiating Volumes," as well as sets of the other versions of the Pentagon Papers, are all available together in the microfiche research set *U.S. Policy in the Vietnam War*, vol. 2, *1969–1975*.[15]

Hedrick Smith

Why was I in that hotel room with Neil Sheehan and then later on Butterfield and going through this massive mound of papers? Neil and I had met in Vietnam in 1963 when I took Dave Halberstam's place. I had come back to Washington in 1964 and reported on Vietnam. I had actually begun reporting on Vietnam from Washington in early 1963; then I went to Vietnam in late 1963. I had a two-year assignment in Cairo, came back, and Vietnam had escalated as a political topic in Washington. I was, primarily, a diplomatic correspondent. I covered the State Department and Congress while Neil Sheehan covered the Pentagon. And I went to work. And that's just about what I did every single day of my life, as everybody did, Murray Marder and Don Oberdorfer and Chalmers Roberts, everybody else, that's what we were obsessed with. That's all we did.

So, by the time we came to the Pentagon Papers, we had been through a lot. I think what we had been through had disillusioned all of us. Had [Dan Ellsberg] come forward with those papers in 1968 or 1969, I think they would have been published then. I think the damage had been done in terms of the government's credibility with the major papers by that time. [The] comment that seventeen papers made the judgment that they would go with their judgment of what was damaging to the national security, not the government's judgment, had been an experience they had all been brought to over a period of five or six years. So, when we started looking at those documents, we had been through a lot.

I can remember personal epiphanies of mine when I had people lie to me, to my face, people that I had trusted. I had experiences where I found the government was literally putting out information that could not be anything but misleading to us as its first consumers then to relay on to our readers. It had had a profound effect. It didn't mean there was hate. It didn't mean there was anger. It meant there was deep, deep mistrust. And I think [Ellsberg is] wrong in saying that had McNamara come forward, and certainly if he had come forward in 1965, he wouldn't have been taken terribly seriously, but by 1967 or 1968, Washington had changed dramatically. I was very struck by coming back to Washington in 1966, late 1966, from a two-year assignment in Cairo, what a totally different place it was.

So, as we looked at those documents, as we considered the question of whether or not to print them and what to do with them, the issue of the government's loss of credibility was a subtext running through everything we thought about our craft and what we were going to do. Remember, by this time, there had been so much debate about the war — there had been so many leaks all throughout the period of the war.

Essentially, most of what Dave Halberstam, Neil Sheehan, Malcolm Brown, and others, myself included, had done in Vietnam was to go talk to captains, lieutenants, majors, sergeants, who were out in the provinces, who were telling us how the war was going. Then we'd go into Saigon and listen to the ambassador and his briefers and MACV [Military Assistance Command Vietnam] and hear totally different facts. All we had done was listen to the government's own reporting system; it just hadn't been ground through the deceptive machine when we got it out in the field.

We knew what was going on. When we saw the documents, we realized, once again, we were in touch with the people at the other end of the line. We had something that was reliable. It was an immense discovery. It was just staggering. But the other thing was that this was like the light being turned on in the room with the elephant. You are on the outside. You are touching some portion of the elephant. When you are outside the bureaucratic state you have some notion of how it operates, but mostly you have to imagine. And you are getting very, very incomplete pictures of what is going on.

Suddenly, with these documents, as you read them, you were able to follow dialogues within the government that went on over months and over years that told you how decisions were made about overthrowing Ngo Dinh Diem, or decisions about sending more troops, or decisions on the bombing. You didn't just get a narrative, but you actually could follow the documents that were going back and forth between the White House and the State Department and the Pentagon or between Washington and MACV, between Washington and the U.S. embassy in Saigon.

It took you inside a world, and what you saw was how one administration after another had misled the American people. [Ellsberg talks] about the necessity of deception; the notion that the public wouldn't buy the depth of the American involvement in the war meant that there was consistent deception. It went back to Truman, Eisenhower, on through Kennedy, Johnson, and then, that's, of course, where [the Pentagon Papers] stopped.

I remember arriving in the hotel room. It took me two solid weeks of reading — two solid weeks of reading just to have a sense of the dimension of what we had. I remember Neil Sheehan and I had adjoining rooms, and we'd go running back and forth to each other, look at this, look at this. This is what Westmoreland said, or, you know, look what Earl Wheeler said back to him. When I showed up, I remember Neil saying to me, man, am I glad to see you. There was so much to do.

He and I had done a number of stories together. In 1968, we reported that Westmoreland had requested 206,000 more troops. It caused a tremendous division within the Johnson administration. We published that, again, on a Sunday morning. The New Hampshire primary was the following Tuesday. That's when McCarthy got 40 percent of the vote. A little while later, Johnson decided not to run again. So, we had collaborated on a lot of important stories in Vietnam. It was very natural for us to do this.

It's interesting; [James Goodale's] idea was the government would stop you once you went public. So, you ought to publish it all in one day, which would have been amazing. To think of the size of the paper we would have had at that point. People literally would have had to bring trucks. James "Scotty" Reston used to say, the *New York Times* is a great doorstop. That one would have been a massive doorstop. It could have held open the doors in the Federal Reserve.

But Sheehan was totally impractical. And Neil had this idea, there was so much information, he said, let's roll out a story every day, two thousand words every day, for about eighty or ninety days. We were each going to do it. I said, Neil, we'll never live [up] to that. I mean, it's crazy. I mean, you have no idea what it is to just look at this much information. We didn't know how to handle it. And very importantly, there was no summary paper. There were forty-seven volumes, and if there ever had been a plan to write an overview, which summarized the findings, it wasn't done. Any press handout from any agencies always got the talking points, the fact sheet. There was no central map to this thing.

We had to go explore all its different provinces. We finally decided to handle it historically. It was set up historically. We did the chunks going back to Truman, Eisenhower, then we went through the Kennedy years, and then the Johnson years, the commitment of the troops and decision to bomb the North, and so forth. I mean, we took it in chunks, and we broke it into about twelve stories.

I remember Neil worrying while we were there that we were going to get wiretapped — and by the way, we stayed in the Hilton Hotel on Sixth Avenue on purpose, because it was a massive hotel. We could be anonymous there. Nobody would pay any particular attention to us. There was some problem with our colleagues explaining that we disappeared. We actually worked in that hotel for three months. So, you explain that we were away.

I was prepared for an assignment to go to Moscow, which I eventually did after the papers were printed. It was not so hard to explain me. I had gone to study Russian language. In fact, while I was in New York, I was studying Russian. Neil was a little bit harder, but Neil had a way of disappearing on assignments, anyway. So people sort of took it. We were very careful about telephone security. Neil said there was going to be a wiretap.

I remember saying to Neil, you are crazy. Our government would never tap working reporters in peacetime unless they suspected us of espionage. I mean, does this tell you how naive we were? Remember we did not have a declared war. Now, this is June of 1971. At that point, I did not know that my home had been wiretapped in 1969.

We did follow phone security. We had an editor who worked with us from time to time and then eventually every day. His name was Jerry Gold. So, whenever we called room service or whenever we asked for anything, we said it was Mr. Gold calling, whether it was Sheehan or me, or whatever it was, always, Mr. Gold ordered. He ordered enormous amounts of food.

Now, a question about this issue about national security, I don't think there was ever a moment that Neil or I had any question in our minds about whether or not we were going to print something from these papers.

There might be a question about what we would print. And this was just loaded with top-secret, secret, top-secret eyes only, I mean, I had never seen anywhere near this many documents since I had left the air force many years earlier. But as a professional judgment, what we knew about the war, we were simply going to try to bring more information to the public. I mean, that was our attitude. So, there was not a question. But there were massive amounts of classified material.

So, that did raise a question about what to use. We had, in that exercise, the same standards we had in any exercise when we dealt with national security. We had been dealing with it now on this issue for seven or eight years.

Number one, you don't do anything in print that will expose a current military operation, or endanger troops, or present the military order of battle that would be of use to the enemy. This was the absolute, flat-out, straight, clear rule that came right out of the experience of reporting in Vietnam.

Second, you don't report any intelligence information, any communications codes that would betray operations or methods and sources and expose codes. We were absolutely clear about that.

Three, we would never expose anything in which there was ongoing secret diplomacy. And there was a good deal of diplomacy going on in terms of trying to find a peace agreement — nothing that would expose channels, current channels, past channels, channels that were potentially useful that were unknown, nothing of that kind. In other words, we had very clear ideas of what the limits would be.

Now, actually, we were spared difficult decisions because this was history. It began with Truman, and it cut off with Johnson in the middle of 1968. We were looking at it in the middle of 1971, so any data that was in there, even the most recent, was at least three years old. Current order of battle, all that kind of stuff, those questions went out.

There was no current intelligence information, as I recall. I do not remember seeing any comment, no communications intelligence data. There was no NSA [code-breaking] data in there and that kind of stuff. This was strictly State Department, Pentagon, White House, what you might call the political agencies, as opposed to the intelligence agencies dealing with foreign policy.

Finally, we had no problem in terms of exposing diplomacy, because the four volumes dealing with diplomacy were not in the papers that we were dealing with. They had been withheld, destroyed, dropped, I don't know what, but in any case, they weren't there. So, we didn't have a problem there.

I remember briefing the *New York Times* lawyers, and I don't remember any problem with [Jim Goodale], but I remember other people being very skeptical that there were no military disclosures, that we did not make hay. I had a distinct impression, even without hearing [Goodale] say that Harding Bancroft was extraordinarily uncomfortable, if not outright opposed to doing this, and probably quite happy when he got the word from Lord, Day & Lord that we shouldn't do it.

Nonetheless, when we talked to Jim Greenfield, the foreign editor, when we talked to Abe Rosenthal, the executive editor — by the way, [Ellsberg] is absolutely right — Abe was in favor of the war. He was not opposed to the war. And I never, for one second, ever sensed Abe Rosenthal flinching one bit about going ahead with this. This was what had to be done as far as he was concerned. This was a professional judgment about the function of the media. And it was deeply affected by what I said before, the climate of relations between the government and the media. Another thing which may be a little difficult for Dan Ellsberg to hear, another one of our operating rules was absolutely minimum contact with the source or sources of the documents. Now, I want to tell you, I did not know the source. Neil never told me during that whole operation where the papers had come from. I knew he had gotten them. The documents did speak for themselves. There could be absolutely no question whatsoever that these were genuine documents. It would have taken the KGB or anybody else twenty years to have manufactured these documents and this material.

So, it was really the credibility of the documents rather than the credibility of the source. I didn't need to know the source. I knew it was a reliable source from Neil. I had worked with Neil enough. We had, on occasions, worked together. Usually we shared sources, but every once in a while, we didn't share sources. And if we didn't, I had enough faith in Neil; I think Neil had enough faith in me, where it didn't become an issue if you didn't tell me.

We also, to my knowledge, had no discussion with [Ellsberg] about when the *New York Times* would publish. That was part of our journalistic ethic — that we should not be, and it may sound funny to people to hear me say this, in collusion with anybody about trying to manipulate when things were going to be published, how they were going to be published, what the content was going to be. We were having extraordinary internal arguments within the *New York Times* about whether or not we were going to publish and when and what and how much.

Once or twice during the three months that I was with Neil, he went off to see Mr. X, [who] later I learned was Dan Ellsberg. The only thing that I know that Neil communicated was simply that the *Times* was interested. We were working hard on it. We were committed to doing something. And that was the limit of it.

[Ellsberg believes] that maybe one of the things that goaded us on was a sense of competition. I never remember that coming up in the conversations with Neil, that Dan Ellsberg or whoever it was was maybe providing this to other papers or whatnot. I never remember that being a factor.

I've mentioned the various sides inside the *New York Times* and the debate that happened. I do remember a couple of funny episodes. We were going full speed ahead. You can imagine, if you are processing this vast amount of material — by the way, the documents were as much of a problem for us in terms of volume and just getting on top of it as the text, reading through the narration and summarizing the narration, so, a couple of editors had to be assigned to do that. There were all kinds of makeup problems, just simply the processing of this much material. I would guess, probably, the last six weeks we had a couple of editors assigned to us, and then a couple more reporters were brought in to actually finish the writing and to help us with stories that we simply couldn't get to, the two of us. There was just too much to do. Somewhere around two or three weeks before the ultimate publication date, we got the word back through Jim Greenfield that Punch Sulzberger, the publisher, had agreed to publish it, but we were going to have to cut everything in half — that it was so long, we were going to have to cut it.

And Neil and I had to laugh, because the two editors who were working with us were people who had edited our copy for a long time, and they had periodically cut our copy. We had complained about it. And now they were complaining furiously that they were going to have to cut their documents. And they were having more agony over the cutting than we were. We thought that was very funny. It doesn't amuse anybody but another reporter that the editors are in more agony than reporters are, but in any case, I remember that just as an amusing sideline.

By the time we got to the last ten days, the *Times* was extraordinarily worried that our security might be compromised, the government might find out about it, and we might be prevented from publishing. They moved Sheehan and me and the documents into the *New York Times,* so, that, theoretically, the mantle of First Amendment was physically thrown around us. The *Times* would stop any warrant coming in to try to arrest us or get the papers and so forth. The last ten days or so, we slept in the paper, around the clock, and we stayed in there. The other two fellows did not. But the papers were all there.

In summation, I would say that we were certainly convinced, as we went though it, that this publication of the Pentagon Papers did not hurt national security in any way that could be demonstrated. I know the district judge and the Supreme Court asked the government repeatedly to show, specifically, any injury, and the courts were not persuaded of that. So, I would say that's, obviously, one set of judgments at the time, certainly that was our judgment, looking through the documents and looking through the text. This was history.

Second, I would say, had there been any serious jeopardy to national security, you would have thought it would have had some serious consequence on the conduct of the war. There has never been any serious allegation of that. Nixon's conduct of the Vietnamization policy went on. We didn't pull out of Vietnam for another four years. I think the main importance of these papers was history. It was a treasure trove for historians. There's a question in my mind, if they hadn't been declassified then by Dan Ellsberg, effectively, whether or not we would have those documents public today.

I think our whole understanding of that war is affected, the way it went, the way government policy was made. I think our whole understanding is different. I think the argument that [Ellsberg] is offering, which is, officials who disagree with policy, resigning on principle and declaring their opposition to policy — which is common in the British cabinet and happens in other European systems — doesn't happen here. I think that's an open question, whether or not that wouldn't be a healthier form of democracy than what we have. I think all of those things are assisted by the fact that the papers were published, and I think we did the right thing.

Don Oberdorfer

On Sunday morning, June 13, 1971, I must have slept a little late, because I got a telephone call from Ben Bagdikian, who was the national news editor and my friend. He said, have you seen the *New York Times?* I said, no. It's on our front step; we haven't gone out to pick it up yet. He said, look at it and call me back. I picked it up. There was this tremendously long article in big headlines, "Secret History of the War." We had heard that the *Times* was about to drop some big bomb, but we had no idea what it was. I call Bagdikian. And as I remember it, this is a little bit, maybe not true, but this is what I remember, because Ben doesn't remember it that way. I remember saying to him, do you know how to get hold of Dan Ellsberg? I knew Ellsberg in Vietnam, where I had met him. He was a guy who was, when I knew him in 1966, very much in favor of the war. He was going around Saigon with a gun on his hip. He was working for Ed Lansdale. But when I came back to Washington — I went back and forth between Saigon and Washington — I knew Ellsberg as a guy who would tell me more truth about what was going on within the government than anybody else I had encountered. I wouldn't call him, really, a source. He was about half a source, because he would, sort of, point me in a direction.

At any rate, however it happened, Bagdikian got a hold of Ellsberg and the *Times* was enjoined. And several days later, on Thursday, Ben Bagdikian came back from Boston with two cardboard boxes with 4,400 pages of the Pentagon Papers. I was in the newsroom. Gene Patterson, who was the managing editor, came up to me and said, in a very low voice, don't tell anybody, just disappear. Bring a typewriter and come to Ben Bradlee's house in Georgetown. I said, have we got them? He said, you just show up.

Ben Bradlee lived in Georgetown. He had lived next door to John Kennedy before Kennedy became president. In front of his house was his ten-year-old daughter, Marina, who had a lemonade stand set up. She said, I've never seen this many people come to my father's house. Murray Marder, Chalmers Roberts, and myself, several editors, including Phil Geyelin who was the editorial page editor, Meg Greenfield who was his deputy, Howard Simons who was, at that point, an assistant managing editor, Bradlee himself — this was a Thursday, you know, around noon, and we are all converging on his house. We went in to the library at Ben Bradlee's house. It was a long, narrow room with a sofa along one side. And the papers were there, but it was an undifferentiated mess — one chapter wasn't differentiated from another.

It took a while, with some help of some secretaries — including, as I recall, Kitty Kelly, who, at that time, was a secretary to Phil Geyelin of the editorial page — to try to straighten out this thing first, figure out what the hell we had. And then when we figured that out, we, sort of, made a decision as to who was going to start writing what. We wanted to write stories for the next day's paper, if possible, because, we felt, clearly, the *Times* had been enjoined, and as soon as they find out we had the papers, we would be enjoined.

I don't remember any question or comment about whether we should go forward with this. The *Times* had already gone forward with this. Chalmers, Murray, and I had been reporting on Vietnam. Nothing that we saw raised any big flag that said something that we shouldn't be printing, and quite the opposite. So, we went to work. Murray on the Johnson administration, Chal on the beginnings of Vietnam, and I, as I recall it, on the assassination of Ngo Dinh Diem.

I had just completed my book on Tet and had sent it to the publisher, but it hadn't been published. I was afraid that it might get enjoined in this whole process. I talked to one of the *Post* lawyers and explained that I'd finished the book, but it hadn't been published. Could they stop me, or stop the publisher from printing it, if I had access to these papers? He said, you just get your editors in New York at Doubleday to make an affidavit that they've, as of this morning, had all your stuff and they had not made any changes. I think you'll be OK.

Anyway, we all went to work. A few hours later, we had been working away, someone brought in sandwiches and so on. Howard Simons, as I recall, came in and said, you guys ought to be aware of what is going on in the other room, the other room being Ben's living room. We went in there, and there was a huge argument going on between the lawyers for the *Washington Post,* particularly, sided with by Frederick R. Beebe, who was the business chief [CEO] of the *Washington Post,* and the editors, Bradlee and Howard Simons. Gene Patterson was back at the paper trying to get things run, and the editorial page people, about whether to print. They presented to us, what was presented to us, anyway, as a "compromise." The compromise was not that we wouldn't print, but that we would withhold publication for a day, notify the attorney general we had these documents, and we were planning to print them a day later. I said, in an unguarded phrase — that I never in my wildest dreams ever thought would appear in any book, let alone every book that has ever been written on the subject — I think it's the shittiest idea I'd ever heard of.

Murray Marder, who had, in a sense, coined the phrase, credibility gap, in his reporting of the government, said, if we were not to publish, we would lose a great deal of the credibility of the newspaper. Chalmers, who was due to retire, said, if you withhold this, I'm not retiring, I'm quitting. And I'm going to tell the world why.

Well, that, I think, had weighed in fairly heavily, as I'm sure Howard Simons and Bradlee probably could have predicted. Anyway, the argument went on, and finally they got Kay Graham on the phone. Kay Graham was at a party at her house a few blocks away for a retiring business manager of the *Washington Post.* The *Post* was in the process of going public. It had submitted the papers and everything to sell stock on the New York Stock Exchange. This was a $35 million stock issue, and the first time that the *Post* had done this.

Also in the balance was the Nixon administration, we were pretty sure, would go after the *Post* in court, if this was published. And if the *Post* was found guilty of violating espionage laws or any other kind of laws, the administration probably could take away the three television licenses that the *Post* had held, which were estimated to be worth about $100 million a year.

Katharine Graham got on the phone. On one end of the phone at Bradlee's house was Frederick Beebe, who was the very well-respected and well-trusted chief of the business operations, and on the other was Ben Bradlee and some others listening in. Bradlee presented the case, why it had to be published and published now. Kay listened and then asked Beebe to give his side of it. She did this in a very judicious manner, we were told. We weren't privy to this conversation, but we knew it was going on. Mrs. Graham had two minutes to make a decision, on which not only $135 million was floating, but the future of the newspaper. I mean, I can't imagine a situation more difficult for a person who was devoted to the newspaper, also believes in the rule of law, and understood the stakes involved. She listened to the two sides. Then, she said, well, let's go. I think we should publish.

The decision to publish the Pentagon Papers made the *Washington Post* a great newspaper, because it set the stage for everything that happened later. Until that point, the *Washington Post*, I think it is fair to say, was the second paper in national affairs. People in Washington would get the *Post* in the morning, delivered, and they'd look, sort of scan it, to see what was there. And then they would go to their offices, where they'd get the *New York Times*, and they'd read it.

But now, there was a competitive side of this as far as the *Post* was concerned, a very competitive side. The *Post* wanted to be in the same league with the *New York Times* in terms of covering national affairs and being taken seriously. In his memoirs, subsequently published years later, Bradlee wrote, I think none of us truly understood the importance of the decision to publish the Pentagon Papers in the creation of a new *Washington Post*.

I know I didn't. I wanted to publish because we had vital documents explaining the biggest story of the last ten years; that's what newspapers do. They learn, they report, they verify, they write, and they publish. What I didn't understand was how permanently the ethos of the paper changed, how it crystallized for editors and reporters everywhere how independent and determined and confident of its purpose the new *Washington Post* had become.

Kay Graham, in her memoir, said, of the publishing of the Pentagon Papers, that was the key moment in the life of this paper. It was the graduation of the *Post* into the highest ranks. One of our unspoken goals was to get the word to the world to refer to the *Post* and the *New York Times* in the same breath, which they previously hadn't done.

After the Pentagon Papers, they did. This was, from the *Washington Post*'s viewpoint, the significance of this decision. It led to a number of decisions, several years later, regarding Watergate. As you know, Watergate, in a way, flowed out of this. But those decisions that the *Post* made against the extreme hostility of the government and the threats of every kind from the Nixon administration, what made it much easier was that we had gone down this road once before. We did what we thought a newspaper should do . . . publish. That's what newspapers are all about, publishing. And it turned out OK.

I personally don't think the publication of the Pentagon Papers had such a great effect on American policy, American thought, public opinion, toward the Vietnam War. That big change had taken place several years before at Tet. But the government wanted to continue the war. It had a bigger effect on the American press. I would say that was a moment in which the American press, and including the *Washington Post* and the *New York Times* and all the rest of the newspapers, became independent of the government on the war.

Mike Gravel

Thirty years is a good time to pause and look back and begin to assess. We find the same questions are still there. Why? How? What happened? Now we see this even more emotionally. There is something in the subconscious of the nation that has stirred. Whatever has gone on and is still going on, has not been dealt with.

In the introduction to the Pentagon Papers, published by Beacon, I wrote a phrase. In it was a wishful thought, that the release of these papers is really going to give us a chance to improve our governance, to improve ourselves as human beings. I've got a sad confession to make. As I look around today, I do not see anything different in the operation of government or in the operation as human beings than I did thirty years ago with that optimistic approach. That's a sad reflection, yet it is not. Because, once you can begin to understand a problem, you can begin to do something about it. If you are oblivious to understanding the problem, of course, we'll never be able to do anything about it.

As I see it, we have two things to deal with. One, we have to deal with what we did, and we have to deal with how it happened. How did this happen in a great country like ours, a great democracy, that you could trash the principles of democracy so wantonly? How could that happen? I want to share with you some views in that regard.

In order to function properly, that body within the people who occupy it develop a camaraderie, develop the clubbiness. Of course, that's important, particularly in the Senate. If you didn't have the club, if you didn't have that congeniality, it would be a mess. We need that to function. The flip side is you stifle creativity. You stifle integrity. You stifle whatever it takes to step out and do what's right.

I would say this in reflection of the Senate during my term, that, because of the club, which is so necessary to its operations, it incapacitated the Senate to be able to end the war. It had the power to end the war, and it had the conscience and the knowledge to end the war; it was incapacitated in doing it.

How did I get involved with the Pentagon Papers? First off, I was filibustering the end of the draft. The draft was the ability of one administration to use young people without their knowledge or will or political clout.

Second, they also didn't have to go out and call up reserves, which had created a real ruckus when that had been done earlier. They had a free pass, and they just poured the young people into it. Obviously, it made sense. If this is the tool to do the damage, let's kill the tool. That's the reason for the filibuster. Eventually it succeeded.

In the course of that filibuster, myself, like everybody else, on June 13, woke up to the release of the Pentagon Papers. I had never heard of the papers before. I had never heard of Dan Ellsberg before. It really stirred me.

I made up my mind that I would support Ellsberg, if, perchance, I got a phone call. I got a phone call around the eighteenth of June. It went like this. Very brief. I didn't know who it was, and I didn't ask — Senator, would you read the Pentagon Papers as part of your filibuster? Yes. We hung up. End of story. You know who gave me the papers, physically? Ben Bagdikian. I promised him, I'll take that secret to the grave, until ten years ago, when he was doing his memoirs, and he wanted to come visit with me so he could compare notes. He says, well, Gravel, you can start telling the world who gave them to you. So, I've been freed in that regard.

When I got the papers on the Thursday night, it was midnight. I took them home. I brought in staff to help me read them. When I brought them to the floor of the Senate on Tuesday morning, I was afraid. I didn't know what the government knew. I didn't know what moves would be made. I was truly afraid. I was afraid they would interrupt my plan, which was to use these papers on the floor of the Senate. I needed security. I couldn't go to the government, I mean, I'm a United States senator. I'm stuck. Who do I go to? I got on the phone, and I had some credibility with the Vietnam Veterans Against the War, because we had appeared at various antiwar rallies. So, I say, I got a favor to ask, but you can't ask me any questions. I need for you to muster up the most disabled veterans you can find and send them to my office, and I'll brief them at that point. My office was guarded by six, seven, eight of them in wheelchairs. I got to tell you, the sight of those people in wheelchairs, guarding my office, is something I have difficulty, emotionally, handling today. I'll never forget it as long as I live. I took the papers to the floor. I was called and was reading them there. I called a meeting of the subcommittee. We had a group of three attorneys in my office. When I was called, it was around 8:00, and I turned to staff. Do we have a Plan B? We don't have a Plan B. So, I went back to the office, and these attorneys came up with, based on the hearings, that I had the power, legally, to call a subcommittee meeting on the spur of the moment. That's what I did. We called a subcommittee meeting, and the rest is history.

One thing happened which was very unusual. I cried at the meeting. An anchor said that was bizarre. A late-night meeting, U.S. senator cries, release of the Pentagon Papers, just thrown out there to the public. I felt his analysis of it bizarre. I'm going to share with you three things that I think are really bizarre. When the papers were sent to the Congress, the Congress asked for them, they were put in a room, they were put in a booth on a table, and they had an armed guard. A senator could go in and read the papers, but he couldn't take notes. Can you imagine? Now, visualize this. I was a top-secret control officer for the Communications Intelligence Service, and I could classify at will and declassify at will. Think of that scene I just described to you and remember the fact that

I had all that power when I was twenty-two years old — more power than was given to the Congress and was accepted by the Congress of the United States. Now, there's a message there.

I also found it bizarre that the entire government involved in the war had no moral ballast and had no fundamental principles of democracy, that is self-determination.

Alexander Meiklejohn, who is probably the most renowned constitutional scholar in the last century, said, the citizens of this nation shall make and shall obey their own laws, shall be at once their own subjects and their own masters. The only good I can see of what's happened to us is the hope that the legacies of Vietnam will bring forth a moral awakening and lead us to a paradigm shift in human governance to true democracy. If that happens, then the cost of Vietnam will have not been in vain.

CHAPTER THREE

Nixon Intervenes

The legal scholar who has written the most detailed account of the court cases surrounding the Pentagon Papers,[1] David Rudenstine of Benjamin N. Cardozo Law School, notes that when the first installment of the Pentagon Papers appeared in the *New York Times* on Sunday, June 13, 1971, Richard Nixon's reaction was to let the press report all they wanted. Though President Nixon considered the press his enemy, the Pentagon Papers dealt with his Democratic predecessors, not his own administration, so it was John F. Kennedy and Lyndon B. Johnson who stood to be most damaged by the leak (Dwight D. Eisenhower, and Nixon as vice president during Eisenhower's administration, had some vulnerability on the Republican side, but it was far outweighed by the secret study's revelations on the 1961–1968 period). Working from the meeting notes compiled by Nixon's chief of staff, H. R. Haldeman, Rudenstine observes that Nixon emphasized in an early morning meeting in the Oval Office on June 13 that "we need to keep clear of the *Times'* series," and again that the "key is for us to *keep out of it.*"[2]

Closeted with Haldeman, the president did remark that the revelations might hurt the war and cause problems with South Vietnamese allies, but Haldeman's meeting notes convey a sense of Nixon's relish at the prospect of leaks damaging to Presidents Kennedy and Johnson, to Robert McNamara, and making out Walt Rostow to be, in Nixon's phrase, the "key villain."[3]

Dr. Rudenstine asks the right question about the situation: What happened between Sunday morning, June 13, when Nixon took a relaxed view of the Pentagon Papers, and the next afternoon, when the Justice Department began focusing on a legal action against the *New York Times,* to change attitudes in the White House? Drawing from the memoirs of Nixon aides John D. Ehrlichman, Charles Colson, and Henry Kissinger, Rudenstine essentially concludes that national security adviser Kissinger was mainly responsible for driving Nixon to assume a different, far more aggressive position. Rudenstine points to a Sunday afternoon telephone conversation and writes, "Neither Nixon nor Kissinger has publicly disclosed the details of this call."[4]

Since the time when Rudenstine was considering this aspect of the Pentagon Papers affair, the National Archives has declassified and released the tapes that

Richard Nixon recorded of his telephone calls during this period. These have been transcribed and form one basis for this chapter, one that constitutes wholly new evidence. The tapes make clear there is a more nuanced history than envisioned even in 1996 (when Rudenstine published); that Nixon's role was both more central and more sinister than seen earlier; that Kissinger has continued his practice of evading responsibility in this as in other matters, as has his deputy, Alexander Haig; and that newspapers bringing the Pentagon Papers to the American public faced a far more formidable foe than just the Department of Justice.

Alexander Meigs Haig Jr. benefited greatly from his service in the Nixon White House. In 1967 he had been a lieutenant colonel, as seen in our examination of how the Pentagon Papers were made. Four years later, in June 1971, Haig was a brigadier general (on his way to major and then full general) and deputy assistant to the president for national security affairs. Like most of the Nixon administration figures, Haig has left a memoir, one in which he avoids any mention at all of the Pentagon Papers.[5] But at 12:18 P.M. on the afternoon of June 13, 1971, General Haig was the first to emphasize to the president the massiveness of the leak.

Most of that day Nixon spent in his hideaway in the Old Executive Office Building with his businessman friend Bebe Rebozo. That fact has interesting implications of its own since, like all officials with access to classified information, Richard Nixon had a responsibility to preserve the security of that information. Yet he proceeded to have a series of highly sensitive conversations with a private citizen sitting alongside him. In any case, after reporting the latest Vietnam casualty figures to Nixon on the telephone, Haig turned to the "very significant" matter of "this . . . Goddamn *New York Times* exposé of the most highly classified documents of the war." When the president expressed a preference for firing whoever headed the Pentagon office he at first assumed to be the source of the leak, Haig instantly pointed Nixon at the Democrats and to the time when Lyndon Johnson's administration had transitioned to Nixon's. Haig expressed certainty that the documents had been "stolen" and that "they've been holding [them] for a juicy time." Haig also identified the leak for Nixon as being precisely of the McNamara Vietnam study, which he already had known about, and returned repeatedly to the theme that the leak was massive, a devastating security breach, and so on, effectively suggesting that an administration response was necessary.

Barely an hour later, Nixon was on the phone with Secretary of State William P. Rogers, who called to exchange pleasantries on the success of Tricia Nixon's wedding, which had been held the day before, and learn the good news Nixon had on the low number of casualties in Vietnam the previous week. Nixon himself brought up the subject of the Pentagon Papers and called it "a massive security leak from the Pentagon," using almost the identical terms with which Haig had provided him. Nixon had clearly built up a head of steam on the Pentagon Papers leak, but after a few moments of political analysis in his conversation with Rogers, had calmed down considerably. White House staffers, however, saw Nixon privately fulminating at the State Department and demanding that everyone there undergo lie detector tests to see who had leaked the documents. A few senior officials are reported to have actually undergone such tests. For the present though, Rogers had mollified Nixon. That left the field to Henry Kissinger.

It was mid-afternoon when Henry called. Kissinger had three main issues on the front burner at that moment. One was nuclear weapons negotiations with the Russians — the administration was at the point of starting a wide-ranging negotiation on the back channel between Kissinger and the Soviet ambassador in Washington, Anatoli Dobrynin. In fact Henry had taken Dobrynin to Camp David for some unusually intimate face time with the president just five days before. The second was Nixon's opening to China, to prepare for which Kissinger was to leave on a secret visit, the proposal for which the Chinese accepted on June 11. The third was the Vietnam negotiations, where Dr. Kissinger also had secret negotiations going on with Hanoi, in which he had just presented the latest U.S. offer. Indeed, in the telephone transcript that appears in this chapter, you will see that after talking about casualties in Vietnam — politically important to Nixon because lower rates of losses could reduce the heat from antiwar opponents — Kissinger immediately begins speculating to Nixon that a trip to Paris by Hanoi Politburo Le Duc Tho must mean the North Vietnamese are "at least gonna explore" the U.S. peace offer. It is Nixon who raises the matter of the appearance in the *New York Times* of the Pentagon Papers. Kissinger thinks the leak "if anything will help us a little bit, because this is a gold mine of showing how the previous administration got us in there." Kissinger relates the Pentagon Papers show "massive mismanagement" and that it "pins it all on Kennedy and Johnson." Nixon laughs. But the president returns to the idea that Al Haig had planted, that the "bastards that put it out" had done something treasonable (both Haig earlier and Nixon here use that word).

Henry Kissinger was good at fancy footwork. Here he turned on a dime. Kissinger immediately agreed that "it's treasonable, there's no question — it's actionable," the Pentagon Papers was no occasional leak, but everything the Department of Defense had. He suggests that Nixon talk to Attorney General John Mitchell. Nixon tells Kissinger to call Mitchell also, but later tells his national security adviser, "Don't worry about this, uh, *Times* thing." The president correctly anticipates the newspaper's legal defense ("The *Times* will justify it on the basis that it serves the national interest"), and both return to the comforting thought that no records of the Nixon administration are involved. Henry Kissinger reassures Richard Nixon: "All the big things you've done in the White House, and those files will leave with you."

In his memoir *White House Years,* Dr. Kissinger notes that the Pentagon Papers "deflected our attention for much of the time before I left on my mission [to China]."[6] He also writes that the idea of exploiting the Pentagon Papers "as an illustration of the machinations of our predecessors and the difficulties we inherited" was an attitude that "seemed to me against the public interest."[7] And again, "Our system of government would surely lose all trust if each president used his control of the process of declassification to smear his predecessors."[8] He also writes that the idea of seeking to suppress the Pentagon Papers through a court order was not his, though he did not object to it. Readers may judge for themselves whether these fine sentiments correspond to what Henry Kissinger actually told Richard Nixon at the time. Revealingly enough, all this text has disappeared in the compilation of Vietnam material from his memoirs that Kissinger has recently published in the paperback *Ending the Vietnam War.*[9]

Kissinger relates that his and Nixon's nightmare was that the Chinese would conclude from the Pentagon Papers leak that the U.S. government was "too unsteady, too harassed, and too insecure to be a useful partner." The transcript shows that in their telephone conversation, or at least those parts of it that have not been deleted, Kissinger and Nixon discussed only the impact of the leak on Hanoi. Kissinger also throws in that the papers unfairly damaged personal reputations, notably that of John T. McNaughton. The bottom line? "I not only supported Nixon in his opposition to this wholesale theft and unauthorized disclosure; I encouraged him."[10] This passage, too, has disappeared from Kissinger's more recent version of history.

Presidential chief of staff H. R. Haldeman supplies more details on Kissinger's encouragement. According to Haldeman, a Nixon intimate from California who probably spent more time with the president than anyone other than his family, "Kissinger told the President he didn't understand how dangerous the release of the Pentagon Papers was." Haldeman quotes Henry telling Nixon: "It shows you're a weakling, Mr. President." Then the chief of staff remarks, almost parenthetically, "Henry really knew how to get to Nixon."[11] Haldeman goes on, "In four and a half years in the White House, I listened, often with smiles, to many Kissinger rages, but the Pentagon Papers affair so often regarded by the press as a classic example of Nixon's paranoia, was Kissinger's premier performance. Unfortunately for Henry, it was recorded, and may someday be played to standing-room audiences."[12] That day is today.

Haldeman separately published his diaries from the Nixon years in the White House, and these show that for Nixon the Pentagon Papers were "the big deal today" for June 13, 1971.[13] Again it was Al Haig who got to Haldeman before the chief of staff had even seen the *New York Times* story. Haldeman's diary reflects Nixon's initial reaction: "The key for us now is to stay out of it and let the people who are affected cut each other up." Haig's message was different. According to Kissinger's deputy, "It will cause terrible problems with the South Vietnamese . . . it's criminally traitorous that the documents got to the *New York Times*, and even more so that the *Times* is printing them."[14] Haig also took the initiative in calling up Walt W. Rostow in Texas to ask about the papers. Rostow, who had always favored a U.S. invasion of Laos and had busily defended the Nixon administration for this move, had been in close touch with Haig since at least February, sending typescripts of his opinion pieces for comment and speaking at the Army War College at Haig's behest. Lyndon Johnson's adviser was forthcoming when Haig reached him in Texas. Harrison Salisbury reports that in the conversation, which he dates the night before the first *Times* story, Haig had already fingered Dan Ellsberg as the leaker. Rostow cracked that Ellsberg still owed him a term paper.[15]

By Monday morning, when the *New York Times* had its second installment of the Pentagon Papers in print, Kissinger was in high dudgeon. Charles Colson, presidential assistant and hatchet man, arrived at the office for the morning staff meeting to find Henry "pacing the floor as angry as I had ever seen him."[16] He had seen Kissinger's anger flash other times, but never so fiercely. The national security adviser was pounding a Chippendale table with his fists. "There can be no foreign policy in this government, no foreign policy, I tell you. We might just as well turn it all over to the Soviets and get it over with. These leaks are slowly and systematically destroying us," Colson quotes Kissinger. Haldeman was in the room as well. "I tell you Bob, the President must act — today. There is wholesale subversion of this government underway."[17] Kissinger threw down several diplomatic cables, from Great Britain, Australia, and Canada, which questioned the leak. Unknown to Colson, the United States itself had asked its ambassadors to solicit these protests from the countries where they were stationed. Later in the morning, Colson saw White House domestic counselor John Ehrlichman, from whom he heard more concerns, this time from the Justice Department. Colson recalls, "What began in the morning as familiar Kissinger fulminations, exploded by late day into a full-scale governmental crisis."[18]

President Nixon had by now taken the same view as Haig. Amid orders to freeze out the *Times* on White House access for news reporting — fairly typical for Nixon — he instructed Haldeman to speak to Haig about "this bad situation over there." The president apparently assumed at this point that the leaker of the Pentagon Papers was Leslie Gelb, who at this moment was working as a fellow at the Washington think tank called the Brookings Institution.

Nixon told Haldeman to "charge Gelb" and to "smoke out Brookings." Within weeks, even though the hunt for the leaker correctly turned up Daniel Ellsberg, Nixon's instructions of June 14 would lead to discussion of a bizarre plot to fire-bomb Brookings and raid its safes using operatives pretending to be firemen.

Nixon also demanded to know what legal options were available, which led to the issue being handed to John D. Ehrlichman, who formally referred the matter to the Department of Justice. Ehrlichman began holding daily crisis meetings on the Pentagon Papers.

Ehrlichman also called in White House legal counsel John Dean for a more private canvass of the possibilities. Dean writes that Ehrlichman called him and said, "The 'old man' wanted to know how he could put those bastards . . . at the *New York Times* in jail." Dean researched the relevant statutes and annotations, only to conclude the possibilities were zero: "The infamous Sedition Act of 1798 had long expired, and the First Amendment appeared a serious barrier."[19]

The central legal determinations on trying to suppress the newspapers publishing the Pentagon Papers were made in Washington on Monday, June 14. Legal scholar David Rudenstine credits William H. Rehnquist, then chief of the Office of Legal Counsel, and Robert C. Mardian, deputy attorney general in charge of the Internal Security Division, with the arguments and push for prior restraint.[20] By Monday night the essential strategy had been laid down when both Ehrlichman and John Mitchell called the president, as displayed in our next pair of transcripts.

Richard Nixon met with Al Haig and Secretary of State William P. Rogers shortly before noon, but at this writing we do not yet have the details of their encounter. That evening on the telephone Nixon spoke first with Ehrlichman. It was a short conversation, just a couple of minutes. Ehrlichman tells President Nixon that the Justice Department will move but feels it cannot prosecute the *New York Times* without first giving warning. "Hell, I wouldn't prosecute the *Times*," Nixon replies. "My view is to prosecute the Goddamn pricks that gave it to 'em." When the president asks if Justice could wait another day before doing anything, Ehrlichman advises that the president ought to talk with John Mitchell directly. Just six minutes later it is Attorney General Mitchell on the phone with the president. Mitchell tells Nixon that unless the government acts it will "look a little foolish in not following through on our — uh, legal obligations." Mitchell mistakenly tells the president that the U.S. government has previously done things like what he was proposing, and also, strangely enough, sees a warning to the *Times* of legal action as a "low key" move. From an extension Henry Kissinger reports that Walt Rostow has just called on behalf of former President Johnson to say, "It is Johnson's strong view that this is an attack on the whole integrity of government," and that LBJ will support anything the Nixon administration decides to do in the matter.

That Nixon was not entirely focused on the Pentagon Papers is demonstrated by his telephone conversation less than an hour afterward with Bob Haldeman. Suddenly his entire focus is on getting the television networks to rebroadcast their coverage of the marriage of his daughter Tricia that had taken place the day before the Pentagon Papers story first broke.

The morning of June 15 Nixon dictated a five-paragraph "Eyes Only" memorandum for Bob Haldeman, again ordering no contact with reporters for the *New York Times,* indeed advocating an attack upon it. The president wanted to have his cake but eat it too, instructing Haldeman to tell White House personnel that the administration was going to enforce secrecy but that this was really a public washing of the dirty linen of another administration. Nixon handed the paper to Haldeman at their morning meeting, which took place at 9:56 A.M. There the president underlined his points for emphasis: no one was to talk to the *Times,* not to Max Frankel, not to "any of those Jews." Nixon told Haldeman not to make the maneuver too blatant, the White House could say the president was too busy and so on, but Haldeman should give the orders to John Scali, William Safire, and others. There were to be no *Times* reporters on pools, none on *Air Force One,* "no *New York Times* person in my presence."

Bob Haldeman, now with three days' worth of installments of the Pentagon Papers to see, commented on the enormity of the leak. He then told the president, "You've got three suspects on this thing, and you can narrow it to those three. It has to be Gelb, Halperin, or Ellsberg, and if I had to guess which one, I would guess it was Ellsberg." A little later Nixon came back with, "Find out who the liberals are. And Goddamnit, if you've got a guy who's against what you're doing, you've got to threaten him." Haldeman assured the president he was doing just the right thing — in fact, that Nixon could hardly do anything else.[21]

In mid-afternoon John Mitchell came to the White House and met with Haldeman, Ehrlichman, and Nixon. Already Daniel Ellsberg was in the gun sights of this group, and Nixon insisted they had to "get him." The president spoke of a congressional committee, Mitchell of the grand jury he was planning to set up in New York. Ehrlichman raised the issue of public relations, and Nixon declared he wanted either the State or Defense Department to put out a statement, and he wanted to look at it first. This led directly to a William Rogers news conference held later in the day.[22]

At the official level of administration statements to the public, the private plans of the president and his associates remained invisible. On the day of initial publication by the *Times,* Defense Secretary Melvin R. Laird was on the Sunday morning television news show *Face the Nation* but was not asked about the Pentagon Papers and said nothing on his own. The next day Laird was on Capitol Hill for congressional testimony. There he expressed concern about the leak but did not say much. At the Pentagon, Laird was called by Robert Mardian (who also called Henry Kissinger and William Rogers) and was on the phone with John Mitchell. Laird ordered up a paper on the subject. Pentagon Counsel J. Fred Buzhardt prepared the paper after meeting with General Robert Pursley, who remained the senior military assistant to the secretary of defense, for Laird as he had been for McNamara. Pursley, of course, knew where the Pentagon study had originated and advised Buzhardt to talk to General Robert Gard. The latter found himself summoned to Buzhardt's office, where the lawyer had Gard's old recommendation papers to McNamara on the desk. Gard proceeded to answer questions about the Vietnam Task Force and its study. Buzhardt produced a memorandum that explained what the Pentagon Papers were and where they had come from, and made a general argument that the leak represented a breach of the security of classified information.

On Tuesday the fifteenth it was the secretary of state in the batter's box, when Bill Rogers held a press conference and was asked about the Pentagon Papers. As many had been saying inside the administration, Rogers told the reporters that the material was about how the United States had gotten *in* to Vietnam. "We hope," Rogers said, "that when the study is made of this administration it will be entitled 'How President Nixon Got the United States Out of the War in South Vietnam.'"

Secretary Rogers declared that he had seen the Pentagon Papers for the first time the previous day when he took a look at the copy in the files of Johnson administration officials Nicolas deB. Katzenbach and William P. Bundy. Rogers emphasized the seriousness of the security breach. From the State Department perspective, he added, "It's going to cause a great deal of difficulty with governments outside the U.S. . . . Already we have had demarches here . . . asking us about it" (in fact, the United States had sent a cable to all U.S. embassies inviting complaints about the sanctity of diplomatic communications, and as noted elsewhere, the diplomatic volumes of the Pentagon Papers had never been part of the leak). Rogers noted the Justice Department action against the *New York Times* that had begun that morning. He talked around a follow-up question on whether the American people had a right to be informed of this material, coming back to the allegation of secrecy violations. He did say, with regard to the impact of the leak on negotiations with North Vietnam — which had been Henry Kissinger's key claim to Richard Nixon — "I don't believe that it will have any effect on Hanoi's attitude toward peace negotiations."[23]

That evening Rogers had a telephone conversation with the president. Richard Nixon told his secretary of state, "I just think you couldn't have done it better . . . particularly effective was what you said about the fact that, uh, some foreign, uh, governments have raised questions about the security of their own cables and that sort of thing." After a digression to discuss the Washington visit of German leader Willi Brandt, the two returned to the Pentagon Papers, zeroing in on the trial judge in New York, Murray Gurfein. Rogers reported that he knew Gurfein well, and worried the judge, though a Republican, was on the liberal side. Nixon answered that Gurfein might be thinking of promotion among the ranks of the federal judiciary, which is dependent upon presidential appointment, thinking this might lead the judge to guard Nixon administration interests.

This was not Richard Nixon's only comment on Murray Gurfein that night. Ten minutes before talking to the secretary of state, Nixon had been on the telephone with John Mitchell. They had started out on Rogers's willingness to solicit foreign expressions of concern ("Yes, he's agreeable to do it," Mitchell had said), then Nixon had moved on to state what was clearly a political strategy: "I think what is very important . . . is to get out some strong [unclear, "language"?] like 'a massive breach of security,' things of that sort, so that we can get something in the public mind. We're not just interested in making the technical case for the lawyers."

The president was in the battle. "By God, it's one I enjoy," Nixon told Mitchell. "These, these bastards have gone too far this time, don't you think?"

Attorney General Mitchell then told the president about Murray Gurfein, "We've got, uh, a good judge on it." Nixon had said, "I know him well. Smart as hell." And, showing some satisfaction, Mitchell had replied, "He's new, and, uh, he's appreciative."

The other phone conversation the president had that evening was with his political hatchet man, Charles Colson. Nixon had wondered to his aide, "Maybe you could generate some support from some of our, our constituent groups on this." Labor leaders like George Meany of the AFL-CIO could be useful. "I mean this," Nixon had continued, and he also wanted congressional support, he wanted "to build a backfire on these people." Colson replied, "My own feeling is that it will backfire against the *New York Times,* and we can help generate this."

"The main thing," Richard Nixon had said, "is to cast it in terms of doing something disloyal to the country." And again, "What the *Times* has done is placed itself above the law. They say the law provides this but we consider this an immoral war, it's our [the *Times's*] responsibility to print it. Now Goddamnit you can't have that thing in a free country!"

In the closing seconds of Richard Nixon's conversation with Colson, the aide had mentioned getting some favorable editorials into the newspapers. That became a main concern for the president the next day. As Bob Haldeman puts it in his diary entry for June 16, "The P[resident] got into this, on and off all during the day, wanted to make sure we're making an all-out effort on editorials."[24] Nixon clearly went on in the same vein as he had with Chuck Colson the previous evening, as Haldeman notes: "He feels that we have to make the issue that the press is massively endangering our security, paint them as lawbreakers, disloyal, etc."

The other item on Nixon's Pentagon Papers agenda by June 16 was convening a federal grand jury to indict Daniel Ellsberg. As the transcript of Nixon's 8:22 P.M. telephone call with John Ehrlichman makes clear, an important side issue with respect to the court cases against the *New York Times,* and by now the *Washington Post* as well, was the feeling that a finding adverse to the administration could cripple the effort to get Ellsberg. Nixon and Ehrlichman go over in detail the timing of convening a criminal grand jury and eventually decide to start one only after the district courts have completed their action on the injunctions, or prior restraint orders ("PROs" Ehrlichman is by now calling them), on the newspapers. It is also in this conversation that, for the first time in the records available so far, there is an inkling that the administration might not get its way in the Pentagon Papers court cases ("There was [is] a possibility that we could get the kind of an adverse finding on the merits," Ehrlichman tells the president).

"*New York Times* is still the major item of the day," White House chief of staff Haldeman wrote in his diary on June 17.[25] The notion of getting Lyndon Johnson to spearhead the attack fell apart this day, regardless of anything Walt Rostow may have told Al Haig. Ehrlichman on the seventeenth noted a presidential order to check with LBJ, and the next day Republican political operative Bryce Harlow had a long talk with the former president on the telephone. Johnson refused to intervene in any way, worried the newspapers would simply "'re-execute'" him.[26]

Nixon spent time with Haldeman, Ehrlichman, Kissinger, Colson, and press secretary Ron Ziegler in various combinations throughout the day. No longer sure that convening a grand jury should be delayed, he instructed Haldeman to tell Ehrlichman to pass that message along to John Mitchell at the Justice Department (Mitchell delayed for a time, but a grand jury was soon empaneled in Los Angeles and began by conferring immunity on employees of the RAND Corporation for evidence used to indict Ellsberg late in June). "He thinks we have to play boldly and not be afraid of the risks," Haldeman noted. Charles Colson recalls the president telling him of Ellsberg, as Nixon shook his finger, standing next to the doors that led to the Rose Garden: "I want him exposed, Chuck. I want the truth about him known. I don't care how you do it, but get it done. . . . Do you understand me? That's an order."[27] At a National Security Council meeting Nixon declaimed on leaks and threatened dire consequences for leakers. In the evening the president met in the Oval Office with Ziegler and the two discussed the impact of television coverage of the latest development, which was the hearing that day in Murray Gurfein's courtroom in New York City.

Late in the afternoon there occurred an Oval Office meeting with Nixon in high dudgeon. So was Kissinger. According to Ehrlichman's notes, the president growled, "The *New York Times* is finished in the White House." The president wanted to favor the Hearst news syndicate instead (he had noticed that Hearst had refused to run anything about the Pentagon Papers). Nixon also wanted the file on the Kennedy people and the 1963 assassination of South Vietnamese leader Ngo Dinh Diem, with which he fancied he could make political hay. Nixon wanted to win the public relations fight, "not just [the] court case." Kissinger talked of Daniel Ellsberg as unbalanced, a person who "flipped from hawk to peacenik," who had "shot at peasants" in Vietnam and had stolen one of two (Kissinger was in error) sets of the Pentagon Papers held at the RAND Corporation. As for the court case, Nixon engaged in a bit of bombast — he might argue the case before the Supreme Court himself (thus by June 17 the president was already anticipating this case would go all the way to the high court).

It is revealing, as Harrison Salisbury notes, that (in their conversation about the Diem assassination) Nixon and Kissinger were more concerned about material that was not in the Pentagon Papers but which they figured they could use to political advantage, than they were about the supposedly sensitive classified documents in danger of revelation. It is also significant that there was no conversation in the White House about the purported diplomatic disaster of revelation, or about consequences of publication for negotiations with China, Russia, or North Vietnam. Salisbury's judgment is on the mark: "The embryo of almost all that was later to follow was present in that discussion — the institutionalization of paranoia, the creation of extralegal subversive units (the Plumbers), the organization of massive secret reprisals . . . a campaign for the 'discipline of leaks' which would be carried forward (and already had been) by criminal means; the groundwork for an elaborate conspiracy against liberals, intellectuals, and antiwar forces with Ellsberg as its focus; the stirrings of a political scheme to smear the Johnson-Kennedy administrations as architects of failure," and more.[28]

Haldeman for June 18: "Again today the *New York Times* papers is the big story."[29] The administration schemed for Lyndon Johnson to take the lead in denouncing the leak, but suddenly the White House aide comments that the former president "had completely collapsed," nixing that possibility. Most of Nixon's official family favored the LBJ-centered strategy, though Henry Kissinger opposed it "violently." Kissinger indeed expressed himself forcefully right down the line. Sometimes it was directly with the president; on other occasions Kissinger spoke up in the steering group that had begun meeting daily in Ehrlichman's office. This may have been where William Safire gave Ehrlichman the advice he cites from his own White House memoir — to parallel the court cases with some constructive legislative proposals to speed up declassification and (also) set penalties for "lifting demonstrably secret material out of government files."[30]

Transcriptions made from the Ehrlichman group sessions have yet to be released to the public — another time bomb in Kissinger's closet — but Ehrlichman writes of the experience that the national security adviser was a leading participant: "Kissinger was passionate in his denunciation of Daniel Ellsberg. . . . He knew quite a bit about Ellsberg's social proclivities (which Henry deplored) and Ellsberg's conduct in Vietnam. Henry urged that a thorough investigation of Ellsberg be pressed."[31] It was Kissinger, Ehrlichman claims, who "fanned Richard Nixon's flame white hot." Bob Haldeman makes the same point: "Ellsberg, according to Henry, had weird sexual habits, used drugs, and enjoyed helicopter flights in which he would take potshots at the Vietnamese below."[32] Haldeman felt Kissinger's charges "go beyond belief."

Trying to figure out the reasons for Kissinger's heat, Haldeman eventually concluded: "I think there was a personal factor in addition to his more substantive concern. Henry had a problem because Ellsberg had been one of his 'boys.'" Kissinger knew very well that Nixon's paranoia regarding leaks, which had long since focused on Henry's NSC staff as a major conduit, would be stoked by the Pentagon Papers affair. The transcripts that follow show Nixon making that very connection, and the Haldeman diaries have the president making the same point to him as well. By taking the lead on denouncing Ellsberg, Kissinger may have been trying to stay in front of that criticism. None of the versions of Kissinger's memoirs, it should be noted, mentions Ellsberg at all. Yet John Ehrlichman concludes, "Without Henry's stimulus . . . the President and the rest of us might have concluded that the Papers were Lyndon Johnson's problem, not ours."

President Nixon, once involved, stayed on the issue like a terrier pulling on a bone. Haldeman's diaries show Nixon fastened on the Pentagon Papers again on June 18, when the *Washington Post* joined the *Times* in revealing parts of the study, the twentieth and the twenty-second. On the twenty-third, Ehrlichman's notes show, Kissinger urged Nixon to "go on the attack."[33] That morning Nixon breakfasted with Senate Majority Leader Mike Mansfield and promised (as Justice Department lawyers would do in the courts also) that the administration would declassify a version of the papers for Congress. Repeatedly throughout this period, beginning as early as June 17, the president spoke of a wider program to declassify and release other secret records that might have a political impact, specifically including the Kennedy administration files on the assassination of Diem. For different reasons Nixon was thinking along lines similar to William Safire. This intention would carry over into action even after the Pentagon Papers affair itself had ended. On June 29 Nixon spoke to his cabinet about the Pentagon Papers, predictably putting it in the context of government leaking, and mentioning Ellsberg in the same breath with Alger Hiss and the Rosenbergs, notorious cold war spy cases of the 1940s and 1950s. The Hiss theme, too, surfaced repeatedly in Nixon's meetings and telephone conversations both before and after the Supreme Court issued its decision on June 30.

Secretary of State William Rogers made the Supreme Court decision the headline topic for his press conference the next day. He emphasized the need to safeguard secret information and confined his references to the Court's decision to language that acknowledged this need. Rogers claimed the administration had long recognized the need to review past declassification practices and offered: "The Government remains ready to lend its assistance in identifying any documents which, if disclosed, would result in . . . harm [to the national security]." Asked about the alleged study of declassification during the question-and-answer period, Rogers resorted to airy generalities, unable to refer to any ongoing work actually in progress.[34]

Many were the reverberations the Pentagon Papers affair had, and would continue to have, within the Nixon administration. President Nixon's determination, a few months later, to fire J. Edgar Hoover as head of the FBI is partly due to Hoover's lackluster investigation of the leak, according to John Ehrlichman.[35] Nixon also demanded and got the formation under Ehrlichman's supervision of a White House antileak unit that became notorious as "the Plumbers," under Egil Krogh, a lawyer who had come with Ehrlichman from his Seattle law firm. In late July, Plumbers operatives who, with Pentagon and Justice Department officials, had been meeting with House Armed Services Committee in an attempt to get them to mount an investigation of the Pentagon Papers leak itself, reported back to Ehrlichman that "only the FBI is disposed to thinking that Ellsberg is the sole prime mover." The White House operatives claimed substantial evidence could be gathered for criminal indictment of Leslie Gelb, Morton Halperin, Paul Warnke, and RAND Corporation executives as well.[36] An August 1971 reporting memo from Krogh to Ehrlichman is specifically about their "Pentagon Papers Project."

Administration demands of the CIA for a psychological profile of Ellsberg would later number among charges of illegal activities in Watergate. The Plumbers carried out a burglary of the offices of Daniel Ellsberg's psychiatrist on September 3, 1971, and these and other actions related to Daniel Ellsberg would ultimately taint the prosecution of the Pentagon Papers leaker for that act, in addition to contributing mightily to the impeachment of Richard Nixon.

Even on the issue of the president's special concern, leaks of secret materials from his own administration, the Plumbers' activities backfired. On May 8, 1972, in the course of a demonstration against the Vietnam War in front of Congress,

Cuban-American operatives employed by the Plumbers tried to beat up Ellsberg on the Capitol steps. An aide to California congressman Ron Dellums who witnessed this atrocious behavior, and who knew that Senator Mike Gravel had been trying to make public the Nixon administration's secret Vietnam study called "National Security Study Memorandum 1," promptly arranged for its publication in the *Congressional Record*.

Hosting a dinner at the White House for American prisoners returning from Vietnam on May 24, 1973, Richard Nixon denounced people who steal secrets and put them in the press — an obvious reference to Ellsberg — and demanded such person not by made into national heroes.

In summary, investigation into the Nixon administration's inner decisions in the Pentagon Papers affairs fails to establish that there was any overriding national security rationale for the president's actions. Although Nixon resorted to what had become, for him, standard techniques of retaliating by cutting off press access to himself and to his administration, the evidence of White House phone calls and meeting notes does not show participants calculating a strategy of making the Pentagon Papers leak the occasion for an offensive against the media. Similarly, although effects on diplomatic negotiations the United States had under way are cited as a rationale in memoirs of the time, the contemporary evidence of Kissinger's initial telephone conversation with the president, and of Secretary of State Rogers's first news conference, shows that few, if any, diplomatic consequences were anticipated at the time, and also that senior officials were not in agreement on what such consequences might have been (Kissinger felt Hanoi's attitude might be affected; Rogers ruled out any impact on North Vietnamese negotiations). The evidence suggests the arguments on diplomatic consequences were concocted after the fact.

The view that the Pentagon Papers prosecution was about protecting the secrecy of classified documents is belied by President Nixon's interest, sparked at exactly this moment, for seeking out a broad range of historically secret material other than the Pentagon Papers to release to the public. Indeed Nixon's interest led directly to an executive order he issued early in 1972 that liberalized considerably the application of the Freedom of Information Act (5 U.S.C. 50 et seq.) which had originally been passed by Congress in 1966 but had until then been largely a dead letter. The Nixon efforts on declassification policy do provide a clue to the real White House intent here. The main action was an effort to extract political advantage while seeming to be about protecting government institutions.

There was a secondary level of action as well. That was about images. Henry Kissinger's stoking of the fires of Richard Nixon's desire to be perceived as tough led initially to the legal actions against the newspapers, but in the mid- and long-term to a vendetta against Daniel Ellsberg. This was personal. Maybe Nixon *was* incensed at the newspapers; the White House tapes (not just these but through-out the time the Nixon taping system existed) certainly show evidence for his enmity there. But there was more than that. The intensity of the effort to "get" Ellsberg cannot be explained by White House concern at Ellsberg's leaking the Pentagon Papers, documents of another era as everyone around the Oval Office saw immediately, however sensitive the papers might have been. Historians of the period later observed: "There are several reasons for believing that the trial of Ellsberg and Russo[37] — popularly known as the Pentagon Papers Trial — was a case of selective prosecution undertaken for political reasons. . . . The available records of White House discussions of how to proceed against Ellsberg suggest that the decision to prosecute was a political strategy designed to make an example of him."[38] John Ehrlichman's records, or others, may yet yield the truth in this matter.

Whether the action was politically motivated or not, Daniel Ellsberg and Anthony Russo were put on trial in Los Angeles for the Pentagon Papers leak. They were prosecuted under the Espionage Act, in a trial that dragged on for months. The friendship between Ellsberg and Russo buckled under the strain. Russo was leery of Ellsberg's legal defense team and thought Ellsberg's commitment to Gandhian nonviolence somewhat suspect. He saw himself as a disciplined political fighter struggling against a war that was destroying the Vietnamese people.[39] Ellsberg maintains he never held any animosity for Russo and never quite understood what happened to him. The pressures were enormous and unrelenting on both men. The government's prosecution, caught in several questionable instances of denying knowledge to defense lawyers (Brady material), destruction of evidence, and even what amounted to conspiracy, held on into 1973, when the progressive revelations of Watergate touched Ellsberg and showed his private medical records had been the object of a White House extralegal covert operation which the CIA was duped into assisting. On May 11, 1973, the indictment was dismissed by the trial judge for government misconduct.[40]

The materials that follow are transcripts of Richard Nixon's Oval Office telephone calls and one meeting with Bob Haldeman, during the period from June 13 to June 16 on the subject of the Pentagon Papers. The president speaks with such figures as Henry Kissinger, Alexander Haig, Bob Haldeman, John Ehrlichman, John Mitchell, and Charles Colson. Some of the conversations have been quoted to create the foregoing account, but below the full transcripts are available. Many of the individual items were transcribed by Dr. Edward Meadows of George Washington University for the National Security Archive. Several more conversations have been transcribed by historian John Prados especially for the present book.

TELEPHONE CONVERSATIONS

Richard Nixon/Alexander Haig

June 13, 1971; 12:18 P.M.

Nixon: Hello.

Operator: General Haig, sir. Ready.

Nixon: Hello.

Haig: Yes sir!

Nixon: Hi Al. How, uh, what about the casualties last week, you got the figure yet?

Haig: Uh, no sir, but I think it's going to be quite low, uh.

Nixon: Uh-huh.

Haig: It should be as

Nixon: Should be.

Haig: [Unclear] last week or better

Nixon: Yeah, could, should be less than twenty, twenty I would think, yeah.

Haig: So [unclear] be very

Nixon: [Unclear] when do you get that, do you, will you know?

Haig: We don't get it officially until Monday afternoon, but we can get a reading on it.

Nixon: Right, well, Monday afternoon officially, well let's wait till then, fine OK. Nothing else of interest in the world today?

Haig: Yes sir, very significant, this, uh, Goddamn *New York Times* exposé of the most highly classified documents of the war.

Nixon: Oh that, I see —

Haig: [Unclear]

Nixon: I didn't read the story but, uh, you mean that, that was leaked out of the Pentagon?

Haig: Sir, it, uh, the whole study that was done for McNamara, and then carried on after McNamara left by Clifford, and the peaceniks over there. This is a devastating, uh, security breach, of, of the greatest magnitude of anything I've ever seen.

Nixon: Well, well, what, uh, what's being done about it then — I mean I didn't, uh

Haig: [Unclear]

Nixon: Did we know this was coming out?

Haig: No we did not, sir, uh.

Nixon: Yeah.

Haig: There are just a few copies of this multivolume report.

Nixon: Well what about the, well what about the, uh, let me ask you this though, what about the, uh, what about Laird, what's he going to do about it, is, uh, now, I'd, I'd just start right at the top and fire some people. I mean whoever, whatever department it came out of I'd fire the top guy.

Haig: Yes sir, well, I'm sure it came from defense, and I'm sure it was stolen at, uh, at the time of the turnover, of the administration.

Nixon: Oh, it's two years old then.

Haig: I'm sure it is, and they've been holding it for a juicy time, and I think they've thrown it out to affect Hatfield-McGovern, that's my own estimate. But it's, it's something that it's a mixed bag, it's a, it's a tough attack on Kennedy, uh, it shows that the genesis of the war, uh, really occurred during sixty-one.

Nixon: Yeah, yeah, that's Clifford, [unclear, laughing?] — I see

Haig: And, uh, it's brutal on President Johnson; they're gonna end up in a massive gut-fight in the Democratic Party on this thing.

Nixon: Are they?

Haig: It's, uh, there're some, uh, very

Nixon: But also massive against the war.

Haig: Against the war, uh.

Nixon: It's a Pentagon study, huh.

Richard Nixon/William Rogers

June 13, 1971; 1:28 P.M.

Nixon: Hello.

Rogers: Hi Mr. President.

Nixon: Hi Bill.

Rogers: [Unclear] that wedding was just great.

Nixon: Well, it was, uh, the, the, gotta give Pat and Tricia the credit, they really worked, and that White House staff — weren't they great?

Rogers: Everything, it was absolutely superb. And I thought the press coverage was excellent — uh.

Nixon: Th, uh, TV *was,* uh, really, you didn't see it probably.

Rogers: I saw some of it, thought it was [unclear]

Nixon: It was, really, really came out [unclear], all three networks did it, just really couldn't have done better.

Rogers: I don't know how you could have done any better, I mean there were, there were no snide remarks or anything, just [unclear]

Nixon: [Unclear] really, really handled it well.

Both: [Laughter]

Rogers: It couldn't have been better.

Nixon: Yeah.

[Withdrawn Item]

Nixon: Uh, incidentally, uh, one thing I was gonna mention that, uh, we, uh, the, uh, casualties this week are gonna be less than twenty again unless they have some, something they haven't, uh, unless something has come up, unless they have some MIAs that they're putting in, in fact it could be fifteen I think.

Rogers: Is that right?

Nixon: Yeah, so we're, we're now coming into that period [unclear] which we said we would. [laughter]

Rogers: You know, I heard on the radio just a little while ago, that this is the first time that there's been no combat activity involving United States troops in South Vietnam.

Nixon: [Unclear] day

Rogers: [Unclear] last twenty-four hours, no combat at all.

Nixon: Good, good.

Rogers: Wasn't that good.

Nixon: Well there were three days last week apparently, I, I just [unclear] talking to Haig, and he said there were three days, there were no, no, no killed in action at all.

Rogers: Isn't it wonderful!

Nixon: And as [unclear] through Thursday there were only four, so, Friday, Saturday may have picked up some, but as I said they all, they sometimes pick up some who have been missing, and that they just decide that — that they're gone now, and they just let 'em go.

Rogers: Right.

Nixon: Yeah, you know I was, uh, [unclear] I don't know whether you, I didn't read the piece, but Haig was, is, uh, was talking to me about it that, uh, he's, uh, that, that piece in the *Times* is of course a, a massive security leak from the Pentagon you know.

Rogers: [Unclear]

Nixon: It, it all is, it all relates to, it all relates, of course, to everything up until we came in.

Rogers: Yeah.

Nixon: And it's, uh, it's very, it's hard on Johnson; it's hard on Kennedy; it's hard on Lodge. Of course the [unclear], the difficulty from our standpoint, and I suppose the *Times* is running it now because of McGovern-Hatfield, it's also hard on the Vietnamese, and [unclear] covert [unclear], but apparently the, McNamara had the study made, started, and then it was continued through, by Clifford. But, uh, it's really something, they said, according to

Haig, four thousand, uh, secure documents had, were, were apparently just leaked to the *Times.*

Rogers: Isn't it awful.

Nixon: Goddamn.

Rogers: Of course McNamara looks lousy too; he comes out looking [unclear]

Nixon: Yeah. I didn't read the piece, but he looks, apparently, uh, by the time, you see the difficulty was McNamara started then Clifford got in, he makes McNamara look bad.

Rogers: Hmm.

Nixon: And, uh, trying to make him look good.

Rogers: God, they're a bunch of scoundrels aren't they?

Nixon: This Goddamn Clifford you know, his, his, talking around, uh, if he's got something, he ought to say, he ought to tell us.

Rogers: Well, I'll, I'll [unclear]

Nixon: [Unclear] he's going to see, uh, your fellow Wednesday, but, uh

Rogers: Who is? He's going to see who?

Nixon: Clifford. Well I'm sure he's going to, he told, he said, said he was, uh, told the press that he was going to see Sullivan, er, uh, er, uh, may, to report to him, you know, the, [unclear, stammering] we asked for it. In other words we said, "Look if you got anything, what is it?" And he said, "Well I'll, I'll talk to Sullivan."

Rogers: [Unclear]

Nixon: Sullivan called him.

Rogers: I, uh, Christ, I didn't know that Sullivan contacted [unclear]

Nixon: No, no, no, he did, at our suggestion.

Rogers: Oh, at our suggestion.

Nixon: Oh no, sure, sure. Because, see, when it came up, uh, Ron, I didn't want to have any, any interest shown in the White House, so, uh, we just said well, uh, have Sullivan say, "Well look, if we're negotiating here, if you've got something to pass on to Bruce, let us know." But he's a [laughter]

Rogers: Well I thought that, uh. I could take him on a little [unclear] — did Mel, was Mel on television [unclear]?

Nixon: He had, I think he was supposed to have been on one of the talk shows, but I, uh, yes I think he was, yeah, I didn't see it.

Rogers: Maybe [unclear] a chance to talk a bit tomorrow about what I should say Tuesday. I'll take him on as hard as you want me to.

Nixon: Yeah, well I would say this, that the real problem is of course how much we want to build him, but on the other hand, others may build him so that he has to be taken on, but we'll see what Mel did too. Mel may have, Mel said he was gonna do, take him on, but, uh

Rogers: Well, I think that if I take him on, I should do it with a, with a flick of my wrist [unclear]

Nixon: [Unclear] more in sorrow than in anger, my view, the view being, look, uh, after all, he was in this whole thing, and he left us with, uh, 550,000 men there, and so forth, and casualties [unclear] 300 hundred a week, now if he's, uh, we, we, under those circumstances of course, if he's got information that, uh, he should, that, that, that it's, he owes it to pass it on, we, we're, and I think the idea too that my God, we've expl— , we're exploring every possible thing, you know Bruce brings up everything he can, every damn thing [unclear, both talking]

Rogers: [Unclear, both talking] Well I can, I can hit him, I can hit him pretty hard if I have to, because he's, he's very vulnerable.

Nixon: I don't know what he has, [unclear, both talking] probably through, don't you think, through some embassy or something, er, uh

Rogers: Oh I don't know. It's a political move, that's all it is.

Nixon: You think so.

Rogers: Sure.

Nixon: Yeah.

Rogers: He doesn't have anything.

[Withdrawn Item]

Nixon: They told me that Johnson is furious at him now, Johnson was at, uh, in New York, was speaking [unclear] talking [unclear] some sort of a party he was attending, and apparently he, he said, "Dammit," he says, "the trouble with Clifford is that if, says he can, he can talk like this and go [unclear, "burning tree"?], and he says, "The president's got to go back to the damn office, and [unclear] he ought to tell him [unclear, both talking and laughing]

Rogers: That's really pretty good, isn't it.

Nixon: That's so true of Clifford [both laughing]. Uh, well, let's talk about it tomorrow then, and let's see what Mel said. And, uh, get a line where, uh, I'm deliberately having [unclear], uh, Ziegler has played it, as you know, rather cool, and will continue to tomorrow, but, uh

Rogers: Well we can decide, I don't think, and we want to be sure we don't build him up as an individual.

Nixon: No, never [unclear]

Rogers: Because he's not known in the country.

Nixon: He's not known, and the story, uh, from what I have heard, is not getting a helluva a lot of attention nationally; it's more, it's more of a Washington–New York story.

Rogers: Even in Washington though, the papers are sort of criticizing him.

Nixon: Yeah. I understand White took him on [laughter].

Rogers: Well, even, even a fellow like [unclear] Roberts, who's against us took him on.

Nixon: Course he was over there too [unclear, stammering] interview, which

Rogers: Right, which, really when you read that interview [unclear] they've toughened their position.

Nixon: Yeah, [unclear, both talking] they're saying, "Look, we won't do anything unless you stop the aid."

Rogers: That's right.

Nixon: Sure. Well, we'll see you tomorrow.

Rogers: All right, fine, thanks Mr. President.

Richard Nixon/Henry Kissinger

June 13, 1971; 3:09 P.M.

Nixon: Hello.

Operator: Mr. President, I have Dr. Kissinger calling you.

Nixon: OK.

Operator: Thank you.

[Unclear] president

Nixon: Hello.

Kissinger: Mr. President.

Nixon: Hi Henry, how are things in California?

Kissinger: Well I just got here, and I'm gonna leave, uh, very early in the morning, so I'll be back in the early afternoon.

Nixon: Oh, I see. I see.

[Withdrawn Item]

Nixon: OK, fine.

Kissinger: [Unclear] I understand you've talked to

Nixon: Yeah, Haig was, I talked to him about the

Kissinger: To Haig [unclear] I just wanted to, to check in, actually things are fairly quiet, we've got the casualties now.

Nixon: Uh-huh.

Kissinger: And unfortunately they're higher than what I told you yesterday; they're about twenty-three.

Nixon: Uh-huh.

Kissinger: But still that's a low figure.

Nixon: Yeah.

Kissinger: It's just four above what we had.

Nixon: Yeah.

Kissinger: They must have picked up some missing in action. The trouble with the daily casualties is that they don't reflect the ones that died, that were wounded the previous week.

Nixon: Yeah, yeah. Well on the other hand, my God, uh, Henry, nineteen, twenty-three, good heavens. It's just, it's just, uh, just [etc., stammering] down to nothing.

Kissinger: That's right.

Nixon: I mean, that's, uh

Kissinger: And the more I've thought about Le Duc Tho coming west.

Nixon: Uh-huh.

Kissinger: Uh, I'm not saying they're gonna accept it; but if they were just gonna kick us in the teeth, they wouldn't need him there.

Nixon: No, no.

Kissinger: So they're at least gonna explore.

Nixon: Yeah, well I, particularly if, uh, our Chinese friends lean on him a little [unclear, "he"? "they"?] will

Kissinger: [Unclear]

Nixon: And it just m— , they just might lean on him a little, yeah, yeah, yeah, yeah [Kissinger talking in between "yeah's" — unclear]. Well it's, uh, Haig was very disturbed by that *New York Times* thing, I thought that

Kissinger: [Unclear] Mr. President. I think

Nixon: Unconscionable damn thing for them to do.

Kissinger: Unconscionable [unclear]

Nixon: Of course it's, uh, it's [etc., stammering] unconscionable on the part of the people that leaked it. Uh, fortunately it didn't come out in our administration, uh, appar— , according to Haig, it's all relates [*sic*] to the two previous administrations, is that correct?

Kissinger: That is right.

Nixon: But I hope th— , but, but I, my point is if, are any of the people there who participated in this thing, who, in leaking it, that's my point, do we know?

Kissinger: In public opinion, it actually, if anything, will help us a little bit, because this is a gold mine of showing how the previous administration got us in there.

Nixon: I didn't read the thing [unclear], give me your view on that, in, in a word.

Kissinger: It just shows massive mismanagement of how we got there, and it [unclear] pins it all on Kennedy and Johnson.

Nixon: Huh, yeah [laughing?]

Kissinger: And McNamara; so from that point of view it helps us. From the point of view of the relations with Hanoi it hurts a little because it just shows a further weakening of resolve.

Nixon: Yeah.

Kissinger: And a further big issue.

Nixon: I suppose the *Times* ran it, uh [stammering] to try to affect the debate this week or something.

Kissinger: Oh yes, no question [unclear]

Nixon: Well, [stammering] I don't think it's going to have that kind of effect.

Kissinger: No, no because it's — in a way it shows, uh, what they've tried to do, I think they outsmarted themselves, because they had put themselves, they had sort of tried to make it Nixon's war, and what this [unclear, "magically"?] proves is that, if it's anybody's war, it's Kennedy's and Johnson's.

Nixon: Yeah.

Kissinger: So that these Democrats now [unclear, "bleeding"? "bleating"?] about, uh, [unclear], or, uh, what we're doing wrong, this graphically shows that, that, who, who's responsible for the basic mess.

Nixon: Yeah.

Kissinger: So I don't think it's having the effect that they intended.

Nixon: Well you know, uh, [stammering] it may not have the effect they intend, they, the thing though that Henry, that to me is just unconscionable, this is treasonable action on the part of the bastards that put it out.

Kissinger: Exactly, Mr. President.

Nixon: Doesn't it involve secure information, a lot of other things? What kind of, what kind of people would do such things?

Kissinger: [Unclear] it has the most — it has the highest classification [unclear]

Nixon: Yeah, yeah.

Kissinger: It's, it's treasonable, there's no question — it's actionable, I'm absolutely certain that this violates all sorts of security laws.

Nixon: What — what do we do about it — don't we ask for an

Kissinger: I think I, I [unclear, "shall"? "should"?] talk to Mitchell

[Withdrawn Item]

Nixon: No. I, I think you should, you tell Mitchell that, uh

Kissinger: [Unclear] this is not an occasional leak [unclear] it's bad enough, but this is everything the Defense Department [unclear, "possessed"?]

Nixon: Yeah, let me ask this, call Mitchell, I think you should talk to Mitchell and ask him about his just, just, uh, calling this, getting this fellow in, uh, on the purpose of, uh, this was a security leak, and we wanna know what does he have, did he do it; and, uh, put him under oath.

Kissinger: That's right; I think we oughta do that think we ought to wait till after

Nixon: Anoth— , another thing to do would be to — be to have a congressional committee call him in.

Kissinger: I think we oughta do it after Wednesday [unclear]

Nixon: A congressional committee could call him in, put him under oath you know, and then he's guilty of perjury if he lies.

Kissinger: But I think we ought to wait till after the vote, before they get, get it all confused.

Nixon: Oh I agree, well you couldn't do it before then anyway, but you know [stammering] get it all set up [unclear, stammering] because you gotta have the questions, and the investigations, and know what it is. Well we're not gonna get disturbed; these are, these things happen you know, Clifford pops off, and this guy pops off. I would think it would infuriate Johnson, wouldn't you?

Kissinger: Oh [unclear], basically, it doesn't hurt us domestically, I think, I'm no expert on that, but no one reading this can then say, uh, that this president got us into trouble. [Unclear] this is an indictment of the previous administration. It hurts us with Hanoi, because it just shows how far our demoralization has gone.

Nixon: Good God.

Kissinger: But basically, uh, I think they, the decision they have to make is, do they want to settle with you, they know damn well that you are the one who held firm, and, and no matter how far they, much anyone else is demoralized doesn't make any difference.

Nixon: Yeah. Right, right. Well you'll find things out there pleasant enough.

[Withdrawn Item]

Nixon: Well, that's a long trip for you, but I wouldn't, that's [unclear], don't worry about this, uh, *Times* thing; I just think we gotta expect that kind of crap, and, uh, we just plow ahead, plow ahead.

Kissinger: Well Mr. President, if we succeed in two out of three as you said [unclear]

Nixon: Yeah, yeah, yeah [both talking, unclear]. If we can, but boy you're right about one thing: if anything was needed to underline, uh, what we talked about Friday, uh, or Saturday morning, about, uh, about really, uh, really cleaning house when we have the opportunity, by God this underlines it, and, uh, people have gotta be put to the torch for this sort of thing, this is terrible.

Kissinger: Gosden was on that plane with me, and he

Nixon: Freeman?

Kissinger: Yes.

Nixon: Yeah, he's a great fellow.

Kissinger: Oh, he, he worships you [unclear]

Nixon: What did he think about all this, this stuff?

Kissinger: [Unclear] what you have to put up with, he said, he could, could never imagine it. He said well Dulles, he blamed the State Department, which is wrong in this case because [unclear]

Nixon: No, I know.

Kissinger: But he said Dulles always used to say that he had to operate alone because he couldn't trust his own bureaucracy.

Nixon: [Laughing] Yeah. I know.

Kissinger: I said well, that was good for Dulles but we pay for it now, because we are stuck with the bureaucracy.

Nixon: That's right, that's right, well I just wish that, uh, we operated without the bureaucracy.

Kissinger: [Unclear, laughing]

Nixon: We do.

Kissinger: [Still laughing] All the good things that are being done [unclear]

Nixon: Yeah, we do, we do, we do. Well, anyway, uh, I tell you what, on the Mitchell thing, I'd just have them — have him examine what the options are.

[Withdrawn Item]

Nixon: And the di— , the *Times* will justify it on the basis that it serves the national interest, is that right?

Kissinger: [Unclear]

Nixon: My God! My God, you know, can, can you imagine the *New York Times,* uh, doing a thing like this ten years ago, even ten years ago [*sic*]?

Kissinger: Mr. President, if, and then when McCarthy accused them of treason, they were screaming bloody murder [unclear] treason.

Nixon: That's right. No, whatever they may think of the policy, it is treasonable to take this stuff out and uh

Kissinger: Oh, it's one thing [unclear]

Nixon: Serves the enemy.

Kissinger: It's one, another thing to print ten pages of top-secret d— , documents that are only two or three years old. [Unclear] they have nothing from our administration, so actually, I've read this stuff, we are, we come out pretty well in it.

Nixon: [Laughing] Well, somebody over there got the stuff that we got, although we, I asked Haig about that, and, uh, he says well look, our file, as far as the White House is concerned, we, we're pretty damn secure; on the other hand of course, uh, naturally whenever I've had to call Rogers and, and Mel in on some of these on Laos and Cambodia, you can be sure all that's in some file.

Kissinger: But Mr. President, all the big things you've done in the White House, and those files will leave with you.

Nixon: Yeah, that's right.

Kissinger: [Unclear] to the Nixon Library.

Nixon: But, but what I meant though, that's true, the files, but I mean these guys of course will have made in their own records the, they'll indicate what I've ordered, you know.

Kissinger: Oh they'll indicate what you have ordered, but they weren't in on the reason.

Nixon: Yeah, well let's not worry about that.

[Withdrawn Item]

Richard Nixon/Bob Haldeman

June 14, 1971; 3:09 P.M.

Nixon: [Unclear] ask you what you thought about the, I was, I think that story in the *Times* should cause everybody here great concern. [Unclear] bunch of crap. [Unclear] that's the most, that's the most unbelievable thing, well that's, uh. That's treasonable, due to the fact that it's [unclear, "aid to the"?] enemy [unclear] classified documents I can remember how much [unclear] the Hiss case, a few little pumpkin seeds, slipping a little stuff to one guy [unclear], huh? But turning, turning stuff over to the [unclear], this turns it over to the enemy and puts the whole damn thing right out there, in the paper! I'm concerned about Henry's staff [unclear] don't have the confidence, because, I asked him, I said now look here — [unclear] Gelb

Haldeman: Over at, Murray G, I mean, uh

Nixon: [Unclear] Brookings

Haldeman: Yeah, I know, over at Brookings.

Nixon: [Unclear] had all these files, this is the thing, why didn't we go get them?

Haldeman: Well, remember I talked to you about that, a year ago. Tom Huston was all alarmed, and was in here and said they have all this, this file and everything, they've got it over at Brookings, they've moved it out of the Defense Department, copies out of the defense [unclear] Pentagon, took the whole file over there, and he argued, and we had, uh, we had some discussions about it. He argued that what we should do is, is send some people in on a routine, they've moved, they have a secure safe over there, to hold this stuff in, move some people in on a routine security check, find the stuff in it and confiscate it and walk out. And, uh, [unclear]

Nixon: Why didn't we do it, Bob?

Haldeman: I don't know. [Unclear] I'm not sure as a matter of fact, that this is precisely the same material; there is other material there too.

Nixon: [Unclear] this must be the material [unclear]

Haldeman: Yeah, but there's a lot of copies of this [unclear]: there's some other stuff that there're only three copies of, one of which is over at Brookings, according to Huston. Huston is an alarmist, but, uh, Dick Allen was an alarmist when he said we ought to cut out [unclear, "Symington's"?] we didn't do that, and [unclear, both talking] we've been hurt badly by it.

Nixon: We have. [Unclear] another [unclear] involved [unclear] Halperin

Haldeman: I'm sorry?

Nixon: Halperin and Sam Gelb have been working together. How much does Halperin know [unclear] does he know about the [unclear]?

Haldeman: I'm not sure.

Nixon: Henry talks [unclear, "to him"?] an awful lot [unclear] talking to people about what he's doing. [Unclear] that's just four times as great an opportunity for it to leak, you don't need [unclear].

Haldeman: The way to get him on that is just to remind him who he took with him to Paris.

Nixon: Lake.

Haldeman: And is he really happy that Tony Lake is, bouncing around [unclear, both talking]. Plus, and it's more dangerous now; in my view it wasn't this dangerous when he was working for Muskie as it is now, because now he's out of a job. [Unclear] sure he wouldn't leak it; he wouldn't use that information, well bullshit, you know if [unclear, both talking]

Nixon: [Unclear] remember, remember he told me, said he was very bright [unclear], brightest guy we've got; you can't make me fire him [unclear]

Haldeman: [Unclear] we finally did.

Nixon: That's right And he was [unclear]. J. Edgar Hoover was right; [unclear] put the finger on him.

Haldeman: The bugs showed that, the taps showed that, what Halperin

Nixon: Neil Sheehan of the *Times* is a bastard; he's been a bastard for years, on Vietnam. He got this [unclear]

Haldeman: [Unclear] long time; Klein says the team that's on it has been on, on, he, he's [unclear] the team has been on leave, or, or has been submerged for three months.

Nixon: Boy, if I were the publisher [unclear], I wouldn't print this stuff [unclear] top-secret information.

Haldeman: I don't understand why we don't —

Nixon: I, I just, I mean Haig tells us we've gotta not react and all [unclear]

Haldeman: But, uh, if, wh, what's the use of the classification system, why the hell do we classify anything if, if a newspaper feels no compunctions about printing it?

Nixon: [Unclear, both talking] then I think the thing to do is to, see, it's a [unclear], find out what the statute of limitations [unclear]; I think it's plenty long on this sort of thing. I don't think we can do much now, but if the statute of limitations is a year, and we've got a year [unclear] charge them then. And we can just go in and put, uh, subpoena all these bastards and bring the case [unclear]

Nixon: [Unclear] Henry's staff [unclear] and his own, and his people, you know, that [unclear]. . . . He [unclear] and talks to Brookings people himself I warned him about [unclear]; I said "Henry don't go over there," I said, there, those people, that's, that's the Democratic National Committee.

Haldeman: [Unclear]

Nixon: We don't have one friend at Brookings. Bob, no, we [unclear] — we need to remind George Shultz that Charlie Schultz is the guy at Brookings — you understand? So do you still want Charlie Schultz around? They play the game that way Bob; they are a bunch of bastards. They'll lie, cheat, anything, and then squeal when somebody else does. See basically that's what gets back to the whole Hiss syndrome, the intellectual, the intellectuals [unclear] because, basically, they have no morals.

Haldeman: But [unclear, "this thing"?] seems to me it, it hurts us in that it puts the war back up into a high [unclear] tension level, but the facts in it

Nixon: Hurt the other side.

Haldeman: Don't hurt us politically so much, they hurt the others, but what they really hurt, and this is what the intellectuals, and why [unclear] hurts the government. What it says is, Rumsfeld was making this point this morning, what, what it says is, to the ordinary guy, all this is a bunch of gobbledygook. But out of the gobbledygook comes a very clear thing: [unclear] you can't trust the government; you can't believe what they say; and you can't rely on their judgment; and the, the implicit infallibility of presidents, which has been an accepted thing in America, is badly hurt by this, because it shows that people do things the president wants to do even though it's wrong, and the president can be wrong.

Nixon: [Unclear] Roosevelt's involvement [unclear] World War II [unclear] came out [unclear] he knew what was happening and he did it deliberately. Pearl Harbor thing was undoubtedly [unclear]

Haldeman: You had that one, one article by that admiral what's, his, name that, that, uh, U.S. News carried, that, that told that whole story, and, and there was, but it was never official; it was, and it could be discredited because it was just one guy's testimony. This stuff is out of official files; you can't discredit this stuff.

Nixon: Well [unclear "so much for that"?] the story is out; [unclear] nothing you can do about it [unclear] I guess.

Haldeman: [Unclear, "My"?] feeling is that we shouldn't, at least Haig's urging was that, that we shouldn't do anything about it.

Nixon: [Unclear, "why"? "fine"?]

Haldeman: Until we know what, see what we've got, and that by doing anything we would only escalate it more.

Nixon: I think he's right.

Haldeman: It'll be interesting to see now how the, the other papers, and the TV and all pick this up; but I can't imagine [unclear, both talking] I would think they'd be doing white papers on it; and everybody [unclear]; Christ, it's just grist for the mill, that, that, uh

Nixon: Right.

Haldeman: Won't quit [unclear, both talking]. Because the other [unclear, "interest—"?] see what the *Times* decides to print, and what they don't. They picked an interesting time in, chronologically, they didn't start at the beginning; they chronologically started at Tonkin, and, and it's interesting to, contemplate why [unclear] beginning stuff is all there.

Nixon: [Unclear] with regard to what, with regard to our [unclear]. [Unclear] feel that very strongly [unclear]. Just feel that [unclear] Goddamn — don't give 'em anything! Henry talked to that damn Jew Frankel all the time, he's bad, you know, don't give 'em anything! [Unclear] I don't want anything done [unclear, "obviously"?], I want, I just wanna cool it with those damn people, because of their disloyalty to the country. [Unclear, "Kennedy"?] [Unclear, "hard to understand, legal function, left-wingers, trying to do"?] [Unclear] you could imagine a, you could, you could understand, you could justify say a Goldwater trying [unclear]. [Unclear] politically, this, uh [unclear] makes Johnson look terrible.

Haldeman: Johnson and Rostow [unclear]

Nixon: Pretty bad.

Haldeman: Total disaster.

Nixon: Yeah but on the other hand [unclear], this is a bunch of Goddamn left-wingers [unclear] trying to destroy [unclear]

Haldeman: Because of that, there's going to be, uh. I'm sure, uh, a [unclear] that runs through here that, that will say that we put it out, in, in an attempt to

Nixon: [Unclear]

Haldeman: Yeah. [Unclear] surface, the apparent damage here is not to us; it's to the, it's to the Democrats.

Nixon: Yeah.

Haldeman: But the real damage is

Nixon: Well, I'll tell you what to do, I don't agree with these [unclear] around here. Your, your staff doesn't know anything about things like this, Bob.

You know what I mean, they have good intentions, but not good judgment because they haven't been through enough. [Unclear] tell you what I want done: Get [unclear, "the"? "this"?] story out right away to the [unclear]. [Unclear] get Huston, get all the facts together, get Buchanan and get the story, get Lasky to write it [unclear], or anybody else you can get to write it, write a little story. [Unclear] you know, anybody, doesn't make any difference, but get that story out now, that's, that's what to hand in, charge Brookings, let's get Brookings involved in this, get Brookings involved. Another way to do it rather than having to do that is to have [unclear, "a/the senate/senator"?] arrange a speech on the Senate floor [unclear], and, uh, and charge the whole thing [unclear]. That might be better, than have [unclear, "a column"?]

Haldeman: Senator [unclear]

Nixon: Anybody's all right to do it, except Goldwater [unclear]

Haldeman: Goldwater [unclear, "would do it"?]; Dole probably would [unclear]

Nixon: [Unclear, "Dole shouldn't be used"?], but anybody else. [Unclear] a little fun in Congress [unclear] doesn't have to be a senator. [Unclear] oughta do it, make himself famous, but it has to be done. Let's, let's smoke Brookings out, smoke 'em out, [unclear]. [Unclear, "they can't be sued"?] Charge Gelb, use his name, and the information [unclear] he leaked it, [unclear "charges should be brought against him"?] [Unclear] Huston, is he around? All right, put him to work [unclear]. I wanna [unclear] these people [unclear]. [Unclear] now on the other [unclear], [unclear] you talk to, uh, to Haig about, yeah [unclear] this bad situation over there Haig has got to remember now that we've got to watch, we've got all our [unclear "men and papers"?]. [Unclear] reruns of the wedding [unclear] on TV.

Richard Nixon/John Ehrlichman

June 14, 1971; 7:13 P.M.

Nixon: Hello.

Operator: It's Mr. Ehrlichman calling you, sir.

Nixon: Yeah, OK.

Ehrlichman: Hello, Mr., Mr. President, the attorney general has called a couple times, about these *New York Times* stories; and he's advised by his people that unless he puts the *Times* on notice, uh, he's probably gonna waive any right of prosecution against the newspaper; and he is calling now to see if you would approve his, uh, putting them on notice before their first edition for tomorrow comes out.

Nixon: Hmm.

Ehrlichman: I realize there are negatives to this in terms of the vote on the hill.

Nixon: You mean to prosecute the *Times?*

Ehrlichman: Right.

Nixon: Hell, I wouldn't prosecute the *Times*. My view is to prosecute the God-damn pricks that gave it to 'em.

Ehrlichman: Yeah, if you can find out who that is.

Nixon: Yeah. I know, I mean, uh, could the *Times* be prosecuted?

Ehrlichman: Apparently so.

Nixon: Wait a minute, wait a minute, they, uh, on the other hand. They're gonna run another story tomorrow.

Ehrlichman: Right.

Nixon: Why [unclear] just wait until after that one.

Ehrlichman: Well, his, his point is that, uh, uh, he feels he has to give them some sort of advance notice, and then if they go ahead in disregard, why then, uh, uh, there's no, no danger of waiver; but, uh, if he doesn't give them notice then it's almost like entrapment, uh, we sit here and let them go ahead on a course of conduct and don't raise any objection.

Nixon: Well, could he wait one more day, they have, they have one more day after that I don't know, I don't know.

Ehrlichman: He apparently feels under some, some pressure to, uh, either decide to do it or not do it.

Nixon: Hmm, does he have a judgment himself as to whether he wants to or not?

Ehrlichman: Yeah, I think he wants to, uh, you might wanna give him a call and talk with him about it directly, [unclear] I, I'm not very well posted on this whole thing.

Nixon: How do you feel about it?

Ehrlichman: Well, uh, I'd, I'd kinda like to have a cause of action against them in the sack in case we needed it. I'd hate to, I'd hate to waive something as good as that; but, uh, I don't, I don't know what the, uh, ramifications would be in terms of the hill.

Nixon: Oh hell, I'd, it isn't gonna affect the vote, in my opinion, just [long pause]. Uh-huh.

Ehrlichman: Would you wanna take a call from him and

Nixon: Yeah, yeah, I, I'll call him, I'll call him.

Ehrlichman: Good.

Nixon: OK, thank you.

Richard Nixon/John Mitchell

June 14, 1971; 7:19 P.M.

Nixon: Hello.

Mitchell: Mr. President.

Nixon: What is your advice on that, uh, *Times* thing, John? Uh, you w— you would like to do it?

Mitchell: Uh, I would believe so, Mr. President, otherwise we [unclear] look a little foolish in not following through on our — uh, legal obligations, and, uh

Nixon: Has this ever been done before?

Mitchell: Uh, publication like this, or

Nixon: No [stammering] has the government ever done this to a paper before?

Mitchell: Oh yes, advising them of their, yes, we've done this before.

Nixon: Have we, all right.

Mitchell: Yes, sir. Uh, I would think that.

Nixon: How, how do you go about it, you do it sort of low key?

Mitchell: Low key, you call them, and then, uh, send a telegram to confirm it.

Nixon: Uh-huh, uh, uh, say that we're just, uh, we're examining the situation, and we just simply are putting you on notice.

Mitchell: [Unclear] we're putting them on notice that they're violating a statute, because we have a communication from Mel Laird as to the nature of the documents, and they fall within a statute. Now, I don't know whether you've, you've been, noticed it, but this thing was, uh, Mel is working Nixon: Henry, Henry's on the other, I just, he just walked in, I'll put him on the other line, go ahead.

Mitchell: Uh, Mel, uh, had a pretty good go up there before the committee today on it, and it's all over town, and all over everything, and I think we'd look a little silly if we just didn't take this low-key action of advising them about the publication.

Nixon: Did Mel, did Mel take a fairly, uh, hard line on it?

Mitchell: Uh, yes, he, hahaha, gave a legal opinion, and it was a violation of the law, which, uh, of course puts us [unclear, "where we have to get to"?]

Nixon: Well look, look, as far as the *Times* is concerned, hell they're our enemies — I think we just oughta do it, and anyway. Henry tell him what you just heard from Rostow.

Kissinger: Well, Rostow called on behalf of Johnson, and he said that it is Johnson's strong view that this is an attack on the whole integrity of government, that if you, that if whole ca— , if whole file cabinets can be stolen and then made available to the press, uh, you can't have orderly government anymore. And he said if the president defends the integrity, any action we take he will back publicly.

Mitchell: Well, uh, I, I think that we should take this [unclear]; do some, uh, undercover investigation, and then open it up after your McGovern-Hatfield.

Nixon: Yeah.

Mitchell: Uh, we've got some information we've developed as to where these copies are, and who they're likely to, uh, have leaked them, and the prime suspect, according to your friend Rostow, you're quoting, is a gentleman by the name of Ellsberg, who is a left-winger that's now with the Rand Corporation, who also have a set of these documents.

Nixon: Yeah.

Mitchell: So, uh

Nixon: Subpoena them, Christ, get them.

Mitchell: Uh, so I would, I would think that we should advise the *Times* we will start our covert check, uh, and after McGovern-Hatfield just open it up.

Nixon: Right, go ahead.

Mitchell: That [unclear, "does"?] that agree with you?

Nixon: [Unclear, "yeah"? "yep"?]

Mitchell: All right, sir, will do.

Nixon: Yeah, [unclear]

Richard Nixon/Bob Haldeman

June 14, 1971; 7:56 P.M.

Nixon: Hello.

Haldeman: Yes, sir.

Nixon: Uh, I had an idea that, uh, you perhaps have already thought of, but, uh, it occurred to me that this is something we might pull off, if you get Colson, Magruder, and all the rest really to, uh, zero in on it. Why don't you start a campaign, through letters and, and, at the, at the highest levels to, like Don Kendall and others could call people to have, maybe have NBC have a rerun of the wedding in prime time, what do you think?

Haldeman: I think they've already started doing it, because we were.

Nixon: Have they? But what I meant is, if you could have a fellow like Kendall, and, uh, some of their big advertisers call — Pick one network; zero in on them; have the big adver— , say gee this was a fantastic thing; everybody's talking about it; you ought to rerun it; we urge you to rerun it, just that, don't you think so?

Haldeman: Yep.

Nixon: Because — uh, from all accounts everybody, uh, George Schultz was saying even Mrs. George Meany said she sat up and listened, saw it three times, you know.

Haldeman: I'll be darned.

Nixon: ABC, NBC, CBS. But I can't em— , emphasize Bob that if it were the Kennedys [unclear] rerun every night for three weeks, you know. But — uh,

I really think this ought to be done, uh, and, uh. Who, who else could we put on this, who could, who could we recommend — [unclear] we ought to try to get a major network to do it — Just pick one, one major network — [unclear] uh, maybe NBC, they are the ones that're a little [unclear "goosy"?] at the moment.

Haldeman: [Unclear] makes sense.

Nixon: And they did the, they were the pool camera, and so forth, and, and just let NBC run it. But they've got, they've got to get letters; they've got to hear from top people; they, uh, fellow like Colson can, uh, you know, stick it to them, what do you think?

Haldeman: I think it's a very good idea.

Nixon: And, uh, run it about Tuesday or Wednesday of next week, uh, because I, I really think a helluva a lot of people, the women all want to see the damn thing.

Haldeman: Yeah, yeah. Good, we will do it.

Nixon: And nothing really is negative about it, uh, in terms, don't you agree?

Haldeman: Absolutely, oh yeah.

Nixon: [Unclear] the, uh, the reactions I had during the day are really rather astonishing.

Haldeman: [Unclear] a total plus, all the way.

Nixon: People [unclear] you would least expect it from. Well, put it to Colson, he'll figure out some devious way to get at it.

Haldeman: Right, OK, [unclear]

Richard Nixon/Charles Colson

June 15, 1971; 6:21 P.M.

Operator: Mr. President, I have Mr. Colson for you.

Nixon: Yeah.

Colson: Yes, yes sir, Mr. President.

Nixon: I was thinking on our, uh, this, uh, uh, *New York Times* thing. Uh [stammering] maybe you could generate some support from some of our, our constituent groups on this, you know, uh, like for example, uh, I think veterans and, uh, uh

Colson: Yes, sir.

Nixon: And, uh, fellow like Meany ought to pop up on this one, you know.

Colson: Uh-huh.

Nixon: I mean this, and also I think that on the congressional side that what is really needed, here's a great opportunity for a young congressman, or, uh, a vigorous congressman and or senator or so, to really, uh, go, go, go all out on a thing like this. You know now they're, they have the privilege of the, you know, they, they're, what they have is, uh, of course, uh, they can say anything they please, uh, on the floor, uh, and even though the case is gonna be in the courts.

Colson: Right.

Nixon: We're gonna be stuck with it; but on the other hand, uh, uh, we can't say much; but, uh, but I, I think that it's very important to, to, to build a backfire on these people. Understand, I, I personally think that if we [unclear, "cast"?] this in the right direction. Chuck, this could backfire on the *Times,* I [unclear]

Colson: Oh I think absolutely [unclear]

Nixon: They're playing by their own constituency. Now, we've got to get across several points: one, it's the Kennedy-Johnson papers.

Colson: Uh-huh.

Nixon: [Unclear, stammering] basically, that's what we're talking about, the Kennedy-Johnson papers, and that gets it out of our way. Second, it's a family quarrel; we're not gonna comment on [unclear]

Colson: Yes, sir.

Nixon: But what we have is the larger responsibility, to maintain the integrity of government.

Colson: Wholly unrelated to these papers.

Nixon: [Unclear] and, uh, wholly unrelated [unclear] integrity of government, like as Rogers said in his press conferences, he had inquiries from foreign governments today, as to whether their papers were s— , uh, classified, er, you know.

Colson: Right.

Nixon: And that, uh, this also involves, uh, it really, it really does involve this. I mean it really involves the ability to conduct government, how the hell can a president, or a secretary of defense, or anybody do anything.

Colson: That's right.

Nixon: And, uh, how can [unclear, "he"? "they"?] make a contingency plan if it's gonna be taken out in a trunk and given to a Goddamn newspaper.

Colson: Well, I don't think there's any question Mr. President that [unclear], my own feeling is that it will backfire against the *New York Times,* and we can help generate this. I, [unclear] matter of fact we have a meeting going on at the moment, that I, [unclear] that I came out of to talk to you, but [unclear]

Nixon: All right, fine. Well then, go head and meet.

Colson: No, no, the, the purpose of it is to, uh, generate some editorials in the other newspapers, that are highly critical, like the *Chicago Tribune* ought to give us a good play; the *New York Daily News* should

Nixon: Sure, well, uh, Hearst papers refused to print it.

Colson: That's right.

Nixon: And they [unclear "subscribe"?], they ought to take it on, but the papers, the newspaper establishment ought to come, they've got to say whether they're going to approve this kind of thing. Also, I think a network ought to step up for this one.

Colson: Strangely enough, one of the uh, most outspoken fellows in the meeting that we've just been holding on this very subject is Ray Price, who thinks that, uh.

Nixon: [Unclear, "does he"?]

Colson: The newspapers are [unclear], thinks the *New York Times* is totally irresponsible.

Nixon: Well he's a decent man, that's the reason, he's a man of integrity.

Colson: That's right [unclear]. We can certainly get the veterans groups, uh, [unclear]

Nixon: You know, I think some of them should, they ought to put, cast this, [stammering] listen, uh, the main thing is to cast it in terms of doing something disloyal to the country.

Colson: That's right.

Nixon: This risks our men you know, just, uh, all that sort of thing, secret, uh, things that, uh, aid and comfort to the enemy, I mean, after all, [unclear] Jesus, its, uh.

Colson: I think the *Times* position is indefensible; I think that, uh, it's, it's distinguishable from any other case, in that here we went to them and said you can't publish that; it's a violation of security, and they said to hell with you we're going ahead and publish anyway. So we, we, we would have been very, very remiss in our duties had we not taken whatever legal means were available to prevent it, and, uh, I think we [unclear], I think you'll find a great deal of popular support for, uh

Nixon: If we can generate. Now, they're, they're running the line, Chuck, a right to know, b— , raise that with Price; ask him how do you answer "right to know?" That's of course a Goddamn code-word: right to know, the public has no right to know secret documents.

Colson: Well we've been

Nixon: I don't want to know.

Colson: No, of course not. And [unclear, stammering] you can make the point that, that "right to know" does not include things which will compromise the, either the security [unclear, both talking]

Nixon: [Unclear] which will injure the country, and, and right, and, and freedom of the press does not, is not the freedom to, uh, destroy the integrity of the government, to print, uh, well

Colson: [Unclear] there's never a, [unclear] in these kinds of issues, Mr. President, uh you never get into the argument of, of, uh, degree, it's a, you're, you are either a little bit pregnant or you are not.

Nixon: That's right.

Colson: And if you — if it were the battle plan for the withdrawal of troops next week, that could subject boys to attack, [unclear, "why"?] there'd be no argument about it. Now the integrity of the system as a whole is at stake.

Nixon: That's right.

Colson: You simply cannot allow a newspaper to publish classified documents.

Nixon: If they justify this, then in any future ca— , case, then the publisher of a paper will put himself, that was really what Alger Hiss did, you see.

Colson: That's right.

Nixon: He put himself on a higher pedestal, and said well, the Russians are entitled to know this; and he passed the information, and th— , then

Colson: And the *New York Times*

Nixon: [Unclear, "incidentally"?] was among the papers that supported him in that.

Colson: That's right.

Nixon: Now the point is that here, what the *Times* has done, is placed itself above the law. They say the law provides this, but we consider this an immoral war, it's our responsibility to print it. Now Goddamnit you can't have that thing in a free country!

Colson: [Unclear], that's irrelevant, and the right to know issue doesn't really come in there [unclear, both talking]

Nixon: Well, pour it on them.

Colson: We'll, we'll pour it on, we're coming up with

Nixon: Get some congressmen stirred up.

Colson: We'll get the Congress, and some editorials, and [unclear] our groups.

Nixon: Good.

Colson: Yes, sir.

Richard Nixon/John Mitchell

June 15, 1971; 6:35 P.M.

Nixon: Yeah.

Operator: Attorney General.

Mitchell: Yes, Mr. President.

Nixon: I wondered, uh, if you had any, uh, success with Rogers?

Mitchell: Yes, he's agreeable to do it, we've, uh, got the people from [the Department of] Defense, Justice, and his, uh, counsel over there, Stevenson, working on it.

Nixon: Good. Good.

Mitchell: And he understood the point and, uh, was perfectly happy to do it.

Nixon: And he'll get out a sort of a general statement of some sort?

Mitchell: Yes, sir. It will not, uh, be limited solely [Nixon interjects "Yeah"] to the foreign affairs.

Nixon: I think what is very important in this is to find a way to get some strong [unclear, "language"?] like "a massive breach of security," things of that sort, so that we can get something in the public mind. We're not just interested in making the technical case for the lawyers.

Mitchell: Exactly.

Nixon: Something where they can see what is really involved here is, uh, irresponsible, you know, use some really high flown adjectives [laughs]. That's what I'd hope you can get some people to work on that.

Mitchell: We will, and of course Bill [Rogers] has the understanding that, uh, it'll be sent over to the White House to be looked at 'fore it goes out.

Nixon: All right.

Mitchell: So your phrase coiners and wordmakers [Nixon interjects "Yeah, yeah"] can get a crack at it.

Nixon: Well, I tell you, John, it's, uh, one of those fights where you don't know whether you, you don't know how, gonna affects you, but boy it's one we *had* to make, and by God, it's one I enjoy. These, these bastards have gone too far this time, don't you think?

Mitchell: It is certainly my opinion, you had to do it [i.e., suppress the Pentagon Papers through a prior restraint on the press], and the important thing is to work at it like you've suggested, to try and structure it so that the, uh, import of it, and the nature of it gets through to the public.

Nixon: Right.

Mitchell: And I believe that, um, the press is going to be reasonably fair on this. I don't mean the *Times* and the *Post* but I mean the rest of the press.

Nixon: Hmm.

Mitchell: [unclear word] I think

Nixon: I don't know.

Mitchell: I think they'll understand how far they have gone.

Nixon: Yeah, yeah. My God, they're gonna understand there, there, there is no paper in the country that's for us, we're gonna fight it.

Mitchell: OK [amused].

Nixon: Thanks, John [also amused].

Mitchell: We've got, uh, a good judge on it, uh, Murray Gurfein who was

Nixon: [seemingly in wonderment] *Oh yeah.*

Mitchell: Tom Dewey's, uh, counsel up there.

Nixon: I know him well. Smart as hell.

Mitchell: Yeah. And, uh, he's new, and, uh, he's appreciative, so

Nixon: [Guffaws] Good.

Mitchell: We ought to work it out.

Richard Nixon/Secretary of State William P. Rogers

June 15, 1971; 6:44 P.M.

Nixon: Yeah.

Operator: Secretary Rogers, sir.

Rogers: Yeah, hello Mr. President.

Nixon: You had a long day.

Rogers: [Laughs] Sort of. Boy I started at eight o'clock with a congressman who had been going like a, chicken with my head cut off.

Nixon: But I, uh, wanted to tell ya I just, uh, got a chance to go over the, uh, press thing. I just think you couldn't have done it better. And I think, par— , particularly effective was what you said about the fact that, uh, some foreign, uh, governments have raised questions about the security of their own cables and that sort of thing.

Rogers: Right.

Nixon: Because Goddamnit it's true.

Rogers: Right.

Nixon: How can we, uh, how can they, uh, they wonder if, uh, we, if we allow just a wholesale publication of, declassification I should say. Did you know that the documents, uh, with regard to Pearl Harbor have not been de— , declassified yet?

Rogers: Um hmm.

Nixon: Hell, no.

Rogers: Isn't that something? [Laughs]

Nixon: I know. And, and this thing is uh, uh, we can talk about, somebody placing themselves above the law and all that but, on this, uh, statement thing the, my feeling is that, first, I cannot say anything I feel.

Rogers: That's right.

Nixon: Because it's in the courts. I think you can, solely from a, as a, you know, a foreign

Rogers: Sure.

Nixon: Can you, don't you think so?

Rogers: Sure. I'll be glad to say anything that would be helpful.

Nixon: Well, that's. Tonight, could I ask one thing: uh, I don't know how they got the seating arrangement but, uh, I really talked myself out with [West German

Chancellor Willi] Brandt,[41] I think, and, uh, maybe I think I'll try to, uh, when we talk we'll engage the three of us. We'll just sit and, you know, talk around my, I don't know whether you're on his right or left or however.

Rogers: OK, I'll try to do the talking.

Nixon: [Laughs]

Rogers: I, I, I ran out of stuff to talk to him about too, you know.

Nixon: You know, I know, it's just, uh, they, they, a subject, the only subject left is *Vietnam,* and I, uh, you want to talk about that tonight so we'll, uh, talk a little about Vietnam.

Rogers: [Laughs] You know I just sat looking at television that, the picture came over pretty good on television.

Nixon: Oh, did it?

Rogers: Getting better. But uh, the, uh, dammit they never carry the good things. I said that when they talked about this thing, I imagine the papers, I said that I was not going to get involved in, in passing judgment on it. I said, we've got other things to do. We're trying to get this nation out of war.

Nixon: Yeah.

Rogers: I said we, what I would hope is that when President Nixon leaves office we can have a study made of how we got the United States out of Vietnam. Uh.

Nixon: [Laughs]

Rogers: And, uh

Nixon: Also, as I say, basically this is a family quarrel. We, and I, I think the [Pentagon] Papers could well be called the Kennedy-Johnson Papers is what they are, you know.

Rogers: That's right.

Nixon: Not the McNamara, basically it's McNamara and Clifford.

Rogers: Yeah. That's right.

Nixon: Uh, and uh, I told the boys here just call them Kennedy-Johnson. You know? [Laughs]

Rogers: It's uh, it's really a shameful, shameful [words obscured]

Nixon: I just, I just can't really see how the *Times* could do it. Incidentally, [news magnate] George Hearst told [Nixon adviser] Bob Finch, you know they are the, they, they are the *Times,* uh, syndicate in California and he made the decision there not to print it because he considered it not in the national interest. I thought it would be interesting, I told the boys to check around the other *Times* clients to see how many of them might have done the same thing. [Rogers interjects "Yeah" repeatedly] That's uh, that's uh, that's very damn, uh, uh, good of old George to, not to do that.

Rogers: Yeah. I hope this judge we've got in New York is all right. He, uh, he uh, entered a temporary injunction, I mean.

Nixon: Well, you know who it is?

Rogers: Yeah. His name is Murray Gurfein. I know him well. He's

Nixon: Dewey's man, yeah.

Rogers: He used to be in the office.

Nixon: I just appointed him.

Rogers: I know it, but he's also pretty —

Nixon: Liberal?

Rogers: A little liberal, and he's, uh, I'm sure he would like to cultivate the *Times* so he'll have

Nixon: Well he also may be thinking of going up [among the ranks of the judiciary, which is dependent upon presidential appointment], too.

Rogers: Yes.

Nixon: And he damn well better act well. [Laughs] OK.

Rogers: All right, see you later, Mr. President.

Nixon: Bye. Thank you.

Richard Nixon/Domestic Counselor John D. Ehrlichman

June 16, 1971; 8:22 P.M.

Nixon: Uh, well [name]

Operator: Mr. Ehrlichman.

Nixon: Yeah, John, I just reading the memorandum with regard to the grand jury thing, uh, have you talked to [Attorney General John] Mitchell about it?

Ehrlichman: No, I haven't. I thought I'd better clear it with you first [Nixon interjects "Yeah"], because I didn't know what, uh, what you might have been talking with him about.

Nixon: No, I haven't talked to him about it.

Ehrlichman: I'll, I'll give him a call tonight.

Nixon: Fine. [Pauses] Well what, uh, how does uh, y— , y— , your thought is, uh, uh, to, I mean it isn't a question, I mean the delay is one thing, I think in, in terms of, uh, of uh, reconsidering whether we go ahead with it of course is something else, that's something that, uh, has profound implications you know.

Ehrlichman: [Clears throat] Sure. I understand. It just, it occurred to me today as I read the pleading.

Nixon: Yeah.

Ehrlichman: That, uh, there was a possibility that we could get the kind of an adverse finding on the merits.

Nixon: Yeah.

Ehrlichman: In this, uh,

Nixon: Right.

Ehrlichman: Hearing, that we really ought to have a chance to take a look at. If we once launch that grand jury and then

Nixon: Yeah.

Ehrlichman: Get an adverse ruling from the court and stop it, then I think we've got a, a bad face-off.

Nixon: Well, what does it really get down to? If you delay it does that mean that the *Times* goes ahead and the, uh, the uh, temporary restraining order apparently applies for four days only, is that right?

Ehrlichman: It, it expires, eh, by its terms, uh, uh, Saturday at noon, or one o'clock.

Nixon: So they'd go ahead and print.

Ehrlichman: They'd print the Sunday edition anyway, regardless of what the grand jury did.

Nixon: Yeah. [Short pause] I'm not too concerned about what they print *now*. Uh, the point is you don't want to have an adverse, uh

Ehrlichman: I don't want to appear to be calling off a grand jury in mid-flight.

Nixon: Right. Right. That makes a lot of sense. Well, have you talked to [Robert D.] Mardian about it?

Ehrlichman: No, I'll give, uh, I'll give John Mitchell a call.

Nixon: Whoever you think is really in charge. You know, you might call and chat a bit about it.

Ehrlichman: All right.

Nixon: It's imp— , it's imp— , I agree with you it's important not to have an adverse court ruling right in the face of all this. But, uh

Ehrlichman: Well, I'll get his estimate.

Nixon: We have to go, naturally we have to go forward on the, uh [chuckles], one way or another, on the, not only on the *Times* but on the, person who, obviously the FBI thing can go forward I understand.

Ehrlichman: Right.

Nixon: That, that is going forward, is it not?

Ehrlichman: Right. That's, that's very vigorously under way.

Nixon: Don't you have to, on that, does that require a grand jury, or how does that work?

Ehrlichman: It would, uh, you see, but there isn't any reason why they can't go ahead and finish their investigation and then convene the grand jury on Monday [Nixon interjects "Right," then "Yeah"] instead of on Thursday, and then you'll know what the court did on the PRO [prior restraint order].

Nixon: In eff— , in effect, let the *Times* go ahead and print.

Ehrlichman: Sure. If we get an adverse ruling. I think the chances are that the court will grant an, an injunction, pending a trial on the merits.

Nixon: Yeah.

Ehrlichman: Or he'll extend the PRO, one or the other [Nixon interjects "Yeah"] but, uh, that's just a hunch, because the issues are very complex. I'd be very surprised if he could dispose of them Friday or Saturday.

Nixon: They are complex I know. Yeah. All right, well you, uh

Ehrlichman: I'll talk with them.

Nixon: Be sure to talk to John.

Ehrlichman: Right.

Nixon: Kick it around. OK? Thank you.

CHAPTER FOUR

First Amendment Rights

The Papers in Court

The legal aspects of the Pentagon Papers affair became as thorny as the journalistic and historical matters involved. That is what the lawyers for the *New York Times* anticipated, and that is why there was such a battle within the newspaper's corporate offices before the Pentagon Papers ever went to press. The story of the legal fight has its own rallying points and wrinkles, and the end result was important constitutional law, First Amendment law, but also an important lesson. Floyd Abrams, one of the lawyers involved on behalf of the *Times,* put it this way in 1992: "It seems to me that the enduring lesson of the Pentagon Papers case is something other than its result: it is the need for the greatest caution of and dubiety by the judiciary in accepting representations by the government as to the likelihood of harm of publication and the degree of that harm."[1] Government lawyer Whitney North Seymour never came to that view. More recently legal scholar David Rudenstine has gone back to the position federal officials argued in 1971, that real national security was at stake in the Pentagon Papers case.[2] President Nixon's decision to make the Pentagon Papers leak into a federal case, actually a succession of cases (initially against the newspapers and later against Daniel Ellsberg and Anthony Russo), only marked the beginning of what really became the "affair" of the Pentagon Papers. The lawyers did much of the brick building that elevated this episode of opposition to the Vietnam War into a legal and constitutional milestone for America.

This evolution began with Attorney General John Mitchell's Department of Justice. There the assistant attorney general for internal security, Robert C. Mardian, became the point man in organizing the government response beginning with the June 13 revelations by the *New York Times.* Mardian coordinated with Pentagon Counsel J. Fred Buzhardt to establish a claim that the public release of the Pentagon Papers damaged U.S. national security. Through Monday the fourteenth, the inquiry proceeded while the government let the *Times* publish. This established a pattern of the behavior the Nixon administration was going to ask the courts to suppress.

Legal preparations at the Pentagon are worth a word or two. Fred Buzhardt's inquiry seems to have been rather perfunctory. He interviewed military aides Robert Pursley and Robert Gard; looked for authorization documents in DoD files; and surveyed the shelf list of the volumes of the Pentagon Papers. There is no evidence that Buzhardt spoke to anyone who had actually managed the Vietnam Task Force or anyone who had written a portion of the Pentagon Papers. There is no evidence Buzhardt read the Pentagon Papers himself or had any familiarity with their contents. Buzhardt's blanket assertion as to damage to national security was rendered in an affidavit the same day it was asked for, with time taken out for a personal meeting with Robert Mardian at Justice. Accounts of the affair note only one specific portion of the papers cited as a concern, the notorious diplomatic volumes. The *New York Times* had specified in its very first installment from the Pentagon Papers that it did not have the diplomatic volumes. That did not deter Buzhardt from asserting an extravagant claim of damage.

That evening, June 14, after John Mitchell's telephone call to President Nixon, the Justice Department sent a telegram to the *New York Times* containing a demand that the newspaper cease and desist from publication of the Pentagon Papers. Previous accounts have held that Mitchell and Nixon went over the proposed telegram during their conversation and that Nixon approved it. The transcript of their conversation in the previous chapter demonstrates clearly that Mitchell merely reported affirmatively to Nixon that the Justice Department was about to take this action, and he gave the impression that the telegram was to be a "low key" shot across the bow, so to speak.

In reality the Justice Department telegram was more than Mitchell had represented it to be. The telegram declared that "publication of this information is directly prohibited by the provisions of the Espionage Law, Title 18, United States Code, Section 793," and that further publication would cause "irreparable injury to the defense interests of the United States." Mitchell's telegram ended by expecting both a halt in publication and news from the *Times* that it had made arrangements for the return of the documents. Ironically, the Justice Department telegram was first delivered to a fish company in Brooklyn. It had to be retransmitted to the *Times*.[3]

The newspaper received John Mitchell's telegram as it was preparing to go to press for a further installment of the Pentagon Papers scheduled to appear on June 15. Most of the *Times*'s senior executives and editors had left for the day when the telegram found its way to the office and Robert Mardian called to read the text. This telephone call was routed to Executive Vice President Harding Bancroft at home. Bancroft soon drew in key officials and legal advisers, including James C. Goodale, the newspaper's in-house counsel, whose account of his

Pentagon Papers experience from the viewpoint of the paper appears following this introduction. It was sweltering on the fourteenth floor of the *Times*'s building, where the executive offices were located, since the air conditioning was turned off each day at 7 P.M. The *Times* officials talked with Bancroft on one phone line and to the head of the paper's legal counselors, the firm Lord, Day & Lord, on another. There was the question of a response to make to the Nixon Justice Department and the issue of whether to go ahead with publication. The press time for the next day's issue of the paper was fast approaching. Most favored going ahead, but Bancroft and editor Sydney Gruson pressed the option of stopping the series. The key executive missing that night was Arthur Ochs Sulzberger, off visiting London. Through London correspondent Anthony Lewis, the group finally got "Punch" Sulzberger on the phone, and he approved continued publication of the Pentagon Papers. A cheer went up from the *Times* employees assembled in the newsroom awaiting the results of this meeting.

A response to the Mitchell telegram had still to be crafted. James Goodale jotted down language as ideas shot around the room. Eventually the group assembled a draft and tried to find James Reston in Washington. "Scotty" Reston, it turned out, was at dinner at Robert McNamara's home, where he took the call in the library. Reston then went over the proposed language with the former secretary of defense who had ordered the creation of the Pentagon Papers in the first place. McNamara helped the *Times* here, encouraging the newspaper to make clear it would comply with the decision of the *highest* courts — anticipating this case would reach the Supreme Court — not simply offering to follow the order of any court the Nixon Justice Department might resort to. The *Times* changed its draft, partially following McNamara's advice, noting it would comply with the *final* decision of the courts.[4]

Unknown to newspaper executives, Attorney General Mitchell had separately telephoned Herbert Brownell of Lord, Day & Lord and cautioned him about representing the *Times* in this case. Brownell had been attorney general himself during the Eisenhower administration and had helped draft the 1953 presidential executive order that still remained, in 1971, the basic authority for the government secrecy system. Brownell had thus been a colleague of Vice President Richard Nixon at that time also, and he had been one of Mitchell's law partners before the Nixon administration. Now Lord, Day & Lord suddenly told the *Times* that if the paper proceeded with publication, the law firm would not work for it. Goodale suggested hiring Yale law professor Alexander Bickel and the attorney Floyd Abrams. That became the route taken.

Robert Mardian had prepared a complaint against the newspaper and a list of its editors and reporters, which he dispatched by messenger to federal prosecutors in New York City. The complaint was backed up by affidavits sworn by

Mardian himself and by Buzhardt on the issue of damage to national security. Finally the government presented a draft of the court order it desired to have issued that prohibited the *Times* from continuing to publish excerpts from the Pentagon Papers and required the newspapers to surrender to the court all its materials from that study until the legal issues had been resolved, when presumably the government would take over the documents. These legal papers arrived in Manhattan in time for Justice Department lawyer Michael Hess to go before the federal court for the Southern District of New York about noontime. He appeared in the courtroom of Murray I. Gurfein, a brand new judge whose first case was the Pentagon Papers case.

As seen in the previous chapter, where Richard Nixon discussed Gurfein with both John Mitchell and Secretary of State William P. Rogers, the administration hoped for a sympathetic hearing from Gurfein. In fact they got one, at least initially. Alexander Bickel argued for the *Times* that the government had failed to cite any particular part of the Espionage Act on which to base itself and that the demand for prior restraint was a classic application of censorship. The second part of this argument is clear. Without regard to either argument, Gurfein, once the *Times* rejected a temporary restraining order, issued one anyway. He did not require the newspaper to hand over its photocopies from the Pentagon Papers. Judge Gurfein then set June 18 as the date for a hearing on the government's request for a preliminary injunction.

On the date of the hearing the government's legal problem suddenly mushroomed as the *Washington Post* appeared in print with its own materials from the Pentagon Papers. Not only was the government obliged to take action in the District of Columbia federal courts, but the *New York Times* was given an argument to use against any penalties that might be leveled against it and not the Washington newspaper. The government, needless to say, did move immediately against the *Post*, as it would later against the *Boston Globe* and the *St. Louis Post-Dispatch*.

The essential legal issues resolve themselves into several sets. Without attempting any extensive legal analysis, which several of our commentators will touch on later,[5] it is appropriate to at least outline the sets of issues. Most commented upon at the time — and best remembered later — were the First Amendment issues. The federal government under the Constitution has no authority to block publication and could not abridge the freedom of the press. The government was essentially arguing that the fact the information in the newspaper's possession was secret gave it such a right. The newspapers rejected any such argument. The *Washington Post* hinged its defense precisely on the First Amendment issues, and the New York newspaper added arguments about the separation of powers under the Constitution. One such assertion was that the executive branch, in seeking a court injunction against a newspaper, was attempting to embroil a different branch of government in enforcement of its own wishes without the Congress ever having passed legislation authorizing this novel use of the law. This was the "inherent authority" argument. Another assertion started with the doctrine that the courts traditionally leave national security to the executive so that, as a consequence, they had no power to review the executive's contentions in the Pentagon Papers case. A different argument based on national security was that an injunction against publication was not a proper legal remedy for a breach of the national security. According to legal scholar Joel M. Gora, who participated in creating an amicus curiae brief in behalf of the American Civil Liberties Union, "At the core of the cluster of claims was the concept that the primary and substantive power belonged to Congress, that the president's substantive powers were limited, and that the president could neither usurp significant powers from Congress nor impose serious obligations on the judiciary in his attempt to deal with the national security breach." Consequently, in Gora's view, "the very commencement of the lawsuit was both an affront to legislative primacy and an imposition on judicial restraint and independence."[6]

Occasionally mentioned in oral arguments, though not apparently in written legal briefs, is the issue that defeats any analogy drawn between the Pentagon Papers case and some other publishing or newspaper situation — say of plagiarism, or of stealing and printing a scoop in another paper. That is, the U.S. government by law cannot *own* information, cannot have a copyright in it. Thus an injunction against publication (the practical mechanism that would enforce a prior restraint), which would be a logical remedy in the analogous situation of preventing plagiarism, was not similarly applicable to the Pentagon Papers case.

All the legal arguments had scarcely yet been engaged, however, when Murray Gurfein held his hearing on June 18. Before ever getting to the niceties of the legal arguments, the federal government botched the presentation of its claim that the Pentagon Papers represented some highly sensitive, top-secret gold mine that had to kept from the public to prevent irreparable damage to the national security. Having made this dire allegation, the government proceeded to deliver a set of the Pentagon Papers to the Court's offices on Foley Square and then just left it there. No top-secret security vaults, no escort officers left with the documents, no security guards at all, except whatever the district court itself mandated for the Federal Building. At a minimum, this was a violation of the same rules on the security of classified documents the government was claiming to be defending in the case. Then the government behaved as if all it had to do was to show that the Pentagon Papers were classified documents in order to vest

itself with full authority to repress newspaper revelations and repossess the documents themselves — a clear effort to claim "inherent powers."

In addition to these disturbing actions, the government came into court with
general assertions rather than specific claims to secrecy. Vice Admiral Francis J.
Blouin, the senior military witness, who was deputy chief of Naval Operations
for Plans and Policy, testified that publication would be "a disaster," but under
cross-examination retreated to an assertion that "there is an awful lot of stuff
in them that I would just prefer to see sleep a while longer."[7] A Pentagon official, Dennis J. Doolin, testified that the papers were properly classified, that he
had been the official who had made recommendations to Secretary Laird in
regard to Senator Fulbright's repeated requests to have the Pentagon Papers
declassified, and that he had "specific fact situations" in the papers in mind in
advising against declassification. But Doolin represented himself as having arrived
at the Pentagon (from the CIA) before the Pentagon Papers project had been
finished when he had not (he transferred to DoD in May 1969; the papers had
been turned over to their recipients four months earlier), and then he proved
unable to explain to Judge Gurfein how the government's responsibility to act
positively on declassification, as stated in the Eisenhower-era executive order
that regulated this process, even affected the categories of classified, secret,
and top-secret information. Doolin also admitted the government had made
no positive efforts to declassify the Pentagon Papers. Whitney North Seymour,
the federal attorney who had taken over from Michael Hess the courtroom role
in the case, tried to salvage the situation by suggesting that better discussion
of the classification system, and of specific secrets in the Pentagon documents,
could be had in a secret, closed hearing.

But in the closed hearing that afternoon, according to David Rudenstine,
Doolin's "testimony turned into a disaster."[8] Among other things, after relating
a series of subjects included in the Pentagon Papers that Doolin considered sensitive even though their treatment in the documents was historical, the Pentagon official claimed that it would take persons "trained in the trade" to identify
what in the papers was, in fact, historical.[9] He also claimed the disclosure of any
document would harm U.S. diplomacy, and he made essentially the same claim
regarding the Pentagon Papers' analysis of bombing North Vietnam (which had
ended in 1968) and information regarding U.S. troops in South Vietnam (so-
called order of battle information, similarly dated, since by 1971 the United States
was withdrawing forces from the war). Doolin's pigheaded assertions antago-
nized Judge Gurfein. Deputy Undersecretary of State William B. Macomber,
finally, testified on the diplomatic fallout from the papers, and his message was
simply that diplomacy without confidentiality is more difficult. Macomber spoke

of Australia, Canada, and Russia, and commented directly to Judge Gurfein about the classification system.[10]

The government also made repeated arguments based on the four diplomatic volumes of the Pentagon Papers that were never part of the Ellsberg leak and eventually got the courts to stipulate that the case would be decided as if the negotiating papers were in fact among the leaked materials.

Assistant Attorney General Robert Mardian was present in the courtroom. Mardian attempted to prevent the *Times*'s entire defense team from even taking notes in the hearing. That maneuver failed. Floyd Abrams recalls Mardian's "fiery glance" at the lawyers for the newspapers as they went about their business. The senior lawyer, Alexander Bickel, turned to Abrams and whispered, "Every time Mardian looks at me, I think he wants to have me deported."[11]

In sum the U.S. government showed poorly in its presentation of the Pentagon Papers case. That would be reflected in the decision by Judge Gurfein, rendered on Saturday, June 19, which denied the government the prior restraint order it had sought and vacated the temporary restraint Gurfein had himself issued a few days earlier. The government immediately appealed to the U.S. Court of Appeals for the Second Circuit, which covers New York in the federal judicial system. Here the government submitted with its legal brief a "special appendix" that contained numerous assertions labeling particular portions of the text of the Pentagon Papers as being highly sensitive, thus requiring the protection of secrecy. The appendix, which had not been submitted to Judge Gurfein, was accepted by the appeals court, even though, as Rudenstine puts it, "it is highly inappropriate during an appeal to supplement the factual record, since the appeal is supposed to be based on the facts developed at trial."[12] The appeals court found for the government on June 22, sending the case back to Judge Gurfein for reargument.

In the meantime the dam had broken on the Pentagon Papers with publication in the *Washington Post* and, as the court cases began, other places as well (see the discussion in chapter 1). The government moved immediately against the *Post* on the day of its initial publication, the same day as the first court hearing in New York. Assistant Attorney General William H. Rehnquist, today the chief justice of the Supreme Court, called the newspaper to demand that its lawyers appear at the Federal Court for the District of Columbia that afternoon. The Court stayed open late to accommodate this government move, and the case was assigned to Judge Gerhard A. Gesell. After an initial hearing Judge Gesell denied the government a temporary restraining order, but warned the *Post* that it could be vulnerable to criminal prosecution. The government immediately went to the District of Columbia Circuit Court of Appeals, which reversed Gesell's decision, effectively stopping the *Post* from publication, and ordered the lower court to hold a hearing and decide the case on June 21.

At that hearing, still with Judge Gesell presiding, the *Washington Post* relied upon First Amendment arguments. The government continued the obsession with secrecy it had demonstrated in the New York legal proceedings. As *Post* lawyer William R. Glendon recounts, "Some evidence, it was alleged, was so sensitive it could not be shown to defense counsel. Judge Gesell responded that the government need not bother showing it to him either, and we saw the evidence. [The night before the hearing] I was shown some draft government affidavits as part of the discovery, but was told I could not keep my notes derived from them. A public brawl ensued and I kept the notes."[13] At the hearing the government affidavit, from Admiral Noel Gayler, who headed the National Security Agency, did not ultimately impress Judge Gesell very much at all. Gesell found in favor of the newspaper. Again the government appealed immediately to the Circuit Court of Appeals.

Attorney General John Mitchell now decided to bring up the government's biggest guns. He turned to the solicitor general of the United States, Erwin N. Griswold, to argue the Pentagon Papers case before the D.C. Circuit (and then the Supreme Court as well). Griswold tried to avoid the assignment, maintaining he had no familiarity with the documents at issue or with the applicable law. Mitchell insisted and Griswold went before the full Court of Appeals. He made a presentation that once again referenced diplomacy and mixed in the rules of copyright infringement, for at least two questionable elements. In an effort to strengthen their case, as Whitney North Seymour had done in the appeals court in New York, in Washington the government made an effort to strengthen its evidentiary presentation, this time at the argument before the full Court of Appeals on June 23.

During the argument the government, with, as Glendon puts it, "appropriate fanfare," introduced a document into evidence that was a National Security Agency (NSA) communications intercept from the Gulf of Tonkin incident. Glendon recalls, "It was classified top secret, and it was impressive." The Gulf of Tonkin incidents and the congressional resolution that had followed were matters of great controversy in American politics. Congress had investigated the facts of the U.S.-Vietnamese naval encounter, including the NSA intercepts, and had just published a committee report on the matter. To pick up from Glendon: "We were waiting in an anteroom in the Court of Appeals while the Court deliberated. We had with us George Wilson, the *Post*'s Pentagon reporter, who had been puzzling over this dispatch. Finally, George, with a grin on his face, called me over and pointed out the identical dispatch printed in the public section of a Congressional Committee Report he happened to have with him."[14] Glendon sent the document into the panel of jurists to supplement the record like the government had been doing. With so much made of the Tonkin Gulf radio intercepts, here and elsewhere, history should note — and it is recorded here for the first time — that the Pentagon Papers analyst who wrote the study's section on the Gulf of Tonkin incidents, William R. Simons, reports that he had no access to the NSA radio intercepts in his work on the Pentagon Papers.[15]

The D.C. Circuit Court ruled against the government, permitting the *Washington Post* to resume publication of the Pentagon Papers. It also rejected the government's petition for a rehearing of the case. The government had lost in Washington and won in the Second Circuit in New York, but there the *New York Times* appealed to the Supreme Court. The government appealed in the Washington case. The Supreme Court accepted the appeals and joined the cases as *United States v. New York Times Co.* (403 U.S. 713 [1971]). That became the Pentagon Papers case in the Supreme Court. The lawyers had only one day to prepare their briefs and arguments.

Once again, Solicitor General Griswold argued the case for the government. Griswold filed an open brief and a secret one, the latter yet another selection of items from the Pentagon Papers that allegedly required the protection of classification which, for good measure, included also the "Special Appendix" that had been filed with the Second Circuit Court of Appeals. Both newspapers filed open briefs and sealed briefs. The open briefs emphasized the constitutional issues and made general arguments about secrecy, which the Pentagon Papers might require except for its nature as an historical document. The *Washington Post*'s sealed brief spent considerable space refuting the testimony of witnesses at the New York and Washington hearings on the district court level, and the affidavits submitted by diplomats, military officers, and Pentagon officials. The *New York Times*'s sealed brief has apparently been lost.

Oral arguments before the Supreme Court focused on the larger legal issues and on certain features of government secrecy. The question most in the government's favor, to which neither of the newspapers' lawyers could respond adequately, came from Justice Potter Stewart, who asked what the Court should do if it opened up the papers and found something whose "disclosure would result in the sentencing to death of one hundred young men."

In effect, despite its missteps in the presentation of evidence, the government won the argument over whether the Pentagon Papers contained information that was properly classified (we shall take up this matter explicitly in the next chapter). As *Times* attorney Floyd Abrams put it, "A majority — I repeat a majority — of the Supreme Court was persuaded that there was such a threat [that is, a threat to national security posed by publication]."[16] By a six to three margin, the Supreme Court *nevertheless* held, on June 30, 1971, that the government had not met the "heavy burden" of showing justification for a prior restraint, and the *New York Times* and the *Washington Post* could not be stopped from publishing the Pentagon Papers. First Amendment freedom of the press was the decisive factor in the short decision, although the nine accompanying concurring opinions and dissents also cited other matters. The government quickly abandoned its legal actions against the *Boston Globe* and the *St. Louis Post-Dispatch.*

To complete this chapter, we present the commentaries of four individuals who either stood at the center of the legal battles over the Pentagon Papers, observed and reported that fight in the press, or studied it in history. James C. Goodale, the in-house counsel for the *New York Times,* tells of his role in the first stages of the case, when the *Times* decided to defy Attorney General Mitchell and go on publishing, and he had to find new legal representation for the newspaper. William R. Glendon, counsel for the *Washington Post,* gives an overview of the progress of the whole case from the standpoint of his newspaper. Sanford Ungar, at that time the reporter who covered local courts for the *Washington Post,* describes the intricacies of reporting this legal case for the public. Finally, law professor David Rudenstine comments on the legal cases and the issues involved.

James Goodale

This happened so long ago that I feel like I'm ninety years old. I never thought that I was engaging in an act of civil disobedience, and I never had a doubt as to what the law was. I must say, I didn't have much doubt as to the way the case was going to come out, too. But I was one alone.

I was told by the *Times* that they had some classified documents with a wink and a nod. That's all they said. I knew that meant I had to look the law up. And I did. I was staffed with three lawyers who were doing other things. And I had a summer associate from Columbia.

When we looked at the law, we found three things: one, an Espionage Act; a law that says that you stamp documents classified, top-secret, so forth and so on; and last, a famous case called *Near v. Minnesota,* which held, generally speaking, that you can't get injunctions against the press.

I starting parsing the first, the Espionage Act, and I was confused that when I read it; I couldn't seem to fit the facts of what we were doing. I didn't know at that point that when the act had been passed, it was passed to cover espionage. And the testimony on the floor of the Senate made it very clear that the First Amendment would not permit it to do anything else. But since I was staffed with one summer associate, all I had to do was look at the language. And the language told me, regardless of what legislative history was, you can't use it.

The stamping act, where you've been in the army, you stamp documents classified, seemed to be totally irrelevant, applied to the people in the government, didn't apply to the *New York Times.*

And with respect to getting injunctions in court, I had a lot of experience in that. I had been general counsel to the *Times* for seven or eight years; I had read all the cases. I knew there were no federal cases ever granting an injunction against the press in the history of the United States up to that point.

So, I knew what the three sources of the law were. And I then had to figure out where the risks were. And the risks were, number one, I thought, getting an injunction. And number two, there was some slight risk that there would be a criminal prosecution. But I didn't think that was going to be a real risk because when the Pentagon Papers were given to the jury, I didn't think the jury was going to convict. That was just a judgment. It was a risk. I was really worried about the injunction.

But at this point, I hadn't seen the papers. I did all the analysis without seeing the papers. So, one day, they were rolled in to me, cart after cart after cart. And they said, here you are, go read them. Well, I didn't know what to do. But I did start reading them. And I read the first few chapters. They pointed out a history of deception, which had begun so early in the history of what we are talking about, that is to say, right after World War II. And I found that history fascinating, because I didn't know about it. So, I started to ask myself, can the government stop us from publishing this? Then I looked at the sources of the information I was reading: *New York Times, New York Times, New York Times,* see page, *New York Times,* see page. I said, oh, come on, the government is going to go into court and stop the *New York Times* publishing from something it's already published? It can't be.

I then had to take all of the above, which lawyers do. They take the facts, the law; they usually take them the other way around, but my case is a peculiar situation. And I had to make some judgments. Now, I didn't come at this as a naïf. I am an old-time liberal Democrat from age twelve, an FDR fan from age seven, and a Richard Nixon hater from the days that he ran against Jerry Voorhis and Helen Gahagan Douglas. And at one point in time, I could have told you the circulars that Richard Nixon had sent out, either in the Voorhis election or the Douglas election, that brought him the bad reputation that he had in liberal circles. I knew Richard Nixon like a book.

I also had a lot of experience with classification. I knew what the armed services thought and the government thought about classification; I was familiar with the idea of overclassification. My judgment was that if we published this in installments, the government was going to come in and enjoin us, no matter what, because the government had to protect the sanctity of the classification system. They couldn't let a huge leak like this go by.

My theory was the Joint Chiefs would go to Laird. Laird would go to Nixon, and Nixon would let it rip. I'm off a little bit, but I'm not off that much.

I hadn't figured Henry Kissinger's role in this, when he had played a prominent role. But I don't care what Henry Kissinger's role was.

I knew what Richard Nixon had done. I knew what he had done in the Alger Hiss case. By the way, I think he's guilty [in Watergate]. I knew he was going to bring an injunction. I told the *Times* that was going to happen and that they ought to consider publishing it all at once. Because, if they publish it all at once, you can't get an injunction, can you?

And from a criminal point of view, if you go into the grand jury, then you've got a sort of funny case. He's got to show this is what they published. And look at it. And then they can't go to the other parts of the Pentagon Papers and say, look how much this other material hurt national security; they can look at the newspaper itself.

Well, a side point. Did I think the material that I read damaged national security? Well, I confess, I did not read all of the Pentagon Papers. But the material that I read, and more relevantly, the material that was published by the *New York Times,* in my judgment, did not damage the national security, and was, in a sense, a bunch of hokum. However, I will admit, the government certainly could have come to the point of view that it thought it damaged national security. I think that is David Rudenstine's point of view, and that's why I concluded, indeed, that the government was going to take the action that it took.

Well, it seems pretty simple, doesn't it? When I brought this point of view to the management of the *New York Times,* they did not take it kindly . . . and in fact, did an end run around me. They went directly to the law firm where I had started, Lord, Day & Lord, to the ex–attorney general of the United States, Herbert Brownell Jr., and to a former president of the New York City Bar Association, which is a big deal in New York City, and asked them for their advice.

I don't know what they based their advice on. I honestly don't think they could have looked at the law, thought about the First Amendment, or done a lot of other things they should have done. They advised the *Times* it was criminal to publish the Pentagon Papers and that they, the lawyers, would find it a criminal offense to even read the Pentagon Papers.

And what ensued thereafter, was, my superior and I had a series of arguments; we went back and forth, and it really just drove me crazy. I had to leave the *Times* right in the middle of this because my wife had a daughter, I had a daughter. I went to her in the hospital, and I said, I'm sorry to tell you this, because we just have new financial obligations, but I'm going to resign from the *New York Times* unless they publish the Pentagon Papers. There is no point in being there if I'm going to be run around.

Well, I came back after a short respite with my wife. I found that, for reasons not entirely clear to me to this day, all of a sudden, the idea of publishing was going forward, even though outside counsel had advised that it was criminal. I looked at the material to be published. I looked at the documents that went along with the prose. I was worried about publishing the basic documents that went along with the prose. But after I read them, I wasn't so worried, because I really thought they were rather outrageous. And off the publication went to not much of an interested audience on a Sunday before the week in which the litigation began.

I came back on Monday. Guess what? Laird went on television and said, well, our national security system is at risk. And I said, oh, here were go again. I was very lucky that day that Alexander Bickel had come into my office, because we were working on another case involving a *New York Times* reporter called Earl Caldwell. And we went off to lunch with Reuven Frank, who is the head of NBC. On the way over, he said, that was a great thing that you did. And I said, great. He says, in fact, it's a lot easier case than the one you've given me on Earl Caldwell. We had lunch. I went back, waiting for all hell to break loose. And it hadn't. I went home, and it was about 7:00. I said, jeez, you know, Laird went there, I know something is happening. So, I called my superior. I said, anything going on? He said, yeah, we've got a telegram here saying that we ought to stop publication. Well, do you think I better come over? Yes, you better come over. So, I went over to the *New York Times*. I walked into a room where Abe Rosenthal, Harding Bancroft, my superior, and Sydney Gruson were all yelling and screaming at each other as to what they do with respect to obeying or not obeying what was in the telegram. I inserted myself. I said, well, you can't obey a telegram. I mean, there is a question whether you should even obey a temporary restraining order or an injunction. I mean, that's an open question. But in this case it would be foolish not to obey it. But a telegram? And so, we went back and forth. And somebody said, well, let's call Punch Sulzberger. Punch Sulzberger was in London then; he had left just before the publication. We woke him up, got him out of bed. And they screamed and yelled. Finally, Punch turned to me. He said, well, what do you think we should do? Will there be any more liability for us if we go ahead and publish? I said, I think there may be a tiny bit more liability, but I don't think you really have liability for publishing. He said, well, let's go.

And now the question was — since the government had threatened in that telegram to go into court the next day — what we are going to do with respect to legal representation? After a long wrangle, because it took time to make decisions on the top of the *New York Times*, we ended up talking to Herbert Brownell at about 11:00 at night. And I said, Herb, you looked great at the Nixon wedding. The Nixon wedding had been the Saturday before. I said, I expect to see you in court with some of your pals from Lord, Day & Lord. He said, absolutely not. I said, absolutely not? I had a little perspiration on my brow at that point. He said, well, I drafted that classification document that you talked about. If I go into court, I'll have to defend it. I can't, because I drew it.

I said, well, OK. But I didn't really believe him. I don't think he wanted to have anything to do with the case. He received a call from John Mitchell earlier in the day, effectively telling him that it probably wouldn't be a very good idea for the Republican Party if he were in the case. So, then what to do? Well, Alexander Bickel was their only hope, but they couldn't find him.

It was then midnight, and I knew that we were probably going to be in court the next morning at 10:00 or 11:00. What to do? I said, oh, the hell with it. I know I know as much as they know about it, having been through the attorney general of the United States, the city bar association president, they didn't know anything about it. I had been thinking about it and all these issues for seven or eight years, generally — this one, particularly, for three or four months — I'll argue it myself. There was only one problem with that: I'm not a litigator.

I went out of there, went home, and about 2:00 in the morning, the people in the newsroom called me and said we found Bickel. I said, great. I got Alex on the phone. He said, absolutely, I'll do it. I said, well, if you get this Floyd Abrams at Cahill Gordon to join you, I think we've got a team. And off we went. And the rest is, as they say, history.

William Glendon

When I started thinking about this, I was concerned about recollections of a thirty-year-old matter, particularly at my age. I was reassured, though, by a friend, who told me, it's all right, Bill, the short-term memory goes first. So, I hasten to say, I've drawn heavily on my friends and their very authoritative books.

This case was, you call it a case, it was a constitutional case, it certainly was. It was a very, very difficult experience. The difficulty arose because of the fact that for the first time in our history, for two hundred years, the presses had been stopped by the government. And they'd been stopped by temporary restraining orders, prior restraints, right in the teeth of the First Amendment. That produced the crazy pace that we went through. Our case rocketed from the district court to the Supreme Court in eight days.

Sleep was not considered a palatable subject. Everybody suffered. The judges, the lawyers, the witnesses were all under terrible pressure — pressure because of these prior restraints, which held up publication. On the other hand, you have to say, well, if they hadn't held them up, the case might have become moot. I'm not trying to justify them. It put a terrible onus on everybody and it was very difficult.

I came down from New York on a Saturday. The injunction, the temporary restraining order issued by the court, said we would go to trial on Monday morning, and it would be completed by 5:00 that night, a rather unusual provision. I contemplated, I saw a number of problems; we all did.

The first problem that occurred was, there was a large attitude, a substantial portion of the country thought the papers had been stolen. That was the popular word at the time — and that we were indeed destroying the national security. I can illustrate that point by a remark of an old uncle of mine whom I was very fond of, who, when I later inquired on his attitude on the subject, said, you ought to be locked up, the whole lot of you. That, I think, was an attitude that prevailed around the country.

Among the problems we had, and I'm not trying to exaggerate to make it any more difficult than it was, the government didn't know what we had, and we didn't know what the government was talking about. That really was what we got from the government, and I'm not trying to criticize here, so, my view is the bad guy here was the classification system. It was massive overclassification. None of the Pentagon Papers had been declassified. Many of them went back to the 1940s.

The government believed its own rhetoric. Secrecy was a way of life in the South. We had to deal with that. The government had an obsession with secrecy. Everything was secret; the hearings were secret; the briefs were secret. For example, one trial in the district court, we had an open hearing and we had a secret hearing. When we had a secret hearing, the doors were locked and the windows were blacked out. I remember saying to the government lawyer, I don't quite understand this blacking out of the windows, is there a Russian spy who can lip-read, because it made no sense.

There were a series of substantial problems we had to face. There was no legal help. When you went to the books to try to get some legal help, the closest we came was the *Near v. Minnesota* case that's been mentioned by Jim. The *Near* case really wasn't on point, but there was some language in there that said there could be prior restraints in wartime for such things as obstructions to the recruiting service, sailing dates of transports, things like that.

But it was dicta: it wasn't necessarily a decision. However, it did come from the Supreme Court. That was the only guideline we lawyers had to worry about as to how we would go forward and how we would handle the case.

The problem of problems with the documents was pervasive, because Ellsberg, in his wisdom, had not turned over all the papers, but the *Times* had more papers than we did. He had held back from both of us a serious part of the Pentagon Papers. The government didn't know, and we wouldn't tell them what we had. We had to finally give an inventory so that the government could get some idea of what they were. The government wouldn't tell us what they were so hot and bothered about, and it was a real problem.

When I came down here, my first thought was, we got to find out what this is all about. We got to get what we lawyers call discovery. We had to go to the judge (they wouldn't do it voluntarily) and get an order requiring them to turn over their draft affidavits. There were a lot of problems. We went to trial at 8:00 on a Monday morning. We went down to the Department of Justice on Sunday night to review the discovery that the government had been forced to disclose. They didn't disclose much. They gave us a draft affidavit, which, essentially, could be changed. I was sitting there trying to take some notes, and I was told, after, I could take the notes but I couldn't keep them. Something snapped. I said, I'm going to keep these notes. So, it was a big FBI agent assigned to me, he had the biggest arms I have ever seen in my life. I said, I'm going to keep these notes. I'm going to leave here. I know you are going to try to stop me. There is going to be a hell of a fight. I'll lose it. And when I get to court on Monday morning, I'm going to tell the judge I was beat up by the Department of Justice. So, I got the notes. We made a compromise, which I was very glad to do, that I would get the notes, but I would be responsible for their security. I lost them, I suppose, someplace.

We went to trial, a Monday morning, rather unprepared — not the way a lawyer likes to go to trial. Right from the start, the government exasperated Judge Gerhard Gesell. They took positions, and I don't mean this critically. They took it because of the nature of the claim. Everything was classified; nothing could be discussed. Nothing could be printed, although, as has been stated, there were presidential speeches, which, generally, are in the public domain, newspaper articles, etc. But everything was classified.

That was their opening gun. They retreated throughout the trial a series of retreats. At one point they initially said, well, maybe we could take a look and see if we could declassify it and so forth, but that's where we came from.

One of the government's rather strained positions, I thought, was they had an affidavit. This affidavit was so secret, I was reminded of the British security system. They have something called hush most secret, and this one should have been hush most secret. It was so secret I couldn't see it. They couldn't show it to me. I had a security clearance, I was cleared, I couldn't see it. Judge Gesell handled the problem rather briskly. He said, don't bother showing it to me either.

Again, I saw the affidavit. The government took, again, I think, through force, rather than because they wanted to, some strange positions, which did bother the judge. They said that the defendants, the individual defendants, Mrs. Graham, the editors, the reporters who wrote the story, couldn't be in the courtroom because it was top secret. The judge rejected that. They took other positions; it just didn't make any sense.

Their first witness [Dennis J. Doolin] really ended the case for them. He was a gentleman who had testified in a New York hearing, and we had some information about him. We had the advantage, a real advantage. The government didn't put on any witnesses only; they just put in affidavits. That allowed us to sort of cherry pick who we would like to interview, depose, question, cross-examine. And this witness had not done very well in New York, and he didn't do well in Washington either, because he exaggerated the claims.

There were six blue chips [most sensitive secrets] referred to in the Pentagon Papers. These six blue chips were the negotiating position that the United States would take if it [were to] withdraw from Vietnam. His position was this would destroy, impact, damage the national security. The six positions, I won't name them all, were such brilliant thoughts as, cease the bombing, withdraw our troops from Vietnam, so, this annoyed Judge Gesell enormously. He said, a high school senior could figure this one out. And that was the end of that.

They talked about serious impact on troop movements. Now, remember, this is 1971; the papers ended in 1968. How do you talk about current troop movements in 1968? It turned out, what the witness was talking about was movement of troops from the United States to Vietnam, top secret. That annoyed the judge. In other words, things like that. So, that part of the case went well.

They had a very good witness on diplomacy [William B. Macomber]. He proved that diplomats like to deal in secrecy — that diplomacy needs secrecy. That foreign nations, people who don't have the First Amendment, would be upset, because we couldn't keep a secret. There was not much dispute about that. At some point during the trial, the government started this retreat and announced they might be able to consider declassifying.

Well, anyway, Judge Gesell had about a half an hour to pull together his thoughts and issue an opinion. He did a good job. He declined to issue an injunction. He used the standard that the government would have to prove that there was going to be a breach in diplomatic relations, a war, an armed attack; this was the definition of what top secret was at the time. He used that, and said, none of that is here, so, no injunction.

Then we were up in the Court of Appeals. There, I should mention, my thought was that the government created a miasma of secrecy — that everything they did was designed to make it look as though the fate of the nation was probably at risk. This was the thing they were trying to do.

In the Court of Appeals, who shows up but the distinguished, and I mean this seriously, Erwin Griswold, solicitor general of the United States. He doesn't appear in the courts of appeals. He argues cases in the Supreme Court. But that showed the importance of the matter. Well, the poor man, and I don't use that in any pejorative sense, because I had great respect for him. He had been assigned — I thought I was in trouble and was harassed and badgered by the time constraints — the case that morning by the attorney general. He had time to walk down to the courthouse and think what he was going to argue. And he argued things that I was glad to hear him argue, because they didn't have anything to do with the case, like the copyright laws.

He was still arguing that in the Court of Appeals, that's, as we know, not much to do with the First Amendment.

A couple of things happened, though, in the Court of Appeals that were interesting. General Griswold announced that the government was prepared to conduct a joint task force to study what could be printed by the papers. They would go right up right away if we would agree not to publish during that interim. I didn't have to consult with my clients to reject that. I said that was the government by handout, and we wouldn't do it.

Another interesting thing that really impacted, I think, quite substantially, on the government's case: while the court was deliberating, we were summoned down to sit in an anteroom in case they needed to talk to us. There had been a document introduced at the district court that was troublesome. It was a top-secret document. It was a dispatch [about the Gulf of Tonkin affair] and it gave us a lot of problems. We couldn't do anything about it. We are sitting in the anteroom and we had with us George Wilson, the *Post* Pentagon reporter. George had been troubled by this, and he had been worrying about it. All of a sudden he called me over, big grin on his face. He had a book, public hearings and congressional public hearings. In the public hearings of the congressional, whatever, committee, is, guess what, the top-secret document that had been played before us and was giving us so much trouble. I grabbed it and drafted a motion to supplement the record, which you really shouldn't do, you can't do, because you try cases in the district court and the record in the Court of Appeals. I showed it to the government attorney, who was too shocked to object, I guess, and shipped it in to the judges, via the clerk. I think it probably helped.

The Court of Appeals, on Wednesday, came down with a five to two decision, saying, the government hadn't met its heavy burden, and therefore, they affirmed Judge Gesell. There was a dissent by two judges. Judge Wilkie said that his reading of the papers showed he thought there could be a lot of loss of lives, serious damage to the national security.

This bothered the majority, who do the unusual stuff; they were coming out the next day with an amendment to their opinion on which they said, we disagree with Judge Wilkie. Obviously, there were some tensions going on in the Court of Appeals.

So, after that, we headed for the Supreme Court. We were told on Friday afternoon that we would be there on Saturday at 11:00 with our briefs, secret, and open at the ready. We knew from the proceedings that there was a sharp division in the Court. Four had voted to affirm, let the papers print, and four had wanted to hold a hearing until September. That would have been a terrible defeat, because we would have lost momentum; public interest would have lost, the cases probably would have become moot. Justice Stewart saved the day by saying unless they had immediate hearing, he would vote to let the papers print it right away. So, that took care of that.

We got to the Supreme Court; the argument went reasonably well. I had always thought there was a lot of legality. There were issues about power, and how could the government sue, and was there a statute. But it always seemed to me this was really a fat case.

If there was something really bad, something akin to a terrible thing that happened in World War II when the paper published it, we were breaking the Japanese code, something like that nature. We were in trouble. Otherwise, I felt confident we'd win.

We got out there, and we got into trouble in another score. Professor Bickel was arguing first. Justice Stewart said to him, supposing, after we look at these documents, we find something that surely convinces us publication of these papers will lead to the deaths of one hundred young men whose only fault was, they were twenty-one years old and had a low draft number. What do we do? I was sitting close to Bickel, and I heard a "uph," and I did the same thing to myself. So, I turned to my partner, Roger Clark, and I said, I got to keep listening to this argument, see if you can figure out an answer. That's called delegation. So, when I got up, there was no way to answer the question. It was a miserable question, a brilliant question. We weren't about to give way and say, oh, just don't print it. The other side of you said, oh, you are going to die, you are just a callous theoretician. So, as I got up, I turned to Roger, who had been sitting there. I said, well, and he said, punt. That was about what happened. I was a little lucky. I was just able to say, well, there's nothing like that in the record, and I kept at that. The court came down with a six to three decision, per curiam, just saying again, it [the government] hadn't met a heavy burden. Each justice wrote his own opinion, and you probably all are familiar with them. Several of them, I think probably the majority, spoke of their enthusiasm for the government concerning criminal prosecution, although they did say there wasn't anything had been published so far that was criminally liable. I think that was a caveat to the press to watch your step, you know, from what you report.

Anyhow, that was the end of the case. One final postscript: two weeks after the case was over, I had turned to other things. I got a call from Roger Cliff. It was a brief [unintelligible] and he says, guess what? I said, what? We had agreed to turn the papers back to the government after we finished with them. So, Roger says, "The *Washington Post* has lost the Pentagon Papers." I hung up and I never inquired whether they've ever found them again.

Sanford Ungar

Ten years from now, on the fortieth anniversary of the publication of the Pentagon Papers, God willing, we'll all be together and talk about them again. I have, since I got the call this time, tried to do some original thinking, if there be room for that, about why people still assemble around this issue and this topic that occurred, for me, at least, more than half a life ago. And why it is so important to do this.

I actually made an attempt at explaining this to my seventeen-year-old son last night when he said, are you still talking about that? My own personal relationship to this issue has uniquely to do with the conflict between the government and the press. I had never been to Vietnam until last year, when I finally got to go as the director of Voice of America, and that was a very meaningful opportunity for me.

I'm still, like so many other people, working on understanding what happened to all of us in that Vietnam War period. To quote Dan Ellsberg quoting Bill Buckley, I was very young at the time. I was twenty-six years old by just a few days when the Pentagon Papers were published. The main meaning of the Vietnam War for me, at that time, quite apart from everything else, was that a lot of my friends and classmates were going to fight in Vietnam, and they were being killed. It was a profound thing.

I was draft exempt because my brother had been killed in World War II. There were many times when I felt guilty about being draft exempt because so many of my friends were affected by it.

I had been at the *Washington Post* less than two years at the time the Pentagon Papers were published. I had this extraordinary good fortune of being assigned to a beat, a term you don't hear much anymore. My beat was the U.S. District Court and Court of Appeals, the federal courthouse, down at Third and Constitution. I would go every morning. I'd inherited that beat from somebody else, who, incidentally, went off to cover Vietnam. It was a local beat on the metro staff of the paper.

At that time, if you were assigned to a beat like that, whatever happened on your turf, you were in charge of covering. I mean, if an assassination had happened on the steps of that courthouse, it would have been my story. So, when the *Washington Post,* my newspaper that I had been working for, for less than two years, was sued on my beat, it was my story, and quite a big story, at that.

I was plunged into it. I think there were several nights when I slept one or two hours, if at all, trying to familiarize myself enough with these documents.

Jim Goodale said he doubts very many people have read all of the documents; I'm sure Dan has read them several times, among others. One of the great advantages I had at this time was that I knew the judges, and perhaps more important, I knew their clerks.

I was in a great position. Some of these same people who were law clerks in that courthouse at the time, now, thirty years later, are all in impressive jobs and so on, but I knew them. And that was a real advantage, because I could get material faster than anybody else who had converged on that courtroom.

We had a seedy old pressroom. I don't know whether it has been improved or not. In that time, the couches were overstuffed and split and spilling out. That same Frederick Beebe, who was chairman of the board of the *Post* at the time, hung out in the pressroom while the hearings were taking place, and he looked over my shoulder while I wrote these stories. Now, if you have any doubt that at that time a barely twenty-six-year-old junior reporter at the *Washington Post* didn't generally get to hang out with the chairman of the board in a seedy pressroom where the stuffing was coming out of the couches . . .

It was a very interesting experience to try to explain to him what was going on and when we could expect some information. The interesting thing is that this case, for me, as for so many other people in this room, had a huge impact on my life. This is something I've been thinking about for a long time.

My book on the legal battle [within] the government and [between] the government and the newspapers has now been published four times. I often think of it as one of the two things that happened early in my career as a journalist that really had the biggest effect on me. The other one was being assigned to Paris to work for UPI during the worker student revolt in France in 1968.

I think, for a kid from a small town who thought that the authorities never lied, and the police always protected us, and the public officials always did their best, these two events combined to change my perspective on life a tremendous amount. The one thing that I would stress very hard and really urge people to look at: I think it is very difficult for people today to understand the climate that existed in 1971 in this town between the media and the Nixon administration. It is very easy to make light of it and dismiss it. We really felt it at that time.

I went to work for the *Post* in the fall of 1969, and that was when the really big antiwar demonstrations started. By the spring of 1971, I think we, my very particular generation of cohorts, felt that this city was in a state of siege. I think we felt that there was a serious threat to freedom of the press at that point. The Pentagon Papers were published just about six weeks after the May Day demonstrations. I don't know if people remember those extraordinary events here in Washington.

I wrote a big piece under the guidance from one of the editors at the *Washington Post* about how the law was broken to enforce the law on the occasion of that May Day — hundreds of people were picked up on their way out to or back from lunch because of the way they looked, because they had a beard or had long hair, or were in some way suspect. Jerry Wilson, then the chief of police of Washington, D.C., was thought to be a top, leading candidate to replace J. Edgar Hoover as director of the FBI, if only Hoover could somehow be removed from that position. Nixon wanted desperately to remove Hoover. Wilson was determined that law and order would be preserved during the May Day demonstrations, no matter what it took. They put buses, great big buses, back-to-back, touching each other, entirely around the perimeter of the White House. I've always wondered how they figured it out so there would be no gap at all between the buses. There was no space between those buses in a perimeter around the White House. Nobody could get close to the White House during the May Day demonstration.

Spiro Agnew, later so discredited, was out giving these speeches written by William Safire, Pat Buchanan, and others, you know, exploiting his own speaking skills to stir up hatred against the press, against the media. Reporters were being hauled before grand juries to reveal their sources.

The Earl Caldwell case scared us all to death. Earl Caldwell was a young African-American reporter for the *New York Times* who was able to get inside the Black Panther Party in Oakland, had written stories about them, and the Justice Department was doing an investigation on the Black Panther Party. Earl Caldwell was one of their major vehicles to try to find out what was going on. He was resisting testifying. He was a real hero, let me tell you, for doing that. Because we were all certain he'd end up in jail.

Nothing, today, comes close. There is a lot of stress between government and press today. And nothing since, nothing before, that I'm aware of [this was before September 11], comes close to the sense of what we felt as young reporters in Washington, about the status of freedom of the press. I mean, the lengths that we went to. We all talked, we imagined we were being tapped, and never realized that it actually was happening to some respected, slightly older colleagues, like Rick Smith.

When I did start working on this case, covering the case against the court case against the newspapers, the grand jury investigation of Dan Ellsberg, Tony [Russo], and others, when I covered the trial in Los Angeles, and when I was writing my book, the paranoia that some of us felt at the time was extraordinary. For years, I think for seven or eight years, all of the notes, all of my tapes, all of my notebooks from writing my book, *The Papers and the Papers,* were hidden under the bed of a lawyer friend of mine in Boston.

Actually, they were not under his bed. They were under the bed of someone else he knew. I wanted to be able to say, I didn't know where the materials were. Legally, it was probably totally shaky, but it made me feel better that I didn't know where this stuff was.

So, it was an extraordinary time. I believe that the Pentagon Papers — and we all have slightly different gradations of views of this — helped convince editors and publishers and other people that their worst fears were justified about the war in Vietnam, about the trustworthiness of public officials, going back a long time.

I think my own sense was we, the younger generation, at the time, working for the newspapers, were quite convinced of these things. But it took something else to convince the top echelon, because they could not really accept this had taken place, this kind of lying had occurred. I believe it was immensely courageous for editors and publishers and other executives of these organizations to make the decisions they did.

Dan [Ellsberg] counts seventeen newspapers [that published stories based on the papers]. In a funny way, it took more courage for the other papers than it did for the *New York Times,* because the *Times* knew it had something. The *Times* was going to set the trend with this. But for the other papers to go ahead after seeing what had happened to the *Times,* after seeing that they'd been taken to court, I think, in some ways, even required a little more courage.

Some of us, again, in the younger generation, felt that the court orders, the stays to stop publication temporarily, should have been defied. We felt it was so important that the newspapers should not have stopped, should not have obeyed the courts. I understand, perhaps a little better now, some of the reasons why that decision was not taken. I'm not sure it would have helped. I also think it was courageous for some of the judges who were involved in this case.

Much has been written and said about Judge Murray Gurfein in New York, a brand new judge. As I remember it, his desk was in the hallway of the courthouse in New York. He wrote a brilliant decision, or some clerk wrote a brilliant decision for him, that still has immensely and wonderfully quotable things. Judge Gerhard Gesell, here in district court, was somebody I had covered very closely for about six or nine months. Judge Gesell made a decision that he would not grant a stay. He required the Court of Appeals, here, to grant the stay because he felt so strongly that the case the government had brought against the *Washington Post* was weak.

I covered this Justice Department team later on for the *Washington Post.* I moved from the courthouse beat, to the national staff, and to covering the Justice Department and the FBI, and I became persuaded that the Nixon administration's decisions in this case were almost totally political. I believe their national security claims were an utter and complete sham.

I don't think the Nixon administration believed its own arguments in this case. I believe they were completely constructed in order to try to score political points. I realize, I think, that Henry Kissinger was driving the show. Dean Erwin N. Griswold told me before he died that he didn't believe the arguments. He was not persuaded by the case that he had to make in the Supreme Court. I think that is something we need to understand more, and we need to get to more of the players on the Nixon administration side.

The last couple of points: the long-term significance, there is absolutely no doubt that Watergate would not have happened without the Pentagon Papers case. My students at American University used to accuse me of some kind of self-aggrandizement — because I was so affected by the Pentagon Papers case — when I would claim, but there's an absolutely clear line, if it hadn't been for the Pentagon Papers, maybe Watergate would have occurred later, maybe it would have been different, but the abuses would not have been so great.

You have to remember it was the Pentagon Papers case. This gets into things in Pat Ellsberg's family and her father's friendship with J. Edgar Hoover, or alleged friendship with J. Edgar Hoover. The Nixon administration believed that J. Edgar Hoover would not do a good enough job investigating Dan Ellsberg and the Pentagon Papers case; that was why they created the White House Plumbers, to do the real investigation. They couldn't trust Hoover, because supposedly, Pat's father gave Hoover toys at the holidays to give to his employees so that Hoover wouldn't have to pay for them. He was such a cheapskate.

The good news about it all is the press stood up for what was right, as one person after another here has testified. The bad news is the system did work, in a legal, constitutional way, to stop the presses for two weeks. I think that was unfortunate and something we've had to live with ever since.

I agree with Dan Ellsberg that unauthorized disclosure is essential to American public life, and having been a minor government official, for the last two years, I see it and believe it even more than I did before. I hope the media today would take this kind of courageous step that they did thirty years ago, in publishing the Pentagon Papers, but I have to say, in conclusion, I'm not sure they would.

David Rudenstine

I think I'm the only one who really was a total observer from the beginning of this case until today. I would first like to say, I have a lot of admiration for everyone who participated in this case as an activist, as well as all of the other newspapers. This was a moment of great national courage by many individuals and institutions.

I want to make it clear that I was not part of that. When this case broke, I shared the view of many people — that the Pentagon Papers was basically a historical document containing nothing that was of any vital importance to the national security in 1971, and that the Nixon administration's decision to sue was mainly an effort to get back at political enemies — what better enemy did Nixon have than the *New York Times* — and that the ultimate victory, the U.S. Supreme Court, was a slam dunk. That was my view in 1971. By that time, I was out of law school for two years. I promptly went off and I bought my Bantam edition of the Pentagon Papers. I started to read it, and I quickly put it on the shelf and went on to things which were more interesting to read.

I did, during that time, go to the courthouse. I wasn't covering the courthouse, as Sandy Ungar was. I was taking time out from my duties as a legal services lawyer because this was the case of the century as far as I could tell. And on Friday, June 18, by that time, Judge Murray Gurfein had already issued a temporary restraining order. He did that on Tuesday. On Friday, he said, we are going to have a hearing on the facts to determine whether or not a preliminary injunction is justified.

I went into the courthouse at 10:00 in the morning, and I had never seen a courthouse that was so crammed with lawyers and government officials and distinguished individuals. This motion of the government was being held in the largest single room in the courthouse in Foley Square in Manhattan.

There were some preliminary statements made, and then suddenly, Mr. Bickel stood up on behalf of the *New York Times* and said he had a motion to make. He wanted to make the motion to dissolve the temporary restraining order forthwith. The judge said, why? And he said, well, we've been told all week long that if there was another installment of the Pentagon Papers case reports that the government would be gravely injured and national security would be severely harmed.

And I'm here to report, mind you, there is an outstanding preliminary injunction against the *New York Times,* that there has been another installment of the Pentagon Papers. And that has been done by the *Washington Post.* As far as I can tell, Bickel said, the republic still stands. At that particular moment, the hundreds of people in the courtroom exploded into applause, clearly sympathetic to what the *New York Times* was trying to do in this particular case. Gurfein, the new judge — you know how new of a judge he was? Brand new, first case.

He gavels down the crowd and tries to bring order to the courtroom and does. He denies Bickel's motion. That afternoon they went in, and the Court had a four- or five-hour secret hearing. It was the first of several secret hearings in this particular case. The next day, he dissolved the temporary restraining order, denied the preliminary injunction, and he, in fact, wrote the opinion himself.

Mel Barkin was his law clerk. He got to the courthouse at 6:00 in the morning. He had a habit of dictating things to his secretary who was there at 6:00 in the morning. He told Mel to come in at 9:00 because he wouldn't need him before that. He issued the opinion at 2:00 in the afternoon. That was, I suppose, the first hook of the case in me.

The second hook happened in 1986. I had always been interested in the case, and I wanted to see some of the original documents. I asked two law clerks to go to Foley Square, the U.S. District Court, and bring me the complaint, bring me the various motions, bring me the documents that went up to the Second Circuit, and I was going to make a collection of them.

I did not know, at that time, that Jim Goodale had already published these in a limited edition. I was going to get them together and make them available for a course I might teach. They came back that day and said, they are not there. I said, well, where are they? Well, they are in Bayonne, New Jersey. They are in deep storage. I said, well, do you have a car? They said, yes.

I said, well, go tomorrow. They came back the next day and said, you know, there is something funny in Bayonne, New Jersey. There's a lot of documents in this file that are marked top secret, yet we were able to read them. They said, I think you ought to come to Bayonne, New Jersey. The government had a huge warehouse in Bayonne, New Jersey. As soon as we saw it, I thought, oh, this is going to take forever. Well, it didn't take forever. Within a matter of moments we had access to two or three cardboard boxes containing the files of the Pentagon Papers litigation that went up to the Second Circuit — none of the Supreme Court documents, just the district court and the circuit court documents of the *New York Times* case only, not the *Washington Post* case. There were literally hundreds of pages marked top secret.

After studying the boxes for about three or four hours, it became clear what happened. Tony Lewis, the *New York Times* columnist, in the 1970s, made a Freedom of Information Act request and got many of these documents declassified. They ended up in deep storage in Bayonne, New Jersey. We asked, can we make a copy of these declassified papers? And the answer was, yes.

One of the very first documents that I read of that group was the transcript of the secret hearing before Judge Murray Gurfein on that Friday, June 18. It ran a couple hundred pages. The government presented three witnesses. The witnesses, basically, were saying, look, if you present another installment of this series, there is going to be grave harm to national security. It's going to affect diplomatic efforts to end the war, to get better conditions for the POWs. There are intelligence matters involved. Yes, the war plans are stale, but the real estate involved in this hot war is limited, and even a stale war plan can reveal how we think about how we will use troops and so on and so forth.

Right? Well, I'm reading all this stuff, not with a particular tilt one way or the other, but I'm looking at it from the point of view of Gurfein, a brand new judge. I know by this particular point that he issued his decision the next day. I also know that he left the courthouse at about 11:00 that Friday night, and the hearing didn't end until 8:00.

So, I'm sitting there trying to figure out how did a brand new judge have the courage, in the face of allegations being made by three government witnesses, to deny the preliminary injunction after, clearly, only a few hours of study, from 10:00 P.M. to when he left, until the next morning when he sat down to dictate the opinion. During that time, he really didn't agonize. He, by his own record, went home. Where did he get the courage to put aside the allegations without ever trying to reassure himself that there was nothing in the documents themselves, and he didn't have time to go back to those documents, because they were forty-seven volumes, seven thousand pages, and they weighed sixty pounds.

Anyway, that was the second big hook that got into me, because, by that time, I had read Sandy's [Ungar] wonderful book. I had read a lot of the news reports. And I thought, maybe there is more here than people have thought.

Maybe there is more here than I thought, because I was a Nixon hater. I thought Nixon sued the *New York Times* because he hated the *New York Times*. I thought this was, simply, a political vendetta. So, I got involved with all of this particular study that resulted in the book I wrote.

Erwin Griswold got notice on a Friday afternoon about 3:00, this is on June 25, that the Court had accepted certiorari. The briefs were due the next morning at 8:00 in the U.S. Supreme Court. So, he had, roughly, seventeen hours to write the brief. He got the first set of the Pentagon Papers in his office that afternoon about 4:00.

He called in three government officials. He said, tell me the worst. I have only a few hours. Tell me the absolute worst. He's sitting there, beginning to take notes with his secretary, and the FBI is there — because every time classified information is being passed, the FBI was monitoring the communications. The FBI agent turns to Griswold and says, Mr. Solicitor General, I'm not questioning your security clearance, but what about your secretary? Is your secretary cleared? He asked the secretary, are you cleared? She said, no. The FBI agent said, I'm sorry, Mr. Griswold, you are not going to be allowed to have this secretary. Well, Mr. Griswold was not a particularly large person. But the way he told the story was that he stood up to the FBI agent and said, I am going to use this secretary for the rest of the afternoon and the evening, as long as I need to, and you can get out of here right now. Go and tell your superiors what I said and don't come back.

The next anecdote involved the difficulties Whitney North Seymour Jr. had in trying to figure out what was involved in this case, not too dissimilar than some of the experiences the press lawyers had. Whitney North Seymour was at a conference in Washington the day the government got an injunction, which was Tuesday the fifteenth. He stayed in Washington, despite being beseeched by Michael D. Hess to come back to handle this case. And he said, no, no, you can handle this case. Mike was in his early thirties at the time, and he felt like, I really shouldn't be handling this case.

Anyway, Seymour returns to New York on Thursday night, the night before the hearing before Gurfein. Robert Mardian came to New York from Washington with the government's three witnesses. They met in the U.S. attorney's office, Thursday night, twelve hours before the trial was to start. Seymour says to them, well, tell me what is so terrible, I need to know, and there is silence.

Seymour turns to one of them, in particular, well, why don't you start with you. And there is silence. Finally, Mardian pops in, and he says, they can't tell you. What do you mean, Seymour says, they can't tell me? Well, it's classified. You are not entitled to hear it.

He and Mardian had a really serious argument, because Mardian wanted to make extreme law in this case. Mardian wanted the U.S. Supreme Court to be put in a position where it either adopted a rule of constitution, which was similar to the British Official Secrets Act [if it's classified, you are not allowed to publish it], or the alternative was going to be that the government would lose, and Mardian didn't think the Supreme Court would hand a loss to the Supreme Court if those were the only two choices.

The best way to make sure the Court didn't have any room to wiggle between them was to deny the Court any evidence at all. All you are going to do is present the Court with a factual situation where the documents were classified properly, according to the procedures that were authorized by rules. Therefore, the Court was going to be told, you are not allowed to appear between the volumes.

Well the result of that was, the next day in court, Seymour managed to get a little information out of the three witnesses, but as the transcript reveals, very, very little. Every time anything went beyond the general allegation to the specific, the witnesses refused to speak. Gurfein, during the course of the four hours, became utterly frustrated with the witnesses. The dam broke because more evidence was eventually brought to the Court's attention. It broke on Sunday, the day after Gurfein denied the preliminary injunction. Washington had a change in mind. Therefore, some of the more specific allegations that were made in the *Washington Post* case and also in the *New York Times* case then came forward that Sunday and Monday of the next week.

One of the great ironies of this whole historical episode, as far as I can tell from the press's point of view, is after having shown enormous courage in going forward, great fortitude in fighting the Court, or fighting the government down to the bitter end, and actually having achieved a somewhat historic victory, many of the lawyers turn around and say, it was a slam dunk. They should have never brought the case in the first place. They were all historical documents. The precedent was clearly on our side. There was no meaningful evidence in the record. And the Court really reached the only legitimate outcome that was in accordance with our constitutional traditions that it could have reached. But what's the big deal? Why are we here every ten years? So, why are we celebrating a slam-dunk decision? I think the answer is that the press, to some extent, has it wrong. This was a tough case. Mr. Glendon said, no precedent, he could find no meaningful award. That, I think, is a really true statement. Jim Goodale takes a slightly different position. He says he went to the books, and he thought for sure the government would seek a prior injunction, but for sure, the government was going to lose. I guess if I had a tilt, I would tilt more toward Mr. Glendon on that one than Jim Goodale.

Near v. Minnesota was the only case that spoke to the issue, and that was a civil matter, not a criminal matter. The government of the United States was not involved. It was not national security. There was no hot war. Nobody claimed that the documents or what was going to be published affected national security. Those are big differences, it seems to me. This was a case of first impression in terms of our constitutional law. Never before had the U.S. government sued a newspaper to try to get a prior restraint to bar it from publishing information that it already had.

CHAPTER FIVE

What Was So Secret?

There is no question that the Pentagon Papers represented a massive, authoritative study of how the Vietnam War was conducted by the United States. It covered the period from after World War II to March 1968, supplying a lengthy narrative and many "exhibits," or illustrations in the form of the full texts of documents. As discussed in previous chapters, the U.S. government made a strenuous effort to convince U.S. courts, right up to the Supreme Court, that the Pentagon Papers were so sensitive that protecting them justified a major abridgement of rights protected by the First Amendment to the Constitution of the United States.

In the heat of the moment, neither the newspapers nor the lawyers or the courts made much of an effort to see for themselves just how sensitive the Pentagon Papers might be, given the exact national security information they contained. Years later Solicitor General Erwin N. Griswold, the government's lead lawyer before the Supreme Court, revealed an important index of the secrecy with which the Department of Justice wanted to invest the Pentagon Papers — he himself was not permitted to view some items. In 1989 Griswold wrote: "It quickly becomes apparent to any person who has considerable experience with classified material that there is massive over-classification and that the principal concern of the classifiers is not with national security, but rather with governmental embarrassment of one sort or another." He continued, specifically with regard to the Pentagon Papers, "I have never seen any trace of a threat to the national security from the publication. Indeed, I have never seen it even suggested that there was such an actual threat."[1]

At the time Griswold wrote, his actual presentation to the Supreme Court, as well as the "Special Appendix" that government lawyers had given to the Federal Court of Appeals for the Second Circuit, were documents that remained secret. There were also various affidavits that had been sworn by government officials declaring the Pentagon Papers documents of great sensitivity. These, too, were secret or lost. Some of the documents were declassified in 1992, others were found by law professor David Rudenstine in records of the Second Circuit Court during the course of his research into a monograph on the Pentagon Papers.[2]

Among the main points Rudenstine made upon publishing his study of the Pentagon Papers case, although he expressed himself somewhat ambivalently (see below), is that there were real secrets in the Pentagon Papers that if revealed would cause — in the words of the U.S. government's own original telegram to the *New York Times* — "irreparable damage" to the national security of the United States. The federal government's lead lawyer in the New York portion of the case, Whitney North Seymour Jr., immediately seized upon the Rudenstine study to argue, "At Last the Truth is Out," that is, that "the revelations . . . debunk the Big Lie that has been repeated [by those who] have asserted that the *Times* editors were only publishing 'history' and posed no threat to the national security of the U.S. Rudenstine's disclosures prove exactly the contrary."[3]

Because arguments such as these have carried weight in certain circles, no doubt enhanced by publication in a law review, and because it seems fashionable in some places to revise our understanding of the Vietnam experience by assertions that effectively maintain that the conventional wisdom of the moment is the real story, the time is far past that a proper analysis of the "secrecy" issue with respect to the Pentagon Papers be carried out. That is the purpose of this chapter.

In both his book and a subsequent article,[4] as well as in comments at the 2001 conference recorded here, Dr. Rudenstine agreed with the basic decision of the courts in the Pentagon Papers case. Like *New York Times* lawyer Floyd Abrams, who notes that a majority of the Supreme Court believed there were real secrets in the Pentagon Papers,[5] Rudenstine thinks the courts did the right thing. What gives secrecy cultists running room, however, is the notion that the secrets were real, which at least suggests the Pentagon Papers decision could have been mistaken (three members of the six-vote majority on the Supreme Court in this case held that there *could be* secrets significant enough to warrant approval of a prior restraint on publication). In his study of the case, Rudenstine actually speaks ambiguously. Early in Rudenstine's book, he writes, "Indeed, it now appears that the Pentagon Papers did contain some information that could have inflicted some injury — at least to a degree that makes the concerns of national security officials understandable."[6] Much later in his conclusion the author notes, "There is no evidence that the newspapers' publication of the Pentagon Papers, followed by the three books in the summer and fall of 1971, harmed the U.S. military, defense, intelligence, or international affairs interests."[7] The latter judgment reflects the consensus among historians; the former one was novel and formed a perfect basis for latter-day attempts to buck the consensus. The truth is different, however. In fact, Rudenstine never performed the evidentiary analysis necessary to sustain a judgment that the Pentagon Papers contained information that would cause "irreparable damage" to the national security.

In his law review reprise of the book, David Rudenstine writes that his treatment persuaded most book reviewers, if not "a handful of prominent *New York Times* officials," that "the Pentagon Papers did contain information that could have injured national security if disclosed."[8] If so, that was unfortunate. In his article, Dr. Rudenstine identified the passages from his book that discussed the evidence of damage accruing from the Pentagon Papers. These add up to about twenty pages in four major passages.[9] The actual material in those sections of the monograph successively describes the initial inquiry by Robert C. Mardian; the testimony at the Gurfein hearing in the New York case; the government's "Special Appendix" of allegations filed with the Court of Appeals, again in the New York case; and the secret brief written by Solicitor General Griswold and filed with the Supreme Court. In every instance, Dr. Rudenstine summarizes the government's testimony or its claims regarding the data, not the data proper.[10] Of the roughly thirty footnotes appended to this material the overwhelming majority are to interviews with government lawyers, briefs, and affidavits. There are only two substantive citations to the Pentagon Papers (and one more referring the reader to this source), both to the collection of the diplomatic volumes published by George Herring, and both of those to Herring's introduction, not to any of the substance. There are four references to specific passages of the Pentagon Papers, which formed part of the Ellsberg leak, in each case merely to note that "this information remains excised and thus is not publicly available."[11] As the evidentiary analysis below makes crystal clear, tracking the relevant passages among the different editions of the Pentagon Papers leads to each of the original substantive sources. They were, in fact, available, and have been since 1972. In two instances Rudenstine refers to the papers and notes the absence of only some of the original substantive material (in one, "a relatively small passage on Page 52"), but in neither case does the author attempt actually to evaluate the material in the Pentagon Papers against the claims made in the government briefs. In short, the Rudenstine account provides *no* basis upon which to judge the merits of claims that revealing the Pentagon Papers would damage national security, irreparably or otherwise.

Whitney North Seymour Jr. and others who have joined in asserting the truth is out have really been engaged in circumlocution. The government's claims in the Pentagon Papers case are summarized, no evaluation of the merits is made, and then the details of the claims that were made are taken as the proof that the government's original assertions were justified.

Not only is this circular logic, but everything about the Pentagon Papers affair calls out to proceed with caution regarding Nixon administration actions. We have established that the prosecution was based on factors that were only incidentally about the protection of classified information. The original inquiry by

Robert Mardian at Justice and Fred Buzhardt at the Pentagon was not an investigation but simply an enabling action. Government witnesses misspoke, misled, or proved ignorant on key issues of substance or made blanket assertions not based on fact. The government sought a judgment on the basis of secret negotiating material that was never part of the Ellsberg leak and which the newspapers had reported from the beginning they did not possess. The government initially had no idea of what specific claims to make, then attempted to snow the courts under with lengthy laundry lists of supposed secrets. It subverted legal procedures by doing this in appellate court, amending the record of a trial in which it had lost. In the incident of the Gulf of Tonkin radio intercept introduced — again at the appellate level — in the *Washington Post* trial, the government was claiming a secret that was not part of the Pentagon Papers and hawking the secrecy of a document that was printed and public in a congressional hearing record. Even if the fact was not known at the time, that the man who wrote the relevant section of the Pentagon Papers had not used the radio intercept, the fact that the intercept was already in the public record was.

These facts generate no confidence that the government's specific assertions of what was secret in the Pentagon Papers ought to be taken at face value.

The manner in which the special claims to secrecy were produced is also important and relevant. The "Special Appendix" that was submitted to the Court of Appeals for the Second Circuit was produced between the afternoon of Saturday, June 19, when Judge Gurfein rendered his decision against the government in the *New York Times* case, and Monday the twenty-first, when the document went to the Court of Appeals. Since, until the Saturday, federal lawyers had been operating under instructions *not* to produce specific claims of secrecy, not only was the document confected in a very short time, but also the drafting had to be done starting almost from scratch. The long list of allegedly sensitive material in the Pentagon Papers that is framed in the "Special Appendix" thus begs the question of where and when anyone had the time to make a considered judgment in this matter.

This point can be drawn even more sharply in the case of the sealed (secret) brief to the Supreme Court, where Solicitor General Erwin Griswold has left an account of exactly how the brief was drawn up. It was noontime on Friday, June 24, 1971, when Chief Justice Warren Burger of the Supreme Court informed Griswold that the case would be argued the next day. "At that time," the solicitor recounts, "no briefs had been written, and, indeed, I had never seen the outside of the Pentagon Papers." Once a set was brought to him, Griswold saw it would be impossible to read through the materials in the time available. Instead he got the Defense Department, State Department, and National Security Council staff each to send over one person to brief him, and Griswold asked each official which items should be included in his brief. The solicitor general finished with a list of forty or so passages or documents, and that was the set with which he began reading in detail. Then Griswold began to consider the basis for claiming a breach of national security in the revelation of each of the listed items, but "quickly came to the conclusion that most of them presented no serious threat." He pared the set down to the eleven particular items that would be included in the secret brief, then stayed up through the night to write the paper, while assigning Deputy Solicitor Daniel M. Friedman to draft the government's "open" brief, which would make the legal arguments while he focused on the secrecy issues.

About an hour before he was actually to appear before the Supreme Court, Solicitor General Griswold telephoned Attorney General John Mitchell to report what he had done. Griswold plainly stated he intended to give up secrecy claims ("waiving objections to the printing of the documents") in all but his set of eleven in the secret brief. John Mitchell did not approve, but he had put Griswold in charge of the case. "If you think that is the way it should be handled, you have my complete support," Mitchell told Griswold.

To recapitulate, the secret brief, with its purported set of super-sensitive materials, was assembled in less than twenty-four hours, by an official who knew nothing of the Pentagon Papers and had never seen them before, had only hearsay knowledge from national security specialists, and was pulling an all-nighter so that he could make a presentation at a key court hearing. No historian or observer should take Griswold's list of State secrets at face value except *after* determining what exactly was being talked about.

To make this picture of the upper reaches of the Nixon administration complete, this is what John Mitchell told Griswold regarding his own knowledge: "You know, I have never seen these papers. I don't know what is in them."[12] Mitchell, of course, had from the beginning been with Nixon in calling the shots on the government's actions in the Pentagon Papers affair.

The Ellsberg-Russo trial record contains at least some evidence of a previous attempt at evaluating the actual sensitivity of the Pentagon Papers from the perspective of secrecy. Apparently in December 1971 a National Security Agency employee, William D. Gerhard (who reported to Fred Buzhardt and to the federal prosecutor in the case, David R. Nissen), was instructed to conduct a damage assessment of the twenty volumes of the papers then in evidence for the trial. Gerhard found nine volumes completely free of truly secret material, though others, he felt, might still have been sensitive in 1969. Their secrecy status for 1971–1972 Gerhard apparently did not comment upon, but it had to be less due to the fact that the entire United States strategy had by that time changed. No detailed studies are available, only fragments of conclusions. At the

Ellsberg-Russo trial the government took the position that this damage assessment was not an official one, that it represented merely the opinion of one person.[13] Trial testimony obscured the matter of these assessments, but knowledge of them should at least have served to emphasize the importance of making a fresh evaluation on the secrecy question.

This chapter performs the analysis of evidence that we have been suggesting is necessary. To do so we reproduce both the solicitor general's sealed brief and the "Special Appendix" document that was given to the Federal Court of Appeals for the Second Circuit. Both of these briefs cite materials in the Pentagon Papers by means of the very awkward delineation of volumes that the Vietnam Task Force actually used for the list of its studies (for example, V-B-4(a), which corresponds to the collection of documents assembled from the Kennedy administration). In each case, roman numerals indicate the overall part of the study referred to, and the capital letter leads to a major title. Sometimes these titles are "volumes" in their own right; sometimes several volumes contribute to the material covered by the major title. There are instances (denoted by small letters) where several studies add up to a piece, several of which make up a "volume." This confusing use of the word "volume" explains why the forty-three volumes of the Pentagon Papers could appear in four books from the Beacon Press and be published in twelve books by the Government Printing Office. In any case, this chapter reproduces the volume list of the Pentagon Papers. Readers may refer to it as a way to identify the specific part of the Pentagon Papers being cited each time the government legal briefs allege an item of information is sensitive.

Because of the way the Pentagon Papers materials are cited in the briefs, the analyses of individual items follow the same method so that analyses can correspond to allegations. Thus the entries in the paper "Evidentiary Analysis" are keyed to the entries in the Griswold sealed brief and in the "Special Appendix" for the Second Circuit. In each case the analysis describes the Pentagon Papers material that is called into question, notes the specific claims to secrecy made by the government in the briefs, and considers whether the material meets the standard of "irreparable damage" claimed by the government. In a number of cases where the text of the Pentagon Papers refers to source documents or materials the Pentagon Papers authors themselves were using, the analysis below also accesses the source documents and discusses these questions with respect to those materials as well. The analysis also deals with general questions raised by the briefs before launching into their lists of sensitive items.[14]

In writing his account of the secret brief for the Pentagon Papers case, Solicitor General Erwin Griswold also gave his assessment of the consequences of the ultimate revelation of the documents. Though Griswold has been quoted earlier in a different context, his words are worth repeating here: "I have never seen any trace of a threat to the national security from the publication. Indeed, I have never seen it suggested that there was such an actual threat."[15] The results of this formal analysis of the claims to secrecy on the Pentagon Papers reinforce that judgment.

OSD Vietnam Task Force

January 10, 1969
Outline of Studies
Index (1 vol.)
I. Vietnam and the U.S., 1940–1950 (1 vol.)
    A. U.S. Policy, 1940–1950
    B. The Character and Power of the Viet Minh
    C. Ho Chi Minh: Asian Tito?
II. U.S. Involvement in the Franco–Viet Minh War, 1950–1954 (1 vol.)
    A. U.S., France, and Vietnamese Nationalism
    B. Toward a Negotiated Settlement
III. The Geneva Accords (1 vol.)
    A. U.S. Military Planning and Diplomatic Maneuver
    B. Role and Obligations of State of Vietnam
    C. Viet Minh Position and Sino-Soviet Strategy
    D. The Intent of the Geneva Accords
IV. Evolution of the War (26 vols.)
    A. U.S. MAP for Diem: The Eisenhower Commitments, 1954–1960 (5 vols.)
        1. NATO and SEATO: A Comparison
        2. Aid for France in Indochina, 1950–1954
        3. U.S. and France's Withdrawal from Vietnam, 1954–1956
        4. U.S. Training of Vietnamese National Army, 1954–1959
        5. Origins of the Insurgency
    B. Counterinsurgency: The Kennedy Commitments, 1961–1963 (5 vols.)
        1. The Kennedy Commitments and Programs, 1961
        2. Strategic Hamlet Program, 1961–1963
        3. The Advisory Buildup, 1961–1967
        4. Phased Withdrawal of U.S. Forces in Vietnam, 1962–1964
        5. The Overthrow of Ngo Dinh Diem, May–November 1963
    C. Direct Action: The Johnson Commitments, 1964–1968 (16 vols.)
        1. U.S. Programs in South Vietnam, November 1963–April 1965: NSAM 273 — NSAM 288 — Honolulu
        2. Military Pressures against NVN (3 vols.)

a. February–June 1964

b. July–October 1964

c. November–December 1964

3. ROLLING THUNDER Program Begins: January–June 1965

4. Marine Combat Units Go to DaNang, March 1965

5. Phase I in the Buildup of U.S. Forces: March–July 1965

6. U.S. Ground Strategy and Force Deployments: 1965–1967 (3 vols.)

a. Volume I: Phase II, Program 3, Program 4

b. Volume II: Program 5

c. Volume III: Program 6

7. Air War in the North: 1965–1968 (2 vols.)

a. Volume I

b. Volume II

8. Re-emphasis on Pacification: 1965–1967

9. U.S.-GVN Relations (2 vols.)

a. Volume 1: December 1963–June 1965

b. Volume 2: July 1965–December 1967

10. Statistical Survey of the War, North and South: 1965–1967

V. Justification of the War (11 vols.)

A. Public Statements (2 vols.)

1. Volume I:

a. The Truman Administration

b. The Eisenhower Administration

c. The Kennedy Administration

2. Volume II:

d. The Johnson Administration

B. Internal Documents (9 vols.)

1. The Roosevelt Administration

2. The Truman Administration: (2 vols.)

a. Volume I: 1945–1949

b. Volume II: 1950–1952

3. The Eisenhower Administration: (4 vols.)

a. Volume I: 1953

b. Volume II: 1954–Geneva

c. Volume III: Geneva Accords–15 March 1956

d. Volume IV: 1956 French Withdrawal–1960

4. The Kennedy Administration (2 vols.)

a. Book I

b. Book II

VI. Settlement of the Conflict (6 vols.)

    A. Negotiations, 1965–1967: The Public Record

    B. Negotiations, 1965–1967: Announced Position Statements

    C. Histories of Contacts (4 vols.)

        1. 1965–1966

        2. Polish Track

        3. Moscow-London Track

        4. 1967–1968

Leslie H. Gelb

Chairman, OSD Task Force

Declassified E.O. 12958 Sec. 3.5

MLJ-S-98001

Griswold Secret Briefs

NOS. 1873 AND 1885

IN THE SUPREME COURT OF THE UNITED STATES

OCTOBER TERM, 1970

NEW YORK TIMES COMPANY, PETITIONER

    V.

UNITED STATES OF AMERICA

UNITED STATES OF AMERICA, PETITIONER

    V.

THE WASHINGTON POST COMPANY, ET AL.

ON WRITS OF CERTIORARI

TO THE UNITED STATES COURT OF APPEALS FOR THE SECOND CIRCUIT AND THE
    UNITED STATES COURT OF APPEALS FOR THE DISTRICT OF COLUMBIA CIRCUIT

BRIEF FOR THE UNITED STATES (SECRET PORTION)

ERWIN N. GRISWOLD, *Solicitor General.*

Department of Justice, Washington, D.C. 20530.

IN THE SUPREME COURT OF THE UNITED STATES

OCTOBER TERM, 1970

NO. 1873

NEW YORK TIMES COMPANY,

PETITIONER

    V.

UNITED STATES OF AMERICA

NO. 1885

UNITED STATES OF AMERICA, PETITIONER

V.

THE WASHINGTON POST COMPANY, ET AL.

ON WRITS OF CERTIORARI

TO THE UNITED STATES COURT OF APPEALS FOR THE SECOND CIRCUIT AND THE
  UNITED STATES COURT OF APPEALS FOR THE DISTRICT OF COLUMBIA CIRCUIT

BRIEF FOR THE UNITED STATES (SECRET PORTION)

There have been great difficulties in the presentation of this case. The United
States does not know what materials are in the possession of the *New York Times*
or the *Washington Post,* and neither District Court below was willing to require
disclosure of these papers, even in camera, without representatives of the United
States present. It would appear in evidence that the papers already published by
the two newspapers bear some relation to a compilation of forty-seven volumes
entitled "United States–Vietnam Relations — 1945–1967," prepared by a Vietnam task force in the Office of the Secretary of Defense. The covers and every
page in this compilation are marked "Top Secret — Sensitive."

It was obviously impossible for the United States to prove directly that the
publication of the papers held by the two newspapers would involve immediate and irreparable injury to the security of the United States. The only method
by which the United States could proceed was to seek to show that there were
items in the forty-seven-volume study which would have this consequence.

When it appeared to be impracticable for the *Washington Post* to produce in
camera the papers it had, the District Court said:

> THE COURT: I think if you feel that way, because of your problems, I can pro-
> ceed on the assumption that you have all the documents the government is
> referring to. We will proceed on that basis. If you want to show that there are
> some documents you don't have, you can prove it. I will proceed on the
> assumption you do.

Accordingly, the government introduced evidence through witnesses, and
through affidavits, which made specific reference to items in the forty-seven-
volume compilation. The forty-seven volumes were available in the courtroom
in the District of Columbia, the relevant portions being regarded as incorporated by reference in the testimony and the affidavits considered by the District
Court. The forty-seven volumes are a part of the record in the *New York Times*
case in the Southern District of New York and have been transmitted to this
Court as a part of the record here.

It is to those forty-seven volumes that references have been made in the "Special Appendix" mentioned in the decision of the United States Court of Appeals

for the Second Circuit, and in the orders entered by this Court in these cases on June 25, 1971. This is likewise true of the items included in the "supplemental list" which was filed (in accordance with the decision of the Court of Appeals for the Second Circuit, and with the orders of this Court) by 5:00 P.M. on June 25, 1971.

The purpose of this portion of the Brief for the United States is to refer to a selected few of these items and to endeavor to show that the publication of these items could have the effect of causing immediate and irreparable harm to the security of the United States. A number of these items were considered hastily by Judge Gesell during the hearing before him on Monday, June 21, 1971. No trace of criticism is intended by the observation that Judge Gesell's consideration was hasty. This was inevitable under the circumstances. Nevertheless, the consideration was necessarily hasty, and the presentation with respect to it was inevitably extremely difficult since no one knows yet what documents either of the newspapers actually have. It is true that they have provided "Inventories." However, these are not very helpful, and they do not, in general, identify particular documents. There are various versions of some of these documents, and the inventories do not show which version the papers have. It is also clear that they have some items which are included in the forty-seven volumes.

We now turn to a few selected items from the forty-seven volumes which we submit involve a serious risk of immediate and irreparable harm to the United States and its security.

1. There are four volumes in the forty-seven-volume compilation which are designated in their entirety. They are: Volume VI-C-1, VI-C-2, VI-C-3, and VI-C-4. These contain a comprehensive detailed history of the so-called negotiating track. Negotiations were carried on through third parties, both governments and individuals. These included the Canadian, Polish, Italian, Rumanian, and Norwegian governments. They also included individuals, some holding public office, and some private citizens, sometimes with the knowledge of their governments, and sometimes without their government's being informed.

These negotiations, or negotiations of this sort, are being continued. It is obvious that the hope of the termination of the war turns to a large extent on the success of negotiations of this sort. One never knows where the break may come, and it is of crucial importance to keep open every possible line of communication. Reference may be made to recent developments with respect to China as an instance of a line of communication among many which turned out to be fruitful.

The materials in these four volumes include derogatory comments about the perfidiousness of specific persons involved, and statements, which might be offensive to nations or governments. The publication of this material is likely to close up channels of communication which might otherwise have some opportunity of facilitating the closing of the Vietnam War.

2. Closely related to this is the fact that there is much material in these volumes which might give offense to South Korea, to Thailand, and to South Vietnam, just as serious offense has already been given to Australia and Canada. South Korea, South Vietnam, and Australia have troops in Vietnam, and Thailand allows the use of airfields from which 65 percent of our sorties are launched.

For the past many months, we have been steadily withdrawing troops from Vietnam. The rate at which we can continue this withdrawal depends upon the extent to which we can continue to rely on the support of other nations, notably South Vietnam, Korea, Thailand, and Australia. If the publication of this material gives offense to these countries, and some of them are notably sensitive, the rate at which our own troops can be withdrawn will be diminished. This would be an immediate military impact, having direct bearing on the security of the United States and its citizens.

There are further references to these items in the "Special Appendix" filed in the United States Court of Appeals for the Second Circuit in the *New York Times* case and in this Court.

3. There are specific references to the names and activities of CIA agents still active in Southeast Asia. There are references to the activities of the National Security Agency.

The items designated are specific references to persons or activities, which are currently continuing. No designation has been made of any general references to CIA activities.

This may not be exactly equivalent to the disclosure of troop movements, but it is very close to it.

4. Volume V-B-4 (a), pages 249–57, 259–311, contains specific reference to SEATO Contingency Plan 5 dealing with communist armed aggression in Laos. This discloses what the military plans are. The SEATO plans are continuing plans. This involves not only the disclosure of military plans, but a breach of faith with other friendly nations.

Similarly, Volume IV-A-1, pages A26 [*sic*] to A-31, discloses SEATO Operations Plans 4 and 6 dealing with military dispositions with respect to Laos, Cambodia, Thailand, and Pakistan. These are continuing military plans made by us jointly in association with the other nations which are parties to SEATO. Such publication not only discloses the plans to possible enemies, but also involves risk of loss of the support of friendly nations.

5. Volume IV-C-6 (b), page 129, sets forth the United States intelligence community's estimate of the Soviet reaction to the Vietnam War. This was made in 1967, but is in large part still applicable. The disclosure of this information

will give Soviet intelligence insights into the capacity of our intelligence operations, and may strengthen them both by giving them better understanding of us, and by leading them to correct matters on their side.

6. Closely related is Volume IV-C-6 (b), page 157. This is a United States intelligence board estimate of Soviet capacity to provide various types of weapons to North Vietnam. There is much about it that is current and its disclosure to the Soviet Union would give them information which could lead to serious consequences for the United States.

7. Volume IV-C-6 (b), page 168, is an internal memorandum of the Joints Chief of Staff on May 27, 1967, containing a recommendation that [remainder of line deleted]
[line deleted]

Although such a recommendation was never formally made, the disclosure that this was considered as a possibility, though in an internal memorandum, could have very serious consequences to the security of the United States.

8. Volume IV-C-7 (b), pages 161–63, contains the full text of a telegram from Llewellyn Thompson when he was Ambassador to Moscow in 1968. This gives the assessment of one of our most experiences [sic] diplomats of Soviet reaction to United States course of action in Vietnam.

The publication of this telegram would provide valuable intelligence information for the Russians. It is important to them to know what we think about them. Moreover, we cannot have an effective ambassador abroad if he is not able to report candidly and in confidence to the Secretary of State and the President.

The publication of this telegram would impair Mr. Llewellyn's continuing effectiveness. He is now an important and valuable member of our SALT talks delegation dealing with strategic arms limitation, which surely directly affects the security of the United States.

9. Volume IV-C-9 (b), page 52, contains reference to extremely confidential discussions which took place between the military staffs of South Vietnam and Laos, given to us in confidence, relating to possible South Vietnamese military action in Laos with the consent of Laos military authorities. The publication of this not only involves a breach of confidence, but also involves grave risk of reactions from the other nations involved.

10. [remainder of page and following page deleted]

11. Finally, reference should be made to prisoners of war. We are currently engaged in discussions on the prisoner of war issue, in some cases with governments which are not wholly friendly, such as Sweden and Russia [?]. It is obvious that these conversations are conducted on the understanding that they will be confidential, and they are not very likely to be fruitful if that confidence is broken. This is covered by the oral testimony of Mr. Doolin in both cases.

There is one of these in particular which it is very likely that we will not be able to proceed further with as a result of the publication of the papers which has already been made by the *New York Times* and the *Washington Post*. The longer prisoners are held, the more will die.

There is, finally, the whole question of the institution of the Presidency — the power constitutionally inhering in the President as Chief Executive and as Commander-in-Chief of the Army and Navy to conduct the foreign affairs of the United States in a way which will not be unduly hindered, to protect the lives and safety of men in Vietnam, and to be able to assure his top military aides, the Joint Chiefs of Staff, that the lives and safety of men in Vietnam, for whom they, and the President, and the Nation are responsible, will not be endangered or subjected to unnecessary risk. The Federal Judiciary has been referred to as "the least dangerous branch." The Presidency can go to great lengths to provide for such protection by establishing security classification schemes, and by using great care in the selection of its personnel. But, in a nation as large and complicated as this one is, there will inevitably be weak spots in any system. When such weak spots occur, the Presidency is powerless to provide the required protection except with the aid of the courts. In a proper allocation of powers, under the separation of powers, each branch should support the other, in appropriate circumstances. Just as the executive has used its power, through United States marshals, and through military force, to enforce the judgments of the courts, the courts should support the Presidency in a narrow and limited area where such protection is needed in the effective meeting of the President's responsibility, and in the safeguarding of American lives. This is not a question of exception to the First Amendment, but of rational interpretation of that provision wholly consistent with its history and purpose.

Since the publication of materials by the *Times* and *Post*, a considerable number of communications have been received from foreign governments. Reference will be made to two of these.

On June 25, 1971, there was received from the American Ambassador to a friendly country a telegram stating that the principal minister of that country

> informed me last night (June 24) that [the head of state] had instructed him
> to express privately and confidentially grave concern over the unauthorized
> publication of the classified Pentagon documents relating to Vietnam. [The
> minister] indicated that it was not the substance of these documents which
> upset the [head of state], but rather the principle involved, namely that highly
> classified confidential documents which might contain information or secret
> exchanges between the United States government and other governments,
> might irresponsibly find their way into the press. [The minister] pointed

out that in his relations with us the [head of state] is completely frank in his discussion of highly sensitive confidential matters.

However, he has felt able to be frank with us because he felt that we would tightly guard the substance of confidential discussions and exchanges with him. If we are not able to do this, said [the Minister], it would obviously have a very inhibiting effect on [this nation's] ability to exchange views with us on confidential matters with full frankness.

A formal message has also been addressed to the Secretary of State by the British Ambassador, the Rt. Hon. the Earl of Cromer, in which the Ambassador says:

[quotation deleted]

This is a great and free country. It must remain a great and free country. It has a remarkable Constitution, of which the First Amendment is surely an important part. But it is, as Chief Justice Marshall so wisely observed in the formative days of our republic, a *Constitution* which the court is expounding. It is a Constitution which has worked, and which must continue to work. Long experience has shown that sound constitutional construction is not to be found in absolutist or doctrinaire constructions of any of the provisions of the Constitution. It is not suggested that the First Amendment must yield to any other provision of the Constitution. It is suggested that the First Amendment must be construed in the light of the fact that it is a part of a constitution, particularly where foreign affairs are so directly involved, and where, in a very real sense, the workability and the integrity of the institution of the Presidency may be seriously impaired. The Constitution should be construed in such a way as genuinely to preserve a free press, while likewise leaving to the Presidency the protection which it requires for the free flow of information from foreign nations and for the free development of thought and ideas between the President and his immediate advisors.

Respectfully submitted.
Erwin N. Griswold, Solicitor General
June 1971

Special Appendix to Griswold Secret Briefs

UNITED STATES COURT OF APPEALS FOR THE SECOND CIRCUIT

DOCKET NO.

UNITED STATES OF AMERICA,

PLAINTIFF-APPELLANT,

—V—

NEW YORK TIMES COMPANY, ARTHUR OCHS SULZBERGER, HARDING F. BANCROFT, IVAN VEIT, FRANCIS A. COX, JAMES C. GOODALE, SYDNEY GRUSON, WALTER MATTSON, JOHN MCCABE, JOHN MORTIMER, JAMES RESTON, JOHN B. OAKES, A. M. ROSENTHAL, DANIEL SCHWARZ, CLIFTON DANIEL, TOM WICKER, E. W. KENWORTHY, FOX BUTTERFIELD, GERALD GOLD, ALLAN M. SIEGAL, SAMUEL ABT, NEIL SHEEHAN, AND HEDRICK SMITH, DEFENDANTS-APPELLEES.
SPECIAL APPENDIX RELATING TO IN CAMERA PROCEEDINGS
AND SEALED EXHIBITS

SUBMITTED BY APPELLANT UNITED STATES
SEALED BY ORDER
OF THE COURT
JUNE 21, 1971

Preliminary Statement
This Special Appendix contains a brief summary of the testimony in the in camera proceeding in the court below, together with the Government's analysis of the significant portions of the Top Secret study on Vietnam, the publication of which would seriously damage the national security of the United States.

Summary of Testimony
During the in camera proceedings below, the District Court heard testimony from two Defense Department and one State Department official concerning the areas of national security that would be jeopardized by publication of the Top Secret study on Vietnam (Exhibits 7 and 7A). The following is a summary of the highlights of that testimony.

Testimony of Dennis J. Doolin, Deputy Assistant Secretary of Defense for East Asia and Pacific Affairs. Mr. Doolin testified that the disclosure of intergovernmental communications, contained in the A 7 volume study, would affect prisoner of war negotiations being conducted by the United States (p. 5).

He also referred to material bearing on signal intelligence and electronic intelligence in the study (p. 6).

Disclosure of documents in the study, according to Mr. Doolin's testimony, could have an adverse impact on various military forces in Vietnam (p. 8), and on SEATO operational plans (p. 10). Although some of the documents did not seem to be prejudicial to the national defense, when individually examined, Mr. Doolin indicated that in combination the documents might be extremely prejudicial (p. 13).

Mr. Doolin testified that articles from the study published by the *Times* prior to the restraining order had produced expressions of grave concern by the Prime Minister of Australia (p. 25), and that Sweden may no longer be willing to act as an intermediary in the conduct of United States diplomacy (p. 28).

Testimony of Vice Admiral Francis J. Blouin, Deputy Chief of Naval Operations for Plans and Policy. Admiral Blouin testified that the 47-volume study is full of highly sensitive material and war plans (p. 50). It describes air strikes against various targets and numbers of aircraft striking various targets (p. 50). [Deletion] contains information on potential targets for bombing and contingency plans (p. 50). It also discloses our command apparatus (p. 51), and our timing system (p. 51).

Rules of engagement, which do not change drastically, are found in the study (p. 52), as are details regarding use of aircraft against particular targets (p. 57), and the capability of the United States to deploy its ground troops (p. 58). The study contains details of our decision-making processes and our reaction times in making decisions (pp. 61–62). In addition, it describes the involvement of Thai forces in Laos, although the Thai government has publicly denied the presence of its forces in Laos (p. 68).

Testimony of William Macomber, Deputy Under Secretary [of] State for Administration. Mr. Macomber testified that one of the source documents for the study is a telegram from Mr. Seaborn, the Canadian representative to the International Control Commission. The telegram describes statements made by him to North Vietnamese officials on behalf of the United States. Mr. Macomber stated that publication of the telegram makes it "almost impossible for the United States to approach third countries and ask them to do delicate things. . . ." (pp. 75–77).

Mr. Macomber testified that the documents also disclose that Australia sent troops to South Vietnam at the instance of [*sic*] the United States, whereas the public position of the Australian government is that troops had been sent pursuant to a SEATO commitment. This disclosure, Macomber testified, might undermine our relations with Australia (p. 77).

Mr. Macomber referred to a message from [deleted]

He also described an "eyes only" telegram sent by Llewellyn Thompson, the then United States Ambassador to the Soviet Union, in which Ambassador Thompson sets forth his estimates of Soviet reaction to military escalation by the United States (p. 79).

Finally, Mr. Macomber described the possible effects of publication of the study on current prisoner-of-war negotiations (pp. 81–82), and on "domestic advisers to the policy makers in diplomatic matters" (p. 84).

Potential Impact of Publication of Exhibits 7 and 7A on the National
Security of the United States

A. Current Military Operations

For the past eighteen months the United States has been withdrawing United States forces from the Republic of Vietnam at the fastest rate possible consistent with capabilities of the South Vietnamese armed forces in taking over the combat role and consistent with the retention of adequate military security for the United States forces remaining. This withdrawal rate has been and is now planned to continue to be based on certain overall assumptions which are critical, inasmuch as this rate of withdrawal is as fast as possible within the lowest level of prudent risk. One major assumption that is implicit in the current withdrawal rate is that the planned support which we expect from our allies and from the Republic of Vietnam will continue without major change. The delicate military balance which we have been maintaining has a high risk of being upset. Disclosure of the material in this study would impede our current rate of withdrawal and diminish the planned efforts of the Army of the Republic of Vietnam and other free world forces. Additionally, were the Vietnamization program to be weakened, the safety and security of our forces would be seriously jeopardized unless our withdrawal races were slowed to compensate for this weakening.

Publication of "Top Secret" documents concerning Southeast Asia will jeopardize the military support we are receiving from foreign forces because of their political and other consequences. Should the level of allied security in Southeast Asia fall below prudent risk, an adverse snowballing affect could not be ruled out. This is particularly so were the North Vietnamese and Viet Cong forces to mount an initiative and accomplish a major localized or tactical victory over the South Vietnamese forces.

The overall publication of the documents must also be considered in terms of the potential Government of Thailand reaction to a public disclosure of documents which impact upon Thai political attitudes, both within country and without. Thailand bases for stationing United States tactical air units and B-52's are essential to the safety and well-being of the United States forces now deployed in Southeast Asia. Obviously a basic tenet of our planning for the Vietnamization program and troop withdrawal has always been and continues to be that there will be adequate air support for the allied forces during the withdrawal period. The air bases in the Republic of Thailand are of utmost importance to maintaining the level of risk to our troops in Southeast Asia at a prudent level and any loss of freedom of operation from our air bases in Thailand below those which are now currently planned would not give sufficient support to our Southeast Asia campaign for protecting Vietnamization and the remaining United

States forces. The current interdiction program against the enemy supply routes into South Vietnam as well as the air support available to United States and allied forces engaged in combat would be unacceptably crippled in the event the status of these air bases are changed.

Without continued support from the Republic of Thailand, air support missions would be substantially reduced, permitting the North Vietnamese to build major supply bases in preparation for mounting sizeable force attacks against the United States, South Vietnamese, and other free world forces remaining in South Vietnam.

Information contained in the documents could also have an impact upon the attitudes, expectations and interests in South Korea, and there is a possibility that the release of this information might cause the government of Korea to withdraw Korean forces faster than is currently envisioned. Such a change in withdrawal rate would be extremely serious and would require the United States to make a reassessment of her planned withdrawal rates. At the present time, the Republic of Korea is maintaining some 49,000 troops in the Republic of Vietnam, and these troops are providing the security to important population areas.

Publication of documents will also have an impact upon the attitudes, expectations, interests, and allied solidarity of those countries of Southeast Asia, including Korea, Thailand, Japan, and Philippines upon whose bases our troop participating in our current operation planning relies. The military risks and dangers of adverse reactions in those countries are of major military proportions to the stability of the situation in South Vietnam.

Publication of the documents clearly would have some effect upon the internal political processes of the South Vietnamese Government. By stimulating instability in the South Vietnamese armed forces or their current operational planning, the relative threat to South Vietnam itself would be increased. One of the military steps, which the South Vietnamese high command presumably would take would be to terminate their cross-border operations and return their participating forces to bolster the security of the homeland. Particularly in the case of Cambodia, withdrawal of these forces would allow the North Vietnamese and the Viet Cong forces to reestablish the series of base areas along the Cambodian-South Vietnamese border from which they could mount increased military activity throughout South Vietnam. The implication to Vietnamization, the security of the United States forces in Southeast Asia, and our redeployment efforts in such a circumstance is obvious.

    I. Portions of Exhibits 7 and 7A, the disclosure of which would present increased risks to the safety of U.S. forces

        VOL. IV. C. 7 (a), VOL. I, para 1 B, pages 9–10; VOL. I, para II C. 2, page 100 — Specific details on JCS recommendations for an intensified bombing program against NVN. These specifics reveal sensitive details about current contingency plans, such as mining the major ports, cutting bridges on the LOCs from China to Hanoi, and the number of sorties required.

VOL. IV. C. 6, page 52 — Provide CINCPAC and NIE 14.3-66 assessment of enemy force structure in SVN in 1966, and would allow enemy to assess accuracy of U.S. estimates at that time and draw conclusions on the extent to which he was capable of avoiding detection in combat situations.

VOL. IV. B. 3. Chronology, pages 1–23;

VOL. IV. C. 5. Chronology, pages 11–33;

VOL. IV. C. 6. Chronology, pages i–xviii — Detailed chronology of step-by-step development of the advisory buildup in SVN, 1961–1967; buildup of U.S. forces, March–July 1965; and U.S. ground strategy and force developments, 1965–1967, providing insight into U.S. decision-making process and reaction times.

VOL. IV. C. 4, pages vii, xii, 14, 17 and 20;

VOL. IV. C. 5, page 9 — Exposes two major military operational plans which had been used in 1964 and in 1965 for planning of emergency deployments of United States ground combat forces into Southeast Asia. These planned deployments were to be used by the Commander in Chief, Pacific, to meet any military offensive moves against the United States by the armed forces of the People's Republic of China. Although these particular operational plans are no longer in use, the discussions relating to these plans do reveal possible total force commitments and planned areas of operation which appear valid for future operations. Such information, if disclosed to an enemy planner, presumably would, if combined with other intelligence generally held by the intelligence communities of foreign countries, seriously compromise current war planning for Southeast Asia.

VOL. IV. C. 10 — Provides statistical information of operational and intelligence nature which would give the enemy a basis for measuring the allied effort and his (enemy) success in combating that effort.

VOL. V. B. 4, pages 313–20 — Contains a special national intelligence estimate and refer to other pertinent estimates reflecting intelligence community data on the situation.

VOL. V. B. 4, pages 295–311 — Reveal aspects of SEATO contingency war plans and relationships which are still in effect to a considerable extent and could destroy usefulness of SEATO as an occupation, and future alliance between the countries concerned. It could reveal to the communists the limited costs of an all-out effort to take all of Southeast Asia.

VOL. IV. C. 5, pages 11–32; VOL. IV. C. 6 (a), pages i–xvii — Chronologies provide insight into deployment times for major U.S. units, which would be invaluable for a potential enemy in estimating U.S. capability to react to contingencies or in reinforcing committed forces.

VOL.VI. C. 4, pages 21, 22, Summary — Direct quote of Saigon Embassy message 10856 from Lodge to Secretary of State, TS, dated 14 November 66 and Saigon Embassy message 12247 to Secretary of State, TS/NODIS, 30 November 66. Presumably would assist enemy in analyzing and possibly breaking codes employed at that time and thereby all traffic of that period.

VOL.VI. C. 4, pages 1, 2, Ohio — Quotes SECRET-EXDIS message, 10 June 1967 OLS0-4531 to Secretary of State and State SECRET-EXDIS message 213389 to OSLO. Presumably would assist in breaking codes in use during period. Many similar examples are interspread throughout this volume.

II. Portions of Exhibits 7 and 7A the disclosure of which would slow the U.S. program of shifting military responsibility in Vietnam to South Vietnamese forces

VOL. IV. C. 8, pages i–viii, 1, 2, 3, 5, 7, 10, 14 and following pages. VOL. IV. C. 9(a) pages iii, iv. vi–ix, 1, 17, 20, 21, 32, 55–58 and following pages. VOL. IV. C. 9(b), pages ii–iv, vi(ii,7, 15, 17, 23, 25, 33 and following pages — Comments on the Pacification program in the basic volume on Pacification and in volumes on "the Evolution of the War" endanger the essential Government of Vietnam interest in and support of the Pacification program by:

1. Citing overparticipation by the U.S. in a program which should have been essentially Vietnamese in character.

2. Documenting friction and competition between U.S. agencies in Vietnam and Washington to the detriment of the program.

3. Documenting efforts by the U.S. to use foreign aid or U.S. withdrawal as "leverage" to exert pressure on the GVN despite its status as a sovereign state.

4. Criticising the Vietnamese Government for lack of interest and emphasis on Pacification.

5. Describing prominent Vietnamese, many of whom are still active in the government, of corruption, inability, inertia, or lack of interest in the essential program.

Disclosure of these statements in an official Top Secret report presumably could subject GVN and key officials to withdraw; cause the Pacification Program to be considered as U.S. rather than Vietnamese;

result in diversion of GVN emphasis to less critical programs; jeopardize U.S. adviser relations with their Vietnamese counterparts; and endanger other critical programs in Vietnam.

VOL. IV. C. 9 (a) and (b), *U.S./GVN Relations 1963–1967*, parts I and II. VOL. IV. B. 3, page 59 — Recounts in detail U.S. disappointment with GVN efforts in government administration and conduct of the war, and U.S. failure to generate effective leverage on the GVN in behalf of changes felt by the U.S. to be essential. Public revelation of the extent to which the U.S. has criticized Vietnamese efforts and attempted to control GVN decisions would make all facets of relations with the South Vietnamese more complicated at a time when the United States is entering a very delicate phase of the withdrawal process wherein we seek to win GVN support for new programs of utmost significance to their own survival and to the security and effectiveness of U.S. forces which remain in South Vietnam.

Particularly sensitive negotiations involve U.S. efforts to solicit effective actions from the GVN in controlling the drug traffic to U.S. forces. Many key GVN officials who are discussed and criticized in the studies still occupy key positions in the GVN.

VOL. IV. C. 6 (c), U.S. Ground Strategy and Force Deployments 1965–1967, VOL. III — This section covers in great detail the processes involved in U.S. decision making. Of course, there are variations to these processes, but the basic blueprint is there. To know how your advisory things [*sic*] and how he develops his plans provides a substantial advantage to the enemy and most often will tip the scale of victory in his favor. This applies not only to the battlefield but to the political arena as well. With the information provided in the volume noted, the enemy is in a better position to predetermine what your next course of action is most likely to be and therefore be prepared to counter your strategy. The knowledge by the enemy of this information could have a decided detrimental impact upon the present Vietnamization program and U.S. redeployment objectives. At a time when the capabilities of the U.S. forces are being seriously reduced by domestic pressures and fiscal constraints any further aid and comfort provided to our potential enemies can only be dangerous to the security of the United States.

VOL. IV. C. 9 (b), Part II — Discloses GVN weaknesses and U.S. attempts to influence GVN actions, involving many of the current leadership. Provides enemy with much data against GVN government and leadership and would promote communist propaganda against U.S. role. Current GVN leadership is expected to continue. Damage by exposure of their position and efforts would be severe. A loss of leadership at this critical time could collapse the GVN and affect U.S. programs for successful troop withdrawals.

B. Current Diplomatic Relations

The United States has received the cooperation of a number of third countries in carrying out delicate diplomatic missions on sensitive and vital issues. The United States has approached, and continues to approach, governments of other countries, some of them not friendly to the United States, for their assistance in possibly achieving a resolution of the situation of American partners of war in North Vietnam. Some countries have played a useful role in getting food and medicine and other relief packages through to our prisoners of war and in other ways assisting in easing conditions for the prisoners of war and their families in the United States. Those efforts, which the United States Government has made a priority item, necessarily depend on the generous services of other countries as intermediaries. The United States' apparent lack of ability to preserve the confidential character of sensitive communications involved in the publication of Exhibits 7 and 7A would seriously undermine our efforts to make such arrangements.

I. Brief outline of third party diplomatic contacts with Hanoi described in Exhibits 7 and 7A:

II. Portions of Exhibits 7 and 7A the disclosure of which would compromise other foreign relations of the United States.

A. In Section IV. C .7 (b), Volume II, at pages 161–62 of the study is a Top Secret cable dated March 1, 1968, from Ambassador Thompson in Moscow to the Under Secretary of States marked "LITERALLY EYES ONLY" containing Ambassador Thompson's careful and detailed assessment of probable Soviet attitudes toward various possible United States military actions with respect to North Vietnam and possible Soviet countermoves.

B. The classified documents concerning the period of the coup d'état against President Ngo Dinh Diem in November 1963 and United States relations with the successor regimes reveal the degree of direct United States pressures and influence on the Government of Vietnam some years ago, especially in 1963 and 1964. Examples are communications regarding United States support for the coup and an Embassy Saigon airgram of December 24, 1964, which related a brutally frank lecture to Vietnamese generals by the American Ambassador. These United States interventions diminish the stature of present Vietnamese political figures in and out of the Government, who are identified in the secret documents. Among them are President Thieu and Vice President Ky.

C. Deleted

Evidentiary Analysis of the Griswold Secret Briefs

The Griswold secret brief (annotated "Reviewed for Declassification" with dates) identifies the eleven items or sections of the Pentagon Papers disclosure of which would cause irreparable damage to U.S. national security. We have commented upon each of the eleven items in sealed (secret) brief. In the discussion that follows the reader should keep in mind that the relevant legal standard articulated to the Supreme Court by Erwin Griswold, the solicitor general of the United States, is that the identified material would, if revealed, cause irreparable and immediate damage to the national security of the United States.

Note: The first reference in each case refers to relevant paragraphs of Solicitor General Griswold's secret brief. Although that document is reproduced here, its original page numbers are not. Additional references are the relevant portions of the Pentagon Papers study that Griswold cites as evidence in his brief. Since in most cases we have used pages from the Senator Gravel edition of the Pentagon Papers (rather than the version declassified by the House Armed Services Committee), the page references will not always match those cited by Griswold but are, in fact, correct.

Griswold Claim No. 1 (paragraph 1)

The Griswold secret brief starts off with a blanket claim for damage assumed to result from the release of volumes of the Pentagon Papers dealing with the diplomacy of attempts to open negotiations from 1964 to 1968 (shown here as VI-C-1 through VI-C-4 — a two-page summary of the four volumes was included in the June 21, 1971, affidavit by William Macomber, deputy under secretary of state for administration, in the *Washington Post* case). Probably the most important point to be made is that these diplomatic volumes were not part of the leak and were never released by Daniel Ellsberg or anyone else. Ellsberg has made clear in public forums and commentaries that he refused to include these volumes in the leak, because he feared release would give the Nixon administration an excuse to halt ongoing negotiations for a Vietnam settlement. At trial the government professed not to know exactly what portions of the Pentagon Papers had been leaked, and the courts agreed to proceed on the basis of assuming all the original documents were compromised. In point of fact, however, neither specific nor general damage could have resulted here and the argument was moot.

Griswold Claim No. 2 (paragraph 2)

The first specific claim is that the diplomatic volumes contain derogatory comments that might be offensive to nations or governments, in particular U.S. allies

---

These two sections on evidentiary analysis are the work of historian John Prados, who is solely responsible for the contents. No other editor or contributor to this book had any role in the analysis.

with troops in South Vietnam, principally South Korea, Thailand, and Australia. Thailand is singled out as critical because 65 percent of U.S. air sorties over Vietnam were then being launched from U.S. bases in that nation. The diplomatic volumes were, in fact, largely declassified under the Freedom of Information Act in 1978; while there are some significant deletions, probably more than 99 percent of the material was in fact released. In the diplomatic papers as released there are only five references to Australia, two to South Korea, and one to Thailand in a text of more than one thousand pages. Most of them are notations that one or another country had or had not been briefed on some initiative. None is derogatory.

The Griswold brief makes the claim that the pace of U.S. withdrawal from Vietnam would have to become slower if the diplomatic volumes were released. The claim is purely speculative. It is equally likely that, faced with the withdrawal of its allies, the U.S. would have withdrawn more rapidly itself.

Griswold Claim No. 3 (paragraph 3)
The Griswold brief asserts there are specific references to the names and activities of CIA agents "still active in Southeast Asia." Almost all the CIA officers identified in the documents were in fact high-level officials like Richard Helms, John McCone, Allen Dulles, and Richard Bissell, publicly known officials. Richard Helms, the director of the CIA, because he was director, was "still active in Southeast Asia." There was no damage to national security that could result from revelation of Helms's name, which was widely known. The only clandestine services officer identified is Lucien Conein, active in plots to overthrow Ngo Dinh Diem, and by 1971 Conein was no longer with the CIA. If accurate, the assertion in the government's brief can only have referred to South Vietnamese officials who were on the CIA payroll as sources of information. Those persons, however, are referred to in the documents in their actual Saigon government capacities and are discussed taking various actions. They are not identified as CIA agents. The additional claim in the brief that currently continuing CIA operations are referred to in the Pentagon Papers can be true only in the sense that the war, including such features as pacification (which had a CIA component), or efforts to block the Ho Chi Minh Trail, and so on; itself continued.

The Griswold brief additionally claims there are "references to the activities of the National Security Agency." In fact there is a document (cited elsewhere in this paper) that refers to a number of National Security Agency personnel included in a 1961 deployment increment (fifteen men). There is also a statement in the text of the Pentagon Papers that covers the early (1961–1963) part of the war that the United States is monitoring North Vietnamese radio transmissions. But the papers have no detailed discussion of programs, methods, results, procedures, management issues, ongoing efforts, and so on. This is hardly surprising since Pentagon

Papers analysts were not cleared for communications intelligence data nor was the study intended to cover this matter. That radio intelligence was a "currently continuing" activity (Griswold brief, p. 10) is correct, but in the same sense as the last point, this could convey no special knowledge to Hanoi. The North Vietnamese were aware long before 1971 that U.S. forces were listening in on their radio transmissions, and their knowledge of U.S. activities was far more detailed than anything they could learn from the Pentagon Papers.

No locations are given in the brief for material that is actually compromising in either of these areas.

Griswold Claim No. 4 (paragraph 4; ref. to V-B4(a) pp. 249–57, 259–311)
The Griswold brief objects to the disclosure of contingency plans of the Southeast Asia Treaty Organization (SEATO), most specifically SEATO Plan 5. The SEATO plans referred to were 1961 plans for blocking the lower panhandle of Laos. Not only were these not "continuing military plans" as asserted in the brief, but they involved absurdly small numbers of troops, given the North Vietnamese dispositions in Laos in 1971, and would have led to major military debacle if implemented. More important, by 1971 the deployment of any number of U.S. troops into Laos was illegal under United States law. Here the U.S. government was in a position much like President John F. Kennedy with the *New York Times* revelations of CIA preparations for the Bay of Pigs invasion — the press would have been doing the government a favor by publishing the leak. In addition, the U.S. government had just finished supporting a major South Vietnamese invasion of Laos which had been roundly defeated (Lam Son 719); the assertion in the Griswold brief that there was any secret left about this option was disingenuous. Finally, by 1971 the SEATO alliance was moribund, and the claim that any SEATO contingency plan might be taken off the shelf and implemented was farfetched. Notwithstanding its claims that this material must remain secret, the United States government published it in full in its own edition of the Pentagon Papers.

Griswold Claim No. 5 (paragraph 5; ref. to IV-C-6 p. 129)
The Griswold brief fears giving Russian intelligence insight into U.S. intelligence capabilities by revealing a U.S. estimate of Soviet attitudes and intentions toward the Vietnam War. In fact, the Pentagon Papers quotes only one paragraph of the estimate (SNIE 11-11-67, which is not, in fact, identified in the leaked documents) which says that the Russians might send volunteers or crews for aircraft or defense equipment to Vietnam, or break off negotiations with the United States on various subjects. The mining or blockade of the North Vietnamese coast is predicted to challenge Russian leaders. An examination of the underlying document, the SNIE, will demonstrate that it is pitched at a similar high level of

generality. The Griswold brief's assertion that "the estimate is in large part still applicable" is accurate in the sense that any simple enumeration of broad options will always contain the range of actions that are possible in a situation.

Griswold Claim No. 6 (paragraph 7; ref. to IV-C-6(b) p. 157)
The Griswold brief asserts that the revelation of a footnote describing the judgment of the United States Intelligence Board on Russian capacity to supply various types of weapons to North Vietnam "has much about it that is current, and its disclosure . . . could lead to serious consequences for the United States." The source text is a May 19, 1967, draft memorandum from Secretary of Defense Robert McNamara to President Lyndon Johnson which contains a footnote referring to the United States Intelligence Board (USIB) opinion. The "USIB estimate" is actually a reference to SNIE 11-11-67, described above. That estimate cites various kinds of weapons that Russia was capable of giving Hanoi, including artillery, aircraft, rockets, patrol boats, and so on. Again, these are in the nature of an inventory of possibilities. Neither the footnote nor the underlying intelligence estimate contains any numerical predictions whatsoever. It remains an enumeration of broad Russian options. Although Department of Defense censors deleted the offending footnote at the location cited in the Griswold brief, in their own edition of the Pentagon Papers, they permitted publication of the identical note in another passage of the study (see IV-C-7(b) page 47).

Griswold Claim No. 7 (paragraph 7; ref. to IV-C-6 (b) p. 168)
The Griswold brief asserts that disclosing that the United States ever considered a nuclear response in the event of a Chinese attack on Thailand "could have very serious consequences to the security of the United States." The document containing language about nuclear weapons use is not a Joint Chiefs of Staff memo of May 27, 1967, as cited, but JCSM 288-67, of May 20, in which the Joint Chiefs discussed U.S. worldwide military posture. This discrepancy in dates is probably a typographical error in the original legal brief. The statement about nuclear weapons arose in the context of a discussion of a U.S. invasion of Cambodia, which was illegal under U.S. law by 1971. In that study it is postulated that Hanoi might counter with more forces in Laos, leading the United States to send extra troops to Thailand, and China to attack the Thais. All of these possibilities were exceedingly remote.

The language about nuclear weapons in the Joint Chiefs memorandum was not unusual; that is, with limited ground forces in the U.S. military, it was customary for the Joint Chiefs to invoke nuclear weapons in almost all discussions of war with China. Throughout the 1950s, during the Eisenhower administration's "New Look" national security policy, nuclear weapons were deliberately built into the contingency plans. In addition, there were four Sino-American crises during that interval, all of which involved U.S. nuclear threats against China (Korea 1953; Tachen 1954–1955; Taiwan Straits 1958; Quemoy/Matsu 1960), plus the Dien Bien Phu crisis of 1954, in which nuclear weapons were brandished by the U.S. secretary of state with language about retaliation "at places and with means of our own choosing," which became known as the doctrine of massive retaliation. Almost identical language about nuclear weapons occurs in JCS and other documents in the Pentagon Papers about the earlier period, which censors did not bother to delete from the government edition of the Pentagon Papers. In any case, for the Griswold brief in 1971 to argue the serious consequences of this item in the Pentagon Papers requires assuming the Chinese had paid no attention to all these events and public pronouncements by the United States. If there was damage to the national security here, this occurred long before 1971, and the Pentagon Papers were not the source of it.

Griswold Claim No. 8 (paragraph 8; ref to IV-C-7(b) pp. 161–63)
The Griswold brief asserts that revelation of this source material, a cable to Washington by then-ambassador to Moscow Llewellyn C. Thompson in March 1968, would impair Thompson's effectiveness and provide the Russians valuable intelligence information. The source text is Moscow cable 2983 of March 1, 1968, in which Ambassador Thompson comments on the likely Russian response to a range of U.S. options in Vietnam, things from the mining of Haiphong Harbor to possible invasions of North Vietnam, Laos, or Cambodia; to increasing troop levels in the South or more bombing of the North. The intelligence Russians could learn from this cable is the set of options the United States was considering in 1968 plus Thompson's assessments of Russian reaction. The set of options could not have been that useful, because, much like the transparency of Russian options toward Hanoi for U.S. intelligence, American options had not changed since the beginning of the Big Unit war. Moreover, by 1971 every one of those options save the mining of Haiphong had been played out, and U.S. withdrawal was accepted and publicly known policy. Llewellyn Thompson's opinions of the options were possibly useful as an index of his thinking, as an indicator the Russians could use to gauge how well Thompson had understood the Russian position in 1968, or as an indicator to the Russians that Thompson was important enough to Washington that the United States would share with him its most secret Vietnam plans.

None of these possibilities lends any support to the claim in the Griswold brief that publication of the cable would "impair" Thompson's effectiveness as an arms-control negotiator, "which surely directly affects the security of the United States." On the contrary, publication most likely encouraged Russians to a high regard for Ambassador Thompson. In any case, the entire issue was specious, through no fault of Solicitor General Griswold, because the arms-control negotiations were directly run and privately dominated by the White House in the person of National Security Adviser Henry Kissinger. The Russians surely knew that; the effectiveness of Llewellyn Thompson was a false issue.

Griswold Claim No. 9 (paragraph 9; ref. IV-C-9(b) p. 52)
The Griswold brief declares that there was a grave risk of adverse reactions from South Vietnam and Laos if the release of the Pentagon Papers revealed they had held discussions related to possible South Vietnamese military action in Laos. The source text, in its entirety, reads: "In May talks started between Lao and GVN [i.e., South Vietnamese] military staffs. The occasion was planning for barrier extension westward, but Washington realized at once that there was little the U.S. could do to limit the contacts to that subject." There was no explicit discussion in the Pentagon Papers of South Vietnamese action in Laos, and no evident reason the passage would be offensive, other than revealing the fact of the talks. In 1971, however, coming after the (failed) South Vietnamese invasion of Laos in Lam Son 719, the alleged problem of a breach of confidence had only academic importance.

Griswold Claim No. 10 (pp. 8–9)
The Griswold brief threatens grave damage from the revelation of communications intelligence secrets, making the enemy aware of significant U.S. intelligence successes, permitting them to assess U.S. communications intelligence capability and to impair current military operations. This is a strange claim. To begin with, the Pentagon Papers carried a "Top Secret" level of classification within the Department of Defense. By itself, that classification grade usually excludes communications intelligence information, which exists in what the United States terms a "special compartmented" category and carries a separate code word. There was no communications intelligence in the Pentagon Papers in the first place. As for directly affecting U.S. operations, the character and content of U.S. operations had completely changed between 1968 and 1971 from large-unit clearing efforts to small-scale patrols in support of pacification. The specifics were all different by 1971, only the techniques remained the same, but the possibility of damage to national security is mooted by the absence of communications intelligence from the documents.

The U.S. government deleted from the *Washington Post*'s brief commenting on the in camera evidence references to three passages in the documents, and the passages themselves, that refer to organization and administration of communications intelligence. All these references relate to the spring of 1961, when Deputy Secretary of Defense Roswell Gilpatric headed an interagency task force on

Vietnam policy. The deletions occur in successive drafts of the task force report. The first is a recommendation to "expand the current program of interception and direction finding covering Vietnamese Communist communications activities in South Vietnam, as well as North Vietnamese targets," and asks for authority to conduct these activities on a joint basis with South Vietnamese. (The source document was declassified in 1977.) The second deletion has nothing to do with communications intelligence and recommended an additional forty personnel for the CIA station in Saigon — for paramilitary and covert-action programs. The third deletion was of a recommendation to send fifteen communications intelligence specialists to Vietnam to help train South Vietnamese counterparts. No conceivable damage to the national security of the United States would have resulted from the exposure of this material, which had nothing to do with either U.S. codes or foreign code breaking. Only the reflexive desire to keep secret all information related to intelligence could be served by deleting these items from the government edition of the Pentagon Papers. These were also exceedingly thin reasons to keep secret all forty-seven volumes of the Pentagon Papers, as was the government's proposed remedy in this court case.

Griswold Claim No. 11 (paragraph 11)
The Griswold brief mentions prisoners of war to invoke the claim that breaking the confidentiality of diplomatic communications would adversely affect negotiations to bring them home. The confidentiality of diplomacy argument is one that the Nixon administration made very strongly, bringing in diplomat William B. Macomber who made it the centerpiece of his testimony and affidavit, and even actually soliciting comments from foreign governments for use in a legal brief. These were essentially political arguments, however. A wide variety of foreign governments had made public their roles in Vietnam negotiating efforts, and even the secret give-and-take was already on the record in a variety of books and news articles. (In particular, see David Kraslow and Stewart H. Loory, *The Secret Search for Peace in Vietnam,* and Chester Cooper, *The Lost Crusade: America in Vietnam.*) As we now know, moreover, the diplomatic volumes of the Pentagon Papers had never been compromised in the first place. Even if they had, in more than a thousand pages of text the diplomatic volumes have only eight references to prisoners of war. It is difficult to avoid the conclusion that the prisoner issue was incorporated into the U.S. legal brief primarily to invoke an issue that would resonate with the justices.

Evidentiary Analysis of the Special Appendix to the Second Circuit
This "Special Appendix," submitted on June 21, 1971, to the United States Court of Appeals for the Second Circuit by the U.S. government, makes a set of allegations

regarding evidence drawn from the testimony of several U.S. officials who appeared in New York court hearings, followed by claims about the impact on current military operations of publication of the Pentagon Papers. The heart of this document is a list of seventeen references to Pentagon Papers material, each with an explanation of how their publication would reveal secrets of great import. That the U.S. government considered this a vital part of its claim is demonstrated by the fact that Solicitor General Griswold included the same items in his "Supplemental List" to the Supreme Court and also separately submitted the "Special Appendix" document in addition to his court briefs. In this examination of the secret brief, we have identified and commented on each of the seventeen items in the government's "Special Appendix" to the Second Circuit.

Note: The "Special Appendix" divided its assertions of damage to the national security into two sections, the first to represent direct impacts on the United States, the second defined as revelations that would "slow the U.S. program of shifting military responsibility in Vietnam to South Vietnamese forces." In each item below the first indicator (e.g., "Part I, no. 1") shows which group of claims the alleged sensitive material falls into. The second reference in each case is to the relevant portions of the Pentagon Papers.

Part I, No. 1 (IV-C-7(a) et seq.)
The Special Appendix asserts that this discussion of Joint Chiefs of Staff recommendations for bombing North Vietnam in 1967 reveals "sensitive details about current contingency plans," including numbers of sorties required for mining major ports, cutting lines of communications to China, and destroying bridges. The source document is a portion of the Pentagon Papers that describes JCS views as of July 2, 1967. The only number that appears in the text is the statement that an increase of three thousand sorties per month (from two thousand to five thousand) would be needed to carry out the air campaign therein considered. This gross figure in no way conveys the kind of information suggested by the legal brief. Similarly, ports, bridges, lines of communication, and so on are simply mentioned; there is no detail, sensitive or otherwise, in the document. Department of Defense censors did not even see fit to delete this material from the government edition.

Part I, No. 2 (ref. IV-C-6, p. 52)
The Special Appendix declares that this passage, which cites CIA and Pacific Command estimates of North Vietnamese and NLF strength in the South in 1966, would permit the adversary to evaluate the accuracy of U.S. intelligence and "draw conclusions on the extent to which he was capable of avoiding detection in combat situations." The 1966 estimates were detailed in the Pentagon Papers, but they

were like a snapshot at a given point in time. By 1971, the estimates were quite out of date. Most important, the conclusion in the Special Appendix does not follow from the data cited. The estimates were strategic ones, order of battle material. In a tactical combat situation, the ability to avoid detection has nothing to do with strategic intelligence estimates. Department of Defense censors did not bother to delete this information from the government edition.

Part I, No. 3 (ref. IV-B-3 Chronology et seq.)

The Special Appendix cites these detailed chronologies of U.S. activities and decision making on Vietnam as providing insight into the U.S. decision-making process and reaction times. In fact the chronologies are prime examples of the opposite of what government lawyers wished to demonstrate — they were of great historical value but of little current moment. Hanoi, Moscow, Beijing, and everyone else dealing with Washington was well aware the entire action system in the United States had changed with the advent of the Nixon administration. Department of Defense censors did not bother to delete these materials from the government edition.

Part I, No. 4 (IV-C-4 pp. vii et seq.)

The Special Appendix, as well as several affidavits and government officials in their testimony made much of this material, which in their view "exposes two major military operational plans . . . used in 1964 and 1965." This information combined with other intelligence, in this view, could "seriously compromise current war planning for Southeast Asia." Examination of the relevant passages cited will show that the Pentagon Papers did no more than to identify the two plans (OPLAN 32-64, OPLAN 39-65) and say that the initial appearance of U.S. combat troops in South Vietnam conformed to their provisions. The documents contain no overall description of the plans, no detail on what forces might be involved or available to the overall package, no detail on planning provisions of sequencing and movement of forces, no detail on the bases or means involved, and so on. An adversary planner looking at this could not do much of anything. Again, the passages were of principal value to historians.

Part I, No. 5 (ref. IV-C-10)

The Special Appendix claimed that this information, a set of statistics, could provide the adversary with a basis for measuring, and thereby countering, the U.S. and third country/South Vietnamese War effort. In fact the set of statistics covered only the years 1965 to 1967 and had no relevance to the Vietnam War in 1971. The various measures in the tables were of the same sorts military officials trotted out at congressional hearings and press conferences to argue that progress was being made in Vietnam. Department of Defense censors did not bother to delete these materials from the government edition of the Pentagon Papers. Editors at Beacon Press preparing the Senator Mike Gravel Edition found this material of so little interest, they did not bother to include it.

Part I, No. 6 (ref. V-B-4 pp. 313–20)
The Special Appendix notes that this passage "contains a special national intelligence estimate" and makes no specific claim of damage to the national security. The underlying material is an October 1961 estimate (SNIE 10-3-61) projecting anticipated Russian and Chinese reactions if SEATO forces intervened in South Vietnam. Aside from the fact that the Vietnam War had been totally transformed between 1961 and 1971, making the intelligence report wholly irrelevant, by 1971 there was no prospect whatever of SEATO intervention in South Vietnam. The document was of historical, not current operational, interest. Department of Defense censors chose to delete only a few lines from one paragraph of the seven-page paper when printing it in the government edition.

Part I, No. 7 (ref. V-B-4 pp. 295–311)
The Special Appendix claims that these pages "reveal aspects of SEATO contingency war plans and relationships that are still in effect" and could reveal to the adversary "the limited costs of an all-out effort [on his part] to take all of Southeast Asia." The documents in question are an October 9, 1961, Joint Chiefs of Staff memorandum recommending intervention in Laos under SEATO Plan 5 and a memo the next day from William P. Bundy to Robert McNamara, reflecting on his Indochina experience since 1954 and agreeing with the intervention recommendation. Both documents are of prime historical significance, but neither had anything to do with the situation in Indochina in 1971. Indeed, if SEATO Plan 5 was an active plan to be implemented in 1971, that would have been suicidal: the plan called for a total of 22,800 troops under multinational command (with all the problems that entailed) against North Vietnamese forces in excess of 70,000. Moreover, in the wake of the defeat of the South Vietnamese invasion of Laos in February–March 1971 (Lam Son 719), there was zero chance of implementation for anything like the schemes at issue here. Department of Defense censors deleted no more than occasional words from the versions printed in the government edition.

Part I, No. 8 (ref. IV-C-5 pp. 11–32 et seq.)
The Special Appendix already tried to use this material to justify maintaining secrecy of the Pentagon Papers in the action discussed above as Part I, No. 3.

Part I, No. 9 (ref. VI-C-4 pp. 21–22)

The Special Appendix asserts that a direct quote of a Saigon embassy message "would assist the enemy in analyzing and possibly breaking codes employed at that time." Unfortunately, examination of the underlying document shows the cited pages do not in fact contain any of the material claimed by the legal brief. However, on the general question of code breaking, the Special Appendix is making the unstated assumption that the Russians (and any other interested actors) have in fact intercepted the coded version of the cited text with which to compare — not a surety — and that a break of one message would have compromised all traffic. The latter is also less likely in the era of machine codes. In any case, the claim was specious since the capture in 1968 off Korea of the U.S. Navy spy ship *Pueblo* compromised the encryption machinery, forcing the United States to change machines. By 1971, this old coded traffic would have been merely academic. In any case, Department of Defense censors did not bother to delete this material from the government edition.

Part I, No. 10 (ref. VI-C-4, pp. 1–2 Ohio)

The Special Appendix makes the same claim as with the previous item. The same arguments against the government's claims apply. The legal brief extends its claim to include "many similar examples" of other cables interspersed throughout the volume. It is worth noting that declassifiers who released this material under the Freedom of Information Act in 1978 left in the vast majority of the plain texts of diplomatic cables among the 99 percent or more of the contents of the negotiating volumes which were released. In all likelihood, this cable was redacted from the declassified version precisely because it had been made the subject of a claim in this prior restraint case.

General Note: In all the preceding items from the Special Appendix, the overarching claim by the U.S. government was that disclosure of the materials would threaten current U.S. military operations and "present increased risks to the safety of U.S. forces." For the next set of items, the general claim is that disclosure of these "would slow the U.S. program of shifting military responsibility in Vietnam to South Vietnamese forces."

Part II, No. 1 (ref. IV-C-8 pages i–viii et seq.)

The Special Appendix claims that disclosure of these materials on the pacification program would "endanger the essential Government of Vietnam interest" and support of the program by revealing U.S. overparticipation, documenting friction and U.S. efforts to exert influence on Saigon, revealing criticisms of Saigon, including charges of corruption, incompetence, and more on the part of prominent Vietnamese. The most important point is that there was nothing secret about any of the materials here. Charges of corruption and the rest were public, not only in press accounts but in congressional hearings, press briefings by the U.S. government, speeches by senior officials, and public releases by the embassy in Saigon, the State Department, and others. In addition, the substantive content of these passages actually concerns the period 1964–1965, which by 1971, was far into the past. As far as the danger of the Saigon government losing interest in pacification was concerned, that program remained one of its central functions; losing interest in pacification meant giving up the war and accepting defeat. There was no likelihood of that happening. Meanwhile, the Saigon government itself had major task forces and other initiatives underway against corruption, and revelation of related charges in the Pentagon Papers was not going to be any surprise. Department of Defense censors saw no reason to delete any of this material from the government edition.

Part II, No. 2 (ref. IV-C-9(a) et seq.)
The Special Appendix charges that these volumes, which detail U.S. relations with the Saigon government, had to be secret because "public revelation of the extent to which the United States has criticized Vietnamese efforts . . . would make all facets of relations with the South Vietnamese more complicated." As in the discussion of the preceding item, the issues in these volumes were matters of public knowledge on issues which the Saigon government could not, in fact, walk away from. Moreover, the emerging declassified record of the Nixon administration shows that the factors complicating U.S.–South Vietnamese relations in 1971 were not the ones in the Pentagon Papers, but Saigon's fears that its interests were being sold out by the Nixon administration in its peace negotiations with Hanoi, to which the Pentagon Papers were irrelevant. Department of Defense censors saw no need to delete this material from the government edition.

Part II, No. 3 (ref. IV-C-6(c))
The Special Appendix declares that this material, which describes the Washington policy review following the 1968 Tet Offensive, "could have a decidedly detrimental impact upon the present Vietnamization program" and would give aid and comfort to potential enemies. As a description of mechanisms for U.S. decision making, this 1968 volume had clearly been superceded by the changeover from the Johnson administration to that of Richard Nixon. The account of post-Tet decisions on troop levels was detailed but overtaken by the event of the U.S. withdrawal from South Vietnam, which, by the time of the Pentagon Papers case, had been under way for almost two years. The matter of aid and comfort to enemies was subject to interpretation. In any case, Department of Defense

censors chose to make only two minor deletions from this entire volume in the government edition.

Part II, No. 4 (ref. IV-C-9(b) Part II)
The Special Appendix here repeats claims to delete material already made the subject of demands listed above. See the analysis for Part II, Nos. 1 and 2.

Part II, No. 5 (ref. IV-C-7(b) pp. 161–63)
This item was also emphasized by Solicitor General Griswold in his secret brief to the Supreme Court. See the discussion of Griswold No. 8.

Part II, No. 6 (ref. IV-C-3 pp. 77–82)
The declassified portions of the Special Appendix contain no argumentation as to why the presence of this material in the Pentagon Papers should justify keeping secret the entire history. The referenced material is an account of military plans for the conduct of the original air campaign against North Vietnam (code-named Rolling Thunder) that began in February–March 1965 and was expected to last for twelve weeks. By 1971 that account was mostly useful to historians. Department of Defense censors saw no reason to delete any of this material from the government edition.

Part II, No. 7 (refs. VI-C-2 pp. 1–18)
Again the declassified portions of the Special Appendix contain no argumentation as to why the presence of this material in the Pentagon Papers should justify prior restraint of the entire document. The referenced material contains an account of the Tonkin Gulf affair and military pressures against North Vietnam during 1964. The material was politically sensitive in that the veracity of the government's account of the Tonkin Gulf affair was in doubt by 1971, and the document showed both that U.S./South Vietnamese covert raids on the Vietnamese coast had immediately preceded both alleged incidents in the Tonkin Gulf (the U.S. government was maintaining there had been no provocations); and also that as of the time of writing of the Pentagon Papers (1967–1968), it was still not possible for an analyst working inside government to say on paper that the second alleged North Vietnamese attack, which is now believed never to have taken place, was anything other than a real incident. Political sensitivity is not damage to national security and is not valid justification for classification of documents. The material had no relevance to conduct of the Vietnam War in 1971. Department of Defense censors did not delete a single word of this account from the government edition.

CHAPTER SIX

The Impact of the Pentagon Papers

The expressed fears of Nixon and Kissinger, and the basis for the president's attempt to suppress the Pentagon Papers, that this event would disrupt and destroy diplomatic negotiations with Hanoi, Beijing, and Moscow, never came to pass. Instead Secretary of State William Rogers's judgment that the documents would have little foreign policy impact was more nearly on the mark. Kissinger left on his initial visit to China, for crucial negotiations to pave the way for the Nixon visit of 1972, the day following the Supreme Court decision. The only echoes of the Pentagon Papers affair were within his own entourage — instructions from Washington for NSC staffers not to discuss the subject with anyone from the Department of State. As for the talks with the North Vietnamese, Kissinger himself wrote in 1979, "I do not believe now that publication of the Pentagon Papers made the final difference in Hanoi's decision not to conclude an agreement in 1971."[1] The Russians were indelicate enough to mention the papers at the height of the crisis over North Vietnam's Easter Offensive of 1972 — when they reminded the United States that the record shown in the documents of unkept promises and misinformation by Washington was not likely to inspire in Hanoi confidence in American trustworthiness, but in actuality Hanoi had little confidence in Washington anyway. That never mattered.

By far the major impact of the Pentagon Papers has been in America, on Americans. The revelations confirmed what protesters had been saying from impeccably authoritative sources. A few years later Cyrus R. Vance, who had worked for McNamara as deputy secretary of defense, would be appointed as secretary of state in the Carter administration. Vance told his confirmation hearings that the Pentagon Papers had shortened the American war in Vietnam. In American politics, as Floyd Abrams quotes Harvard law professor Charles Nesson, the Pentagon Papers revelation "lent credibility to and finally crystallized the growing consensus that the Vietnam War was wrong and legitimized the radical critique of the war." The leak also began a period of militancy on the part of the press. Abrams quotes former CBS News president Fred W. Friendly: it "stiffened the spines of all journalists." Or again, in the words of Columbia

University journalism professor Benno Schmidt, the Pentagon Papers affair "signaled the passing of a period when newspapers could be expected to play by tacit rules in treating matters that government leaders deem confidential."[2]

We have collected here a series of perspectives on the impact of the Pentagon Papers affair. Some reflections are short comments, others more extended remarks. Several key players of the affair are among our observers, including Daniel Ellsberg, Anthony Russo, and Marcus Raskin. Other participants include noted author Thomas Powers, who covered the antiwar movement as a journalist at the time. Murray Marder is a reporter who worked on the Pentagon Papers coverage in the *Washington Post*. William Crandell is a Vietnam veteran serving at the time and is today a member of Vietnam Veterans of America. John Prados is an author and historian and is one of the editors of this book.

Bill Crandell

Like all other historical analysis, the Pentagon Papers were meant, not simply as a dispassionate discourse on the random facts of an era, but as, how did we get into this mess. Such histories are meant as weapons for winning a battle. The battle of the day was over whether to continue the Vietnam War or end it. The Pentagon Papers hit the streets like a sack full of grenades, which the government wanted to keep out of the hands of the rebels and failed.

I was one of the rebels then, a Vietnam veteran trying to bring my brothers home alive. Vietnam Veterans Against the War used these papers to confirm what we had been saying about how war crimes flowed from policies devised by reasonable men in Washington. That point was generally absent from the recent discussion of Bob Kerrey and his men.

In early 1971, before the release of the papers, Vietnam Veterans Against the War did something called the Winter Soldier Investigation in which they brought forward 125 Vietnam veterans to discuss war crimes emanating from policy as opposed to being a barren behavior by a few GIs. They did it in Detroit for reasons that, by the time it happened, didn't make as much sense as in the early planning.

The *Detroit News* hated the idea and led up to the Winter Soldier Investigation with several articles about how bogus this was going to be. During the course of that investigation, a panel of marine veterans testified to an operation in Laos that was called Dewey Canyon. The Pentagon said there was no such thing as Operation Dewey Canyon in the same week it announced Operation Dewey Canyon II in Laos, which is a South Vietnamese operation. The *Detroit News* decided, "We'll get these guys." They went to a bunch of marine veterans in the Detroit area to get them to say, "Aren't these sons of bitches lying?" Every one of those marine veterans said, "No, I was in that operation. It really happened." The *Detroit News* ended up doing an excellent story on Dewey Canyon because they had news on their pockets.

We are always going to have that dynamic, and we are going to lose some of them, and we are going to win some of them.

Anthony J. Russo Jr.

Dan walked into my office in 1968 and said, "That project you work on, that Vietcong Motivation and Morale Project, that is the top strategic intelligence project of the war done by the RAND Corporation under contract to the Pentagon. That project is the most controversial thing everywhere I go. Will you brief me on it?" I said, "Sure, sit down." He sat down, and we talked every day for the rest of the year.

I briefed him daily for about a year and then, after I left RAND, about once every week. In the context of that, I said, "Dan, you should leak that stuff [the Pentagon Papers]." I kept asking him: "Have you leaked it yet, Dan?" About a year later he called up and said, "I want to come over and see you." When he got there, he said, "All right, I've decided to do it. Can you find a Xerox machine?" I said, "I know the place. There was a Xerox machine at my friend's ad agency." It was a hot little shop on Melrose, at the corner of Melrose and Crescent Heights [in Los Angeles, California].

We went up there that night. There I was, standing at the Xerox machine. In the anteroom of the office there was a glass wall and an oak door. A knock came at the door, I looked up, and there was an LAPD in full regalia. I said, "God, those guys are good." What we had done, we'd gone into Linda Sinay's office, and we'd turned on the burglar alarm. We were supposed to turn it off, but we turned it on. I went to the door. I said, all right guys, cover up these top-secret pages with the glaring phosphorescent covers and cover us, now, because the cops are here. I went to the door, and I said, "Yes, sir?" He said, "Did you know your burglar alarm is on? What are you doing here?" I said, "Well, the owner of the office is right here." She came, she explained it to him, and showed him her ID. We showed him our IDs. He said, "Well, can I come and just walk through?" He did. He walked through the offices and then left. We never heard from him again.

After that, it was pretty smooth sailing. We xeroxed for a long time. Dan would go to Washington and really pedal the stuff, talk to people. He would keep me posted.

So, really, what it amounts to is, there were three stages. At the end of that stage, we saw the president fall. About the impact of the Pentagon Papers, the main impact, the short-term impact was the fall of Nixon. What brought it about was the planning for the liberation of the documents, which started in 1968.

You always see it written as the Ellsberg trial. [It was our trial and] the issue was truth. We should never be afraid of truth. It can hurt, but after a while it makes you feel good. In *Wild Man* [Tom Wells] talks about Ellsberg's Russo problem. Ellsberg had a Russo problem during the trial, because I was very radical. I had been to Vietnam. By radical, I don't mean extreme; I mean, going to the root. It's hard to find the roots sometime, unless you really know what you are doing.

I had been to Vietnam. I had interviewed hundreds of prisoners on the RAND project. I had haunted every bookstore between Phnom Penh, Hong Kong, Bangkok, and Penang. Let me tell you, I found a lot of stuff, stuff you couldn't find here. It was good stuff, a lot of Vietnamese authors. In fact, I looked at a panoply of Vietnamese authors, Vo Nguyen Giap, Ho Chi Minh, Truong Chinh, Le Duan, Nguyen Khac Vien, and others. I looked at what they were writing, and I said, how come our side is not writing? Slowly, I began to learn about the history of that struggle.

At night, after I had finished either interviewing in the field or editing interviews in the RAND villa in Saigon, I was so fascinated by the Vietnamese writings, that I would eat and hurry home to read those books. I don't know of anybody else who did that. What I learned was the incredible history of Vietnam. Vietnam has so many female heroes, going back two thousand years.

I saw that on the one hand; and I saw the American racist attitudes toward the Vietnamese on the other hand. I said, "Oh my God, we are in for big trouble. This is a racist war." That's what I say today, that racism pervades our nation. It is not plain and simple the way some people make it look. It can be very complicated. Some of the people who you'd think would be the last people who would be racist; they are, not through any particular faults of their own, but because of their education, because of their upbringing, because of the givens that are there in our culture.

When I came back, Dan had just come back. He wanted me to brief him on the project. We spent the whole year in a dialogue. That was a dialogue that began in 1968 that set off a chain reaction that ended with the fall of Nixon. You don't hear much about the trial. I'm talking about the Ellsberg-Russo Pentagon Papers trial. The press called it the Ellsberg trial. I say, Dan, you ran a side war exercise against me. You know, Dan and I are both critical of each other, but we get along, because, after all, dialogue is where it's at. You've got to be courageous in dialogue.

You've got to tell the truth. You've got to respect the truth. You are not going to get it right if you are timid. You are not going to get it right if you don't try.

You have to be able to undergo the hardships and the difficulties of that situation we found ourselves in, because when we went to Vietnam, we found ourselves personally, individually, up to here in dilemmas: moral dilemmas, intellectual dilemmas, all kinds of dilemmas. The only way to get out of that is to undertake tough dialogues, some tough facing of realities with ourselves, with our friends, with our colleagues.

Let me just summarize, saying the Pentagon Papers was, the Pentagon Papers action, the Pentagon Papers affair, the Pentagon Papers publication. By the way, the Pentagon Papers was first published on June 13, St. Anthony's Day, 740 years after St. Anthony died. St. Anthony, the patron saint of lost articles, not to mention, champion of truth, patron of the poor, confronter of tyrants. I looked at my cheap, dime-store calendar on June 13, 1971, and said, "My God." I felt a current run through my body. I felt like, well, I'm ready for anything. Whatever comes along, I'm ready.

My approach to it, I learned from interviewing the liberation gentlemen, which American propaganda called the Vietcong — the peasants call the liberation gentlemen.

Well, the liberation gentlemen taught me something about struggle. The principles of struggle are, one, that you have to be pursuing a just cause. Two, when you are the rabbit and you are up against an elephant, you have to protract the struggle. You have to lead the elephant all around in a chase, until finally that elephant steps in a ditch, and you have won. Most important, you have to be ready to undergo the hardships and difficulties. I told myself that, but it was hard. I had two nervous breakdowns around the Pentagon Papers, one going in and one coming out. The trial was torture. Everybody in the trial rejected me and opposed me. My lawyer was an Ellsberg mole. See, like I say, Ellsberg said he had a Russo problem, or, according to Tom Wells in this book, but his Russo problem turned into a Russo solution, because that struggle defense won that case — protracting the struggle. See, I didn't have to testify. I didn't have to go to jail. I did go to jail, but I could have testified and gone back to work. But my conscience would have killed me. After all, I had said, "Dan, you ought to leak it," to begin with.

Sometimes we don't see what we are getting into. It was rough. It was rough as a cob. I was deserted by everybody on the defense. Finally, some people came in off the streets. Black Panthers came in off the streets, and they supported me. They said, we see what is happening to you. They could see from the outside. See, I was a radical in the tradition of my forefathers in Suffolk, Virginia, who beat the British when the British burned our town.

Let me just remind you, and I'll stop, the publication plus our trial, our victory, is what brought down Nixon.

The Ellsberg-Russo Pentagon Papers trial is said by scholars to be 66 percent of the reason Nixon fell; Watergate, the other 33 percent — that was stimulated by the Pentagon Papers, too. So, what I say is, "Where you see Watergate, erase it and put in the Pentagon Papers, and remember, the truth will make you free."

I think it is important to remember there was a de facto precedent set with the Pentagon Papers. For the public's right to know, with all this pulling and hauling about national security. When it was all over, nothing had been harmed. In fact, they were a bunch of cowards at the very top who were criminal, and they were just covering up, and they were not talking rationally.

We set a precedent, a de facto precedent, for the public's right to know. We should be demanding, today, an update of the Pentagon Papers, both temporally and horizontally. We certainly need the Pentagon Papers on our alliance with Pol Pot and the third Indochina War and the terror here at home. We certainly need the Pentagon Papers on the Balkans. We need the Pentagon Papers on Africa, on every continent. Because, you can just imagine what's going on, what kind of nefarious deeds are being done in the shadows. Update the Pentagon Papers.

Marcus Raskin

The reason I, with a colleague, Ralph Stavins, wanted to see [Ben Bradlee of the *Washington Post*], was the way the Pentagon Papers was presented in the *New York Times,* [which], as far as I was concerned, went against the sort of arrangement which they had made with me about the way the papers would be presented. I had given an early copy of the papers to Neil Sheehan, who went through the papers very carefully and worked them through, and then got a good number of them afterward from Dan.

But the way they presented the papers was just raw material. My concern was the papers really showed a pattern and practice of war crimes and imperialism, and they should be played in that way. They should be presented that way, and not in some sort of sanitized version, which gave the appearance that this was all about just knowing what it is that was going on, but really not quite knowing what was going on. Of course, the reality was virtually nobody read the Pentagon Papers, and they were a little bit like the Maltese Falcon in people's minds. It was much more an object for the purpose of reconsidering the nature of American power and the nature of American leadership, as it turned out.

I worked in the White House in 1961. I was called by Benjamin V. Cohen, who is a great counselor to the Department of State, and one of the New Deal brain trusters. I went over to see him in Dupont Circle, and he said, you've got to tell them they are getting into an impossible situation in Vietnam. They don't know what they are doing, and you better get them out. You better tell them that I believe they should get out.

Flash forward. In 1964, Bernard Fall and I got together to work and do *The Vietnam Reader*. *The Vietnam Reader* was an attempt to show what the war was about in a factual, disinterested way. The book came out in 1965. In 1967 he was killed. I was supposed to have gone to Vietnam to be with him. He was killed and I didn't go.

During that period, a colleague of mine, Arthur Waskow, and I wrote something called *The Call to Resist Illegitimate Authority*, which was a takeoff on what French intellectuals did during the Algerian-French crisis during the colonial war [of 1954–1961]. It was to state, as we did, that those who, in good conscience, objected to the war, we would support, that is, the young people. The result of that was we went to see the associate deputy attorney general at the time of the Pentagon march. He was there. There was a group of us there. Very few of us knew each other. One of the people said, you have to indict us. There were 370 or so draft cards, turn-ins. And he refused to take them, he refused to pick up, the fabricoid briefcase it was called.

I knew this was going to lead to big trouble for me, personally. When it was my turn to speak, I said, "Look, you really have to understand what is going on in the streets and in the churches of this country and in the intellectual circles." I handed him a 350-page book, which was called *In The Name of America*, a listing of all the differing alleged activities, which you could look at and see as war crimes in Vietnam. It was all from overt sources. It was from newspapers, both in the United States and Europe. I said, if you are interested in looking at who to indict, you better understand the character of Nuremberg, what was personal responsibility under Nuremberg. The people who should be indicted are the people at the top of the government who undertook to send the young men into a terrible situation.

Nothing really happened about that, except Reverend William Sloane Coffin Jr., Michael Ferber, Mitchell Goodman, Dr. Benjamin Spock, and I were indicted. That was the result of this particular moment. The three of us were acquitted at the district level.

The question became in my mind, this whole thing is a war crime from beginning to end. This is not about secrecy, per se, except as it related to the notion that intelligence is something in a democracy, which is to be shared with all the people. It is not something that should be used against the people. It is a shared conception. That's how you know whether or not a democracy exists. So, the whole nature of secret intelligence and so forth and so on was, from my perspective, beyond the ken.

From my perspective, it led to the notion of let's really look at this war, carefully. We put together a group at the Institute for Policy Studies to undertake a book called *Washington Plans an Aggressive War*, and then another called

Washington Wages an Aggressive War, which was not published. In that 1969, 1970 period, it so happened we had a copy of the Pentagon Papers from Dan Ellsberg.

The people at the institute were looking at, just how should these papers come out? How do we link up the question of war crimes, getting the papers out in terms of changing the whole frame of reference and paradigm that was going on? We went round and round on this. Neil Sheehan wrote a very important article about war crimes [*New York Times Book Review,* March 28, 1971]. It was a review of several books. I was struck, as we all were at the institute, with that review. Two of us, Ralph Stavins and I, met with him. We gave him copies of the papers, of those we had. He began using those, thinking about them, etc.

In the spring of 1971, I began getting pangs of guilt or conscience, whatever you want to call it, and told Dan that what he should do is speak directly to Neil. The fact of the matter is they had, I'm sure, their own relationship.

In my view, the Pentagon Papers did have an effect on bringing down Nixon. But it did not have an effect on ending the war, nor did it have an effect on the nature of the American state in the sense of how we do business. There were a number of interventions afterward. There was the whole notion of an official secrecy act, or intelligence act, as it is called. All of that is still on the table.

The peculiarity of this whole business, in my view, is on the one hand, this was seen as a great accomplishment, because, in some sense, it was, to have the *Times* and the *Post* and other newspapers publish it. But it did not go to the substance of the question.

When I had my discussion with Ben Bradlee about this question in which I said, "Really, this is a war crimes question. What you should do is quote from the Pentagon Papers and our book, because we tie this stuff together. We make clear what it was."

He went back to speak to various people at the *Post,* who then said, no, they didn't want to do that, because they were still supporting the war, as, in part, was the *New York Times.* Because they were still supporting the war, you know, that was their social class, so to speak, and they were hanging together. Their interest was in showing they had some of their own power in publishing but not in attacking the basic nature of what that war was or the structure of the state.

That left all of us in this most peculiar position. Here we thought we had a deal with the *New York Times.* It didn't happen. The book itself, *Washington Plans an Aggressive War,* was trashed in the *New York Times,* although we were allowed a longish response. The book then died. The second book never came out. The book died in a very interesting way. It died because there were eighteen thousand copies printed, but the book was basically recalled by Random House, and that also is a very interesting part of this entire story.

Thomas Powers

I would like to make five reflections on what the significance of the papers was at the time and subsequently.

The first, in my opinion, was the release of the papers was a principled act of moral decision. Any public, moral act always raises the temperature of an argument. It certainly had that effect in this particular case. The administration was kind of shell-shocked for a day or two, and then it reacted with a kind of hysterical fury and anger that led them into rash and dangerous excesses that had long-term effects. I think all of that stems from the nature of the release as a moral act. It narrowed the way people looked at this whole issue at a moment when they had to make a very narrow decision, either to go on with the war or to get out.

The second thought I have about the release of the papers is it leveled the playing field. I wrote a book about the CIA, and it happened that I started to work on the book about ten minutes after the Church Committee Report was released. That leveled the playing field for anybody writing about intelligence matters. They could no longer pretend they did not overthrow governments, or undermine democratic movements, or engage in paramilitary warfare, or plan an attempt, and try, and possibly even succeed, in committing assassinations, so when you were talking to agency people, you were talking at the same level. You were, sort of, both grown-ups here. There wasn't a child's version of the history of the world being fed to you. With the release of the Pentagon Papers, that also became the case. After that point, no one could really say, in the government, we know things that if you knew, would change your mind and make you realize the necessity and importance of us pressing this war forward. That was a very important effect, and I think that's been a particularly lingering effect.

Once you see an example of the level of the field like that, and you see the vast gap that separates claims for the nature of what was going on from the reality of the nature of what was going on, you are likely to be skeptical in the future. I think we live, as a result, in a much more skeptical country than the one I went to high school in.

The release of the papers broke a kind of spell in this country, a notion that the people and the government had to always be in consensus on all the major issues. It trained newspapers not to take the government at its word. At the beginning of that episode, no one could really know if any newspaper would summon the courage to publish the papers.

Once the *New York Times* had and had been enjoined from continuing, no one could know for sure if any other newspaper would do it. Well, as it turned out, seventeen newspapers actually published parts of the papers, knowing they faced the same kinds of troubles. That, I think, was a sign the spell was completely and thoroughly broken. The press had regained its autonomy and its faith in its own ability to judge when an issue was legitimately a question of national security and when it was more likely a question of national convenience or political expedience.

The fourth thought I have about the release of the papers is it took genuine courage to do it. The courage was not wanting in the moment when we got to it. Dan and Tony found the courage to copy the papers. That was dangerous in and of itself. After they had done that, they had the courage to tell people about them. They had the courage to circulate them. Eventually, they had the courage to give them to somebody who would really publish them. When the publication process began, they had the courage to ensure that it didn't stop with the order of a single judge.

I imagine that at every step along the way you could summon the courage, but you weren't really sure it was going to come. The newspaper editors who were faced with the decisions of going forward or submitting also were unsure in the beginning if they would have that courage. The stories that we've heard suggest that at every paper there was a debate between people who said, no, do it, and other people who were more cautious, principally lawyers, and wanted to hold back. But they went forward. They found the courage and they had it. I believe, also, a number of the judges who dealt with the case found the courage to issue strong, clear rulings on matters of substance, because they believed they had the judgment to determine whether these really were issues of national security, and they just weren't willing to allow themselves to be dictated to by the government.

Would all of these actors and participants find the courage today? Would newspaper editors today do it? Would there be somebody in the government willing to do it? Would there be judges who would support them and defend them if they did it? I think that's impossible to answer. One of the aspects of principled acts of public, moral courage is they are rare. They always will be rare events. Their effectiveness depends upon their being rare events. You just don't do it over every little thing. My own faith is, yes, at a future time, facing a similar crisis after years of maturation of the argument, the courage would be found present again, that we would not be found wanting.

The last reflection I have about the release of the papers is the entire process of releasing them was based upon a hopeful premise. That hopeful premise is there is a truth about human affairs, an approximate truth, not an absolute truth, but a kind of truth, a degree of truth to be established about human affairs that you can know the way things really happened, more or less, that people actually care what the truth is and that the truth can make a difference.

We all believe this hopeful premise, sometimes. In this case, three people believed this hopeful premise. The first one who believed the truth could make a difference, the truth was there to be found, and that people cared about it was

Robert McNamara. His decision to make that study in the first place came from some core conviction that the truth about this matter needed to be known. Everything I know about it suggests he was actually in some apprehension that it would be hidden or lost and never known. He believed that that was something worth doing.

Dan Ellsberg and Tony Russo also believed this truth was important, that it should be known, and that it would make a difference if it were. I believe the hopeful premise on which all our political and human discourse is based in this instance was vindicated.

John Prados

There was a body of authoritative information, of inside government deliberations that demonstrated, beyond questioning, the criticisms that antiwar activists had been making for many years, not only were not wrong, but in fact, were not materially different from things that had been argued inside the U.S. government. It gave a new credibility and raised the level of discussion in the antiwar movement to a whole new phase. It was an order of magnitude shift in the antiwar movement.

But I want to go beyond that and follow a different line, and that relates to the question of the ongoing effects of Vietnam, the ongoing operations in the Vietnam War. There's a larger issue, and that's the constitutional one, the issue of prior restraint, and the issue of the action that Robert Mardian tried to take but failed to accomplish. If the U.S. government had succeeded in imposing a prior restraint at the time it moved against the publication of the Pentagon Papers in June of 1971, it would have had a real substantial and immediate impact on the U.S. military efforts in Southeast Asia and in the Vietnam War.

Some of the things we found out in that year and the next few years, if the government had been able to hide them, would have permitted it to continue to pursue the war in a very real way. One of them is air attacks on North Vietnam that were being carried out under the guise of "protective-reaction strikes."

A U.S. Air Force general, John D. "Jack" Lavelle, was relieved for commanding a set of protective-reaction strikes against North Vietnam. Those strikes could have been carried out with impunity. The bombing of Cambodia had been denied. The evidence of it only came out when subordinate air force officers, who had participated in falsifying the records on that bombing, came forth and admitted what they had been doing. That could have been suppressed. The government would still have been in place to resume the kind of Cambodia bombing congressional action, in fact, forced it to abandon.

The mining of Haiphong Harbor in 1972, which was a very sensitive, major escalation of the war in Vietnam, could have been hidden under a government imposition of a prior restraint. In the Laos secret war, because we were running out of Laotians to fight this war, we were using Thai troops. We were secretly using Thai troops as advisers and communications people, liaisons with the CIA, but also as artillerymen and infantrymen. That news emerged during this time. There was also controversy about the American presence in Laos: how many Americans were in Laos and what were they up to — again, issues about which the U.S. government was especially sensitive and which could have been hidden with prior restraint.

Most important of all, in the context of the Paris Peace Agreement in January 1973, there was the question of whether the Nixon administration made a secret undertaking to the Saigon government to resume the bombing of the North. Such a commitment was made to South Vietnamese leaders in Washington, D.C., in November of 1972. When the agreement was signed and a cease-fire took place, in the spring of 1973 there was consideration in Washington of resuming the bombing of the Ho Chi Minh Trail on the supposition that the North Vietnamese had not, in fact, stopped infiltrating materiel into the South.

If there had been a prior-restraint regime in effect in the spring of 1973, a decision to do that could have been made with impunity. Whereas, the calculation made in the spring of 1973 was it was politically too sensitive to resume bombing Southeast Asia at that time.

Regardless of the Johnson administration focus of the Pentagon Papers, the imposition of a prior-restraint capability for the American government had real implications for the conduct of the Vietnam War. By the same token, that was a precedent for freedom of the press. Some of the issues and some of the things that have come out as a result of investigative reporting, as a result of journalistic revelation in the past three decades, show the danger inherent in the existence of a prior-restraint regime.

The Chile CIA operations, for which General Pinochet of Chile came under indictment in his own country, could have been suppressed in the United States, something that was material in the Church Committee Investigation.

In 1975 there was an American CIA covert action in Angola. That, too, was bruited about in the press and that, too, could have been hidden.

During the Carter years there was the question of to what degree did the American administration prop up the Shah of Iran and stoke up the hostility that resulted in the particular way he fell and the takeover of the American embassy in Tehran. Those things could have been hidden.

In the Reagan years, there were the covert operations of the 1980s. There was the Grenada invasion. There was a particular disinformation campaign that was mounted against Mu'ammar Gadhafi in Libya. There was also the bombing of

Tripoli. Implicit in it was an attempt to assassinate a foreign leader, which was, in fact, prohibited under American presidential executive orders at least until 2001.

What could have been more sensitive than the revelation in 1986 that led to the Iran-Contra affair? The dealings between the White House, Nicaraguan rebels, and Iran and the whole ball of wax that was involved could have been suppressed in the American newspapers.

For the Bush years, there was the question of whether chemical weapons were released while Americans were eliminating leftover Iraqi ammunition dumps after the Gulf War in 1991. There was also the Bush intervention in Panama.

In the Clinton years, there's been the particular embarrassment of a raid we mounted in Somalia, attempting to capture a Somali warlord, that backfired in our faces . . . the issues surrounding intervention in Colombia, and now the Iraqi War and the war on terrorism could be hidden by government.

The existence of a prior-restraint regime would have had a policy utility for an American government in power, anytime between 1971, when the Pentagon Papers prior restraint failed, and today. The government made an effort in the late Carter administration when an author attempted to publish a story about the design of hydrogen bombs in a magazine called the *Progressive*. The government failed to win on the merits of that prior restraint, although it did get the injunction in that case. Reinforced by the precedent of the Pentagon Papers, the publisher of the magazine, the *Progressive,* defied the U.S. government and went ahead and published this article. The U.S. government, not able to meet the thresholds that were set in the arguments over the Pentagon Papers and the settlement of that case, lost the case on its merits.

So, today we have stronger freedom of the press, and we have a less oppressive U.S. government, in great part, because of the result of this case in 1971.

Murray Marder

John Prados has made the important point that prior restraint would have had a constant damaging effect on the press in the intervening thirty years. We must remember that in thirty years, we have a new generation of press, a new generation of public. And a great deal has changed during this time. Marc Raskin noted the current passivity of the public.

I was particularly struck at the time of the Gulf War that even though there were still some press people around on active deadline basis then, I had retired in 1985 from the *Washington Post,* that the coverage of the Gulf War was abominable. The press showed none of the skepticism that they should have learned in the years since the end of Vietnam. There was no sign there, visible, that the people were even conscious of the Pentagon Papers. They were making all the same mistakes over again. They were the most gullible group.

The first announcement, I believe, was that there'd be fifty thousand troops involved. Of course, that was preposterous. But the press didn't show any skepticism about the announcement there were going to be fifty thousand troops.

But in every subsequent event I have seen the same thing happen. At the same time, the Pentagon Papers have had on a positive side of the ledger, some very encouraging effects. The government is much more cautious now. But it has learned much more, how to circumvent the press than it ever did before. During the Lewinsky case it reached a point where the government spokesman, officials, were laying down conditions to the press, for the press, that the press was gullibly accepting, namely, not just that you couldn't identify the sources, but that you could not even identify from which direction the sources were coming from. Whether they were pro-Clinton or pro-Lewinsky or pro–the special counsel, and the press was accepting this.

We found that White House reporters, experienced White House reporters were accepting these terms. I could go on and on in this direction. I just think the bottom line has to be that, you know, go back and go over and read what is on the Jefferson Memorial about the price of liberty being eternal vigilance. The press has to be eternally vigilant. The press cannot be overwhelmingly celebrity journalists on the tube, engaging in entertainment, and not engaging in questioning officials. It doesn't matter whether the administration is Republican or Democratic or Green Party or anything else. Any government, as Mr. Russo and others have noted, is going to be restrictive, and is going to learn from what has been hung on its predecessors.

And we still have the great misfortune, as evidenced in the last [2000] election campaign, of not even questioning officials who are running for office as president as to their qualifications to be president. Nobody asked either Bush or Gore what qualifies them to be leaders of the free world. We are finding out now, of course, that nothing qualifies Bush to be leader of the free world. But these are the basic elementary questions that the press must learn to ask. And some of us are engaged in, I hope, it was an unusual thing so far as journalism is concerned, questioning basic principles of American journalism. And if we at least had some cooperation from the education side of the ledger, namely of teaching students that there is a Bill of Rights and what is in it, and that you couldn't pass it today if you submitted it to a referendum. Our fundamental education is in no position to reinforce an act of insensitive press. So, I think we can all learn a great deal from the Pentagon Papers affair.

CHAPTER SEVEN

Legal and Constitutional Issues
Michael J. Gaffney

The history of the Pentagon Papers and the Supreme Court's decision in *New York Times Co. v. United States*, 403 U.S. 713 (1971) (per curiam), illustrate the tension between government secrecy and the First Amendment's command that "Congress shall make no law . . . abridging the freedom of speech, or the press." To look more deeply at how that tension reverberates in the legal system, this chapter describes and analyzes the Supreme Court's decision in the Pentagon Papers case; considers some of the subsequent legal developments in the realm of government secrets and the First Amendment; and reflects briefly on the legacy of the Pentagon Papers case in the wake of the war on terrorism triggered by the events of September 11, 2001. This overview is neither an exhaustive study of the interaction between national security and the First Amendment nor a tactical guide to litigating cases that raise these issues. It is a look at how the issues posed by publication of the Pentagon Papers have arisen in other legal contexts.

The Supreme Court's Decision in the Pentagon Papers Case
Before the Pentagon Papers case, the Supreme Court had not decided a case involving a government request for a court order prohibiting publication of classified information. Forty years earlier, however, in *Near v. Minnesota*, 283 U.S. 697, 701 (1931), the Supreme Court ruled that a state nuisance statute which allowed officials to secure an injunction to bar publication of "a malicious, scandalous, and defamatory newspaper, magazine, or other periodical" violated the First Amendment, as applied to states through the Fourteenth Amendment. The statute made resumption of publication while an injunction was in effect "punishable as a contempt of court by fine or imprisonment."[1]

In *Near*, a county attorney had obtained a state court injunction against any future publication by a periodical that had published several articles linking public officials to gangsters. The Supreme Court's majority opinion noted that "liberty of the press, historically considered and taken up by the Federal Constitution, has meant, principally although not exclusively, immunity from previous restraints or censorship."[2]

The Court held that previous restraints on freedom of the press are presumed to violate the First Amendment, but also noted that the protection against prior restraint is "not absolutely unlimited," and that a limitation of the protection "has been recognized only in exceptional cases."[3] The Court suggested that during war, exceptions might allow the government to "prevent actual obstruction to its recruiting service or the publication of the sailing dates of transports or the number and location of troops."[4]

The forty years between *Near* and the Pentagon Papers case saw World War II and the development and use of nuclear weapons; the cold war and the culture of anticommunism; the rise of a national security state with a massive intelligence establishment and ever-increasing amounts of classified information; the Korean War; the frequent use of covert operations to manipulate political developments or topple other governments; the arms race; the advent of television and the growth of the mass media; and then the Vietnam War.

The many legal developments during this period included the National Security Act of 1947, which created the Department of Defense and the Central Intelligence Agency (CIA); Supreme Court recognition of a powerful "state secrets" privilege that allowed the government to withhold classified information in a civil case even when the information was vital to a plaintiff's case, *United States v. Reynolds,* 345 U.S. 1 (1953);[5] and a growing body of Supreme Court decisions about the First Amendment.

In the Pentagon Papers case the Supreme Court had to decide very quickly whether, notwithstanding the First Amendment, the government was entitled to an injunction to stop newspapers from publishing secrets about the ongoing bloody and divisive war in Vietnam, Laos, and Cambodia. The Court announced its decision in *New York Times Co. v. United States*[6] on June 30, 1971. The three-paragraph per curiam (no written majority opinion) decision was accompanied by separate opinions from each of the nine justices. A majority of the justices agreed that prior restraint on publication of excerpts from the secret study violated the First Amendment. The short decision held that there was a "heavy presumption" against the constitutional validity of prior restraints of expression and that the government had not met its "heavy burden" of showing justification for a prior restraint of the press.[7] The newspapers were free to continue publishing the Pentagon Papers. The decision, however, did not say that the First Amendment would always defeat a government demand for prior restraint of the press when the national security was at issue.

The six justices who concurred did so for varying reasons. The three justices who dissented, including Chief Justice Warren Burger, who greeted two *Washington Post* reporters with gun in hand at his home one evening shortly before the case went to the Supreme Court,[8] also disagreed for a variety of reasons.

Justice Hugo Black, a First Amendment absolutist, thundered in his concurring opinion that "every moment's continuance of the injunctions against these newspapers amounts to a flagrant, indefensible violation of the First Amendment. . . . Some of my Brethren are apparently willing to hold that publication of news may sometimes be enjoined. Such a holding would make a shambles of the First Amendment."[9] Justice Black emphatically rejected the government's argument that the president had inherent authority to restrain the press: "To find that the President has 'inherent power' to halt the publication of news by resort to the courts would wipe out the First Amendment and destroy the fundamental liberty and security of the very people the government hopes to make 'secure.'"[10]

Similarly, Justice William Douglas's opinion declared that the First Amendment leaves "no room for governmental restraint on the press."[11] After reviewing the Espionage Act,[12] Justice Douglas concluded that the statute did not bar publication of the secret study; that "any power the government possesses must come from its 'inherent power'"; and that *Near v. Minnesota* "repudiated that expansive doctrine in no uncertain terms."[13] Noting that the documents were "highly relevant" to the debate about Vietnam, he said: "Secrecy in government is fundamentally anti-democratic, perpetuating bureaucratic errors. Open debate and discussions of public issues are vital to our national health. On public questions, there should be 'uninhibited, robust, and wide-open debate.'"[14]

Justice Brennan's approach was equally forthright, but more nuanced: "the First Amendment stands as an absolute bar to the imposition of judicial restraints in circumstances of the kind presented by these cases."[15] He acknowledged that "the First Amendment's ban on prior judicial restraint may be overridden only when the Nation "'is at war'" and then articulated a legal test for such situations: "only governmental allegation and proof that publication must inevitably, directly, and immediately cause the occurrence of an event kindred to imperiling the safety of a transport already at sea can support even the issuance of an interim restraining order."[16] Measured by that standard, "every restraint issued in this case, whatever its form, has violated the First Amendment."[17]

The three other concurring justices (Justices Stewart, White, and Marshall) agreed that the government had not met its heavy burden of justifying prior restraint of the press, but all three referred to the possibility of criminal prosecutions. Justice Stewart was not persuaded that disclosure of any of the documents would "surely result in direct, immediate, and irreparable damage to our Nation or its people."[18] Justices White and Marshall suggested that they might have let the injunction stand if it had been supported by a narrowly drawn congressional authorization, but no such authorization existed.

The three dissenting justices (Chief Justice Burger, Justices Harlan and Blackmun) bemoaned the Court's "irresponsibly feverish" action and two

(Chief Justice Burger and Justice Harlan) referred to criminal prosecutions.[19] Thus five justices, a majority of the Court, considered criminal prosecutions to be an option for the government.[20] The Court was not deaf to the government's arguments about damage to national security. A majority of the Court thought there might be some degree of harm to national security from publication of the secret study, but, under the circumstances, this concern was not strong enough to justify overriding the First Amendment.

The Pentagon Papers decision, like *Near v. Minnesota*, does not prohibit all national security-based prior restraints of the press. The decision emphasizes the strong presumption against the constitutional validity of prior restraints and the "heavy burden" the government must carry when it seeks to use national security to impose a prior restraint on the press. Since there was no written majority opinion and the nine opinions do not reflect a consensus on how a court should determine whether the government has met its "heavy burden," the decision leaves some room for future courts to maneuver in this area.[21]

Less than a year later, the Pentagon Papers again occupied the Supreme Court's attention, but in a less frantic manner that involved the Constitution's Speech and Debate Clause. This clause provides members of Congress immunity from arrest for speeches and debates in Congress and prohibits questions about such speeches and debates in any place other than Congress.[22] The second Pentagon Papers case flowed from the actions of Senator Mike Gravel (D-Alaska) the night before the decision in the first case.

Senator Gravel, who was chairman of the Subcommittee on Buildings and Grounds, convened a meeting of his subcommittee and read aloud for hours from a copy of the Pentagon Papers he had been given by Ben Bagdikian of the *Washington Post*.[23] Since the senator was the only subcommittee member present at the hastily called hearing, there was no objection when he placed a copy of the Pentagon Papers in the record. Shortly thereafter, he began exploring private publication of the Pentagon Papers.

In the fall of 1971, Beacon Press, which was owned by the Unitarian Universalist Association (UUA), published *The Pentagon Papers: The Senator Gravel Edition*. Government investigators had previously visited Beacon Press, and President Nixon had called Beacon Press director Gobin Stair at home to let him know that he should not publish the Pentagon Papers.[24] Several days after publication, "FBI agents showed up at the UUA's bank asking for the UUA's financial records."[25]

As part of the effort to investigate Daniel Ellsberg, who had already been indicted for violation of the Espionage Act[26] and theft of government property, a grand jury had been convened in Boston, where Beacon Press was located. When the grand jury subpoenaed a member of Senator Gravel's staff and an editor who had been contacted about private publication of the Pentagon Papers, Gravel moved to quash the subpoenas. He argued that his legislative immunity extended to his staff member and to the arrangement to publish the Pentagon Papers.

While Senator Gravel's case was working its way through the lower courts, the government "revised its indictment against Ellsberg, charging him with fifteen counts of conspiracy, conversion of government property and espionage."[27] The indictment also named Anthony Russo, who had urged Ellsberg to leak the Pentagon Papers and had helped him copy them, as a coconspirator. When Senator Gravel's case reached the Supreme Court, the Court held that the Speech and Debate Clause applied to the "legislative acts" of the senator's aide that would have been privileged if done by the senator.[28] The Court read the scope of the privilege afforded by the Speech and Debate Clause narrowly and said that Senator Gravel's immunity did not extend to Beacon Press.[29]

With the advent of Watergate, the Nixon administration's interest in pursuing Beacon Press faded, but the criminal prosecution of Ellsberg and Russo continued until May 11, 1973, when Judge Matthew Byrne dismissed the charges because of "improper Government conduct."[30] Shortly before the dismissal, the government had suddenly disclosed that Ellsberg's telephone conversations had been picked up on wiretaps in late 1969 and early 1970.[31] This disclosure had been preceded by a government admission in April 1973 that two members of the White House Plumbers unit had broken into Ellsberg's psychiatrist's office on September 3, 1971. Shortly after the burglary disclosure, a newspaper reported that, during the trial of Ellsberg and Russo, Judge Byrne had met with Nixon and Ehrlichman "to discuss the possibility of Byrne becoming the director of the FBI" and then met again with Ehrlichman two days later for the same purpose.[32] Judge Byrne's decision dismissing the charges did not mention these meetings, but he did rule that Ellsberg and Russo should not be tried again on charges of stealing and copying the Pentagon Papers.

No damage to national security resulted from publication of the Pentagon Papers in either the newspapers or in the three versions published in 1971 by the *New York Times,* Beacon Press, and the Government Printing Office.[33] Eighteen years later Erwin Griswold, the lawyer who argued the case for the government in the Supreme Court, candidly admitted there had been no negative impact.[34]

The Pentagon Papers exposed more than twenty years of government misinformation, misjudgment, manipulation, and deception. Their publication damaged governmental credibility and reputations, not the national security. Nixon's chief of staff, H. R. Haldeman, who later went to prison for his role in Watergate, understood well what the Pentagon Papers meant. On the day after the *New York Times* published the first articles, he told Nixon: "To the ordinary guy, this is all a bunch of gobbledygook. But out of the gobbledygook comes a very clear thing: you can't trust the government; you can't believe what they say; and you can't rely on their judgment. And the implicit infallibility of presidents, which has been an accepted thing in America, is badly hurt by this, because it shows people do things the president wants to do, even though it's wrong, and the president can be wrong."[35]

Some Subsequent Developments in the Realm of Government Secrets

The Pentagon Papers case did not eradicate the government's interest in prior restraints on publication of classified information and did not diminish the national security state's addiction to classified information. The government's desire to conceal and manipulate significant information about national security and foreign policy, the enduring culture of classified information, massive overclassification, and politically calculated leaks of secret information have continued.

Twenty-six years after the Pentagon Papers decision, the *Report of the Commission on Protecting and Reducing Government Secrecy* noted that "secrecy is a form of government regulation" and found that "some two million Federal officials, civil and military, and another one million persons in industry, have the ability to classify information."[36] The commission said: "The classification and personnel security systems are no longer trusted by many inside and outside the Government. It is now almost routine for American officials of unquestioned loyalty to reveal classified information as part of ongoing policy disputes — with one camp 'leaking' information in support of a particular view, or to the detriment of another — or in support of settled administration policy."[37]

Government secrecy may wax and wane at the margins over time, but its substantial core endures. The years since the Pentagon Papers case have seen the following:

- Periodic changes to executive orders governing classification and declassification of government records as different administrations implement varying policies governing classified information.
- A Supreme Court decision, less than two years after the Pentagon Papers case, holding that the section of the Freedom of Information Act (FOIA) exempting information properly classified under an executive order from disclosure[38] did not allow courts: (1) to review the soundness of executive security classifications or (2) to examine classified documents in camera and decide whether part of a document should be disclosed because it was not secret.[39]
- Congressional amendment of the Freedom of Information Act in 1974 to allow courts: (1) to determine whether a record is properly classified pursuant to an

executive order (and therefore exempt from disclosure); (2) to put the burden on the government to prove a record is exempt from disclosure; and (3) to examine classified records in camera. 5 U.S.C. § 552 (4)(B).

- Congressional creation of oversight committees on intelligence in 1976 and subsequent intelligence authorization acts.
- Hundreds of judicial decisions involving the FOIA exemption for classified information and government claims of damage to national security from disclosure of secrets.[40]
- Disclosure or declassification of massive amounts of previously secret information about the activities of the CIA, NSA, the FBI, other intelligence agencies, and the military.
- Periodic prosecutions of traitors, like John Walker, Aldrich Ames, and Robert Hanssen, who for years and years sold secrets for cash.
- Enactment of the Classified Information Procedures Act and creation of a Foreign Intelligence Surveillance Act Court that meets in secret and has granted thousands of secret government requests for warrants authorizing electronic or other surveillance, or even break-ins, in the United States.
- Advances in information technology and telecommunications that have provided electronic access to some declassified records and have enhanced awareness of how the government attempts to manage classified information.

To illustrate some developments in the law concerning prior restraints on classified information since the Pentagon Papers decision, the sections below briefly describe the following:

- Several notable prior restraint cases, primarily related to the enforcement of secrecy agreements.
- The H-bomb article case where the government succeeded in enjoining publication for more than six months.
- The only criminal conviction for unauthorized disclosure of classified information to the press.
- The government's reflexive claims of classified information in a court case, filed twenty years after the Vietnam War ended, by over two hundred surviving Vietnamese commandos who were dropped into North Vietnam as part of a covert operation; spent years in North Vietnamese prisons; and were abandoned there by the Americans who sent them.
- The Pentagon's demands in 1999 that Scott Ritter, who had been a UN weapons inspector in Iraq for several years, submit his book for prepublication review.
- The recent congressional enactment, vetoed by President Clinton shortly before he left office, that created criminal penalties for unauthorized disclosure of classified information.

Victor Marchetti, the Original CIA Whistleblower

The year after the Pentagon Papers case, the government was back in court seeking an injunction to enforce a secrecy agreement against Victor Marchetti, the original CIA whistleblower, who was about to publish his revealing book, *The CIA and the Cult of Intelligence* (cowritten with John Marks). Marchetti's secrecy agreement did not have a prepublication review clause, but the government succeeded in obtaining an injunction requiring prepublication review and prohibiting publication of classified information.[41] The Court of Appeals said the secrecy agreement did not violate Marchetti's First Amendment rights, but emphasized that the agreement could not be used to prevent disclosure of unclassified information.[42]

Marchetti's publisher subsequently filed suit to challenge certain CIA objections to parts of the manuscript. The Court determined that a secrecy agreement "covers only information learned by [employees] during their employment and in consequence of it. It does not cover information gathered by them outside of their employment or after its termination."[43] When *The CIA and the Cult of Intelligence* was finally published in 1974, the text included white spaces (with the number of lines deleted) to show where the CIA had successfully objected to the publication of classified information and bold type to indicate information that the CIA had failed to get deleted. Marchetti's legal battles with the government continued after the book was published. Subsequent editions over the years show fewer deletions and more bold type, but some information remains deleted.

Philip Agee, the Defiant and Unrepentant CIA Whistleblower

While Marchetti was battling to publish his exposé of the CIA, another former CIA officer, Philip Agee, was writing *Inside the Company: A CIA Diary,* an account of his covert work in Latin America during the twelve years he worked for the agency. As the Supreme Court later noted, "In 1974, Agee called a press conference in London to announce his 'campaign to fight the United States CIA wherever it is operating.' He declared his intent 'to expose CIA officers and agents and to take the measures necessary to drive them out of the countries where they are operating.'"[44]

The CIA could not enjoin publication of Agee's book because he wrote it abroad where U.S. courts did not have jurisdiction. After *Inside the Company* was published in 1975 with a twenty-two-page appendix naming over two hundred individuals and organizations allegedly controlled, supported, or used by the CIA, the government persuaded Great Britain, France, and the Netherlands to expel Agee.[45] In 1978, Agee and Louis Wolf edited *Dirty Work: The CIA in Western Europe,* which included the names and biographies of hundreds of alleged

CIA officers identified by research that included cross-checking unclassified diplomatic lists and State Department Biographic Registers. When _Dirty Work II: The CIA in Africa_ was subsequently published, it named more alleged CIA officers. Agee's name was not on the cover as an editor, but he wrote the introduction.

While living in Germany, Agee made a mistake by filing a Freedom of Information Act case in federal court in Washington. The government filed a counterclaim that sought to enforce his secrecy agreement and to make Agee pay the government his book profits.[46] After Agee's lawyer provided the court with a CIA reading list that labeled books by him and certain other former CIA employees as "critical" of the CIA, the court declined to make Agee pay the government his book profits, but ordered him to submit future writings for prepublication review.[47] The district court found that "Agee has shown a flagrant disregard for the requirements of the Secrecy Agreement" and "has openly flouted his refusal to submit writings and speeches to the CIA for prior approval, and has expressed a clear intention to reveal classified information and bring harm to the agency and its personnel."[48]

The following year the Supreme Court upheld the State Department's revocation of Agee's passport.[49] Then Congress, prodded by the CIA and disputed allegations that dissenters had exposed a CIA station chief in Athens who was assassinated, passed the Intelligence Identities Protection Act of 1982, which makes it a crime to disclose the identity of a "covert agent" to "anyone not authorized to receive classified information."[50] Agee published his memoir, _On the Run,_ in 1987. Still critical of the CIA, he now lives in Cuba where he maintains a tourism website at www.cubalinda.com.

The H-Bomb Article: Enjoined for over Six Months and Then Published
The government's interest in prior restraint of the publication of information it deemed classified was not limited to former government employees. In 1979 the United States was able to enjoin the publication by _The Progressive_ magazine of an article entitled "The H-Bomb Secret: How We Got It and Why We're Telling It."[51] The article, written by Howard Morland, a former air force pilot who became a freelance journalist and an antinuclear activist, used publicly available information and interviews with scientists to describe and diagram the three key concepts underlying the radiation implosion necessary for a hydrogen bomb.[52]

A federal district judge in Wisconsin granted the government's request for an injunction prohibiting publication of the article or communication or disclosure of any "restricted data"[53] in the article. Although the court said the article was probably not "a 'do-it-yourself' guide for the hydrogen bomb," the court noted that the case differed from the Pentagon Papers case because a specific statute, the Atomic Energy Act, defined "restricted data" and authorized an injunction against any person who disclosed restricted data "with reason to believe such data will be utilized to injure the United States or to secure an advantage to any foreign nation."[54]

The court also perceived a difference between the cases in the government claims of damage to national security. According to the court's questionable reading of the Pentagon Papers case, "no cogent reasons were advanced by the government as to why the article affected national security except that publication might cause some embarrassment to the United States."[55] The evidence before the court in the H-bomb article case included assertions from the secretary of state and the secretary of defense that publication of the article would increase nuclear proliferation and that this would "irreparably impair the national security of the United States" or "adversely affect the national security of the United States."[56]

The government argued that "much of the data" was not in the public domain; that it was not determinative whether specific information was in the public domain or had been declassified; and that "the danger lies in the exposition of certain concepts never heretofore disclosed in conjunction with one another."[57] The court was influenced by an affidavit from a prominent physicist who disagreed with the *Progressive*'s experts about whether the disputed information was in the public domain, as evidenced, in part, by an encyclopedia article.

Asserting that "the article could possibly provide sufficient information to allow a medium-size nation to move faster in developing a hydrogen weapon," the court claimed that "a mistake in ruling against the United States could pave the way for thermonuclear annihilation for us all."[58] Balancing "the right to freedom of the press" against "the right to continued life," the court "conclude[d] that publication of the technical information on the hydrogen bomb contained in the article is analogous to publication of troop movements or locations in time of war and falls within the extremely narrow exception to the rule against prior restraint."[59]

The *Progressive* sought reconsideration, which was denied, and then appealed. While the appeal was pending, information about the key concepts was published elsewhere several times, and the government finally realized that the alleged secret was in the public domain.[60] The government decided to drop the case, and the injunction was subsequently vacated.

After being enjoined for over six months, *The Progressive* published the original article intact in its November 1979 issue. Nearly twenty-five years have passed since then. None of the confidently asserted damage to national security has materialized. No medium-size nation has moved faster in developing a hydrogen bomb. Thermonuclear annihilation did not happen.

Frank Snepp Disclosed No CIA Secrets but Failed to Seek
Prepublication Review

Former CIA analyst Frank Snepp published a book about the CIA that was not submitted for prepublication review, but disclosed no classified information. When Snepp went to work for the CIA in 1968, he signed a secrecy agreement promising that he would "not . . . publish . . . any information or material relating to the Agency, its activities or intelligence activities generally, either during or after the term of [his] employment . . . without specific prior approval by the Agency."[61]

During the Vietnam War, Snepp worked in the American embassy in Saigon as the CIA's chief analyst for North Vietnamese affairs. He was there as South Vietnam collapsed in April 1975, and he fled by helicopter with the remaining Americans. When Snepp left the CIA in 1976, he executed a "termination secrecy agreement," which reaffirmed his obligation "never" to reveal "any classified information, or any information concerning intelligence or CIA that has not been made public by CIA . . . without the express written consent of the Director of Central Intelligence or his representative."[62]

Snepp's 1977 book, *Decent Interval,* was a critical and scathing account of the mismanaged American evacuation in South Vietnam. The government sued Snepp for breaching his secrecy agreement by not seeking prepublication review and demanded that he lose all profits from the book and submit any future writings about intelligence matters for prepublication review. The district court found that Snepp had broken his 1968 secrecy agreement by publishing his book without prepublication review; that, even though no classified information had been disclosed, publication of the book had "caused the United States irreparable harm and loss"; that future violations of the secrecy agreement should be enjoined; and that the government could take the profits from the book.[63]

The Court of Appeals agreed with the district court except for allowing the government to take the profits from the book. The appellate court reasoned that Snepp had a First Amendment right to publish unclassified information; that his book did not divulge any classified information; and that his obligation extended only to preserving the confidentiality of classified material.[64] The court therefore limited the government's recovery to nominal damages and to the possibility of punitive damages.

Snepp sought Supreme Court review, but the composition of the Court had changed in the several years since the Pentagon Papers case. Justices Black and Douglas, champions of the First Amendment, had retired. So had Justice Harlan, one of the dissenters. William Rehnquist, who had been the assistant attorney general who called the *Washington Post* to ask that it cease publishing the Pentagon Papers, was now a Supreme Court justice. Also on Court was Justice

Lewis Powell, a former military intelligence officer. And the chief justice was still Warren Burger, a dissenter in the Pentagon Papers case. In the years since that case, CIA whistleblowers like Marchetti and Agee had received extensive media coverage. Their books were still selling, but nowhere near as well as *The Brethren,* a recent best-seller by Bob Woodward and Scott Armstrong that used interviews with dozens of former Supreme Court law clerks to pierce the institutional secrecy of the Court. Into this sensitive context came the former CIA officer seeking review of the government's enforcement of his secrecy agreement.

Snepp's petition, which asked the Court to take his case, challenged the injunction requiring him to submit all future manuscripts for prepublication review and sought reconsideration of whether punitive damages were appropriate. His petition argued that his secrecy agreement was unenforceable because it was a prior restraint on speech protected by the First Amendment. The government opposed Snepp's request and filed its own petition, which it asked be granted if the Court took Snepp's case. At this point, the Court would normally decide whether or not to take a case. If the Court takes a case, it usually orders the parties to submit briefs and sets a date for oral argument. In an extraordinary move, however, the Court proceeded to decide Snepp's case based only on the petitions asking the Court to take the case. There were no briefs on the merits of the case. There was no oral argument.

In a per curiam opinion, the Supreme Court affirmed the lower courts' decisions that, even though Snepp had not disclosed any classified information, he had breached his agreement by not seeking prepublication review and could not publish anything about intelligence matters without prior review by the CIA. The opinion noted the lower courts' finding that Snepp's book had caused "irreparable harm" to "intelligence activities vital to our national security."[65] This finding was significantly influenced by the CIA director's uncontradicted testimony, which the Court summarized as saying "that Snepp's book and others like it have seriously impaired the effectiveness of American intelligence operations."[66] Even though the Court of Appeals had not allowed the government to take Snepp's profits from the book, the Supreme Court did so, which eventually meant that Snepp had to pay the government the $144,931.85 he'd earned from his book.[67]

Snepp's First Amendment right to publish unclassified information without review by the CIA was mentioned but not enforced. The government's interest in secrecy by contract, pursued successfully in *Marchetti,* was reinforced by the decision in *Snepp,* which was based on the law of contracts and trusts, not the First Amendment. Snepp's contentions about prior restraint and the First Amendment were summarily dismissed in a footnote that did not even mention the Pentagon Papers case.

Justice Stevens, joined by Justices Brennan and Marshall, dissented on both substantive and procedural grounds. The dissent argued that, since the government had conceded the book contained no classified information, "the interest in confidentiality that Snepp's contract was designed to protect has not been compromised."[68] Justice Stevens observed that, even if Snepp had submitted the book for prepublication review, there was no classified information to delete and the government "would have been obliged to clear the book for publication in precisely the same form as it now stands."[69] The dissent criticized the "unprecedented and drastic" remedy of allowing the government to take all of Snepp's profits because it was "not supported by statute, by the contract, or by the common law."[70] Justice Stevens also objected to the manner in which the Court disposed of the case summarily based on the petitions asking the Court to take the case. The dissent's conclusion warned that a "drastic new remedy has been fashioned to enforce a species of prior restraint on a citizen's right to criticize his government" and cited the Pentagon Papers case in the final footnote.[71]

Inscribed on a wall in CIA headquarters are the words in the Bible from John 8:32: "And ye shall know the truth, and the truth shall make you free." Frank Snepp's unclassified truth did not make him free. It made him an example of how the law could be twisted to punish him for exercising his First Amendment right to publish unclassified truth.[72]

Ralph McGehee Lost His Faith in the CIA in Vietnam and Became a Critic of the CIA

In 1981, Ralph McGehee, a retired CIA officer who spent twenty-five years with the agency and became disillusioned by his experiences in Vietnam, submitted an article about El Salvador and the CIA for prepublication review. The CIA denied permission to publish parts of the article that allegedly contained classified information. McGehee filed suit seeking a declaratory judgment that the CIA's prepublication and classification procedures violated the First Amendment.

In *McGehee v. Casey*, the Court of Appeals affirmed the district court's rejection of McGehee's First Amendment claim, but ruled that the secrecy "agreement does not extend to unclassified materials or information obtained from public sources. The government may not censor such material, 'contractually or otherwise. . . . ' The government has no legitimate interest in censoring unclassified materials."[73] When there was a dispute about whether information was in the public domain, "an ex-agent should demonstrate . . . , at an appropriate time during the prepublication review, that such information is in the public domain."[74]

McGehee had more prepublication review disagreements with the CIA before he published *Deadly Deceits: My Twenty-five Years in the CIA* in 1983, but he resolved them without additional court action.

CIA Whistleblower John Stockwell Meets United States v. Snepp
John Stockwell, who worked for the CIA in Vietnam and later ran the Angola Task Force, quit the CIA to write a book about what he had seen and done during his years with the agency. He did not submit his book, *In Search of Enemies,* to the CIA for prepublication review. Shortly after the Supreme Court's decision in *Snepp v. United States,* the government sued Stockwell and sought his profits from the book. Stockwell, who had already spent the money from his book, agreed to pay the government future royalties and to submit any future writings about intelligence matters to the CIA for prepublication review.[75]

Former CIA Analyst Pat Eddington Sued the CIA to Challenge CIA Objections to His Book
In 1997, Pat Eddington, a former CIA analyst, published *Gassed in the Gulf: The Inside Story of the Pentagon-CIA Cover-up of Gulf War Syndrome.* The inside title page contains a CIA disclaimer that was inserted at the CIA's request. Prior to publication, Eddington had to file suit to challenge CIA objections. A publisher's note reports that the suit "succeeded in forcing CIA to drop objections to certain material, which is now contained in this book. Other deletions at the demand of CIA are under litigation as this book goes to print."

The Only Criminal Conviction for Unauthorized Disclosure of Classified Information to the Press
Twenty-four years after the Pentagon Papers decision, the government obtained its first (and to date only) conviction under the 1917 Espionage Act for unauthorized disclosure of classified information to the press. Samuel L. Morison, a civilian intelligence analyst, gave Jane's Publications classified spy satellite photographs of a Soviet nuclear powered carrier, and *Jane's Defence Weekly* published them in 1984. The following year Morison was convicted and sentenced to two years' imprisonment for violating the Espionage Act and for theft of government property. The conviction was affirmed on appeal and the Supreme Court declined review.[76] In 2001, President Clinton pardoned Morison at the same time he pardoned former CIA director John Deutch, who had admitted to "mishandling of classified information on unsecure home computers."[77]

Approximately two years after Morison's pardon, Jonathan Randel, a former Drug Enforcement Administration analyst, was convicted of stealing sensitive, unclassified information and leaking it to a British newspaper. Randel, who was sentenced to a year in prison, has appealed his conviction. The theft of government property statute (18 U.S.C. § 641) under which he was convicted had been used against Daniel Ellsberg.

Covert Operations: The Vietnamese Commandos Case and
Classified Information

Parts of the Pentagon Papers describe CIA and military covert operations and clandestine warfare in North Vietnam. U.S. covert operations in North Vietnam began after the Geneva Conference in 1954 when the CIA organized small teams of anticommunist Vietnamese to engage in sabotage and espionage, distribute propaganda, and provide intelligence. Casualties were high and results limited. By the late 1950s, the effort was viewed as a failure.

In 1961, former CIA director William Colby, then chief of the CIA's station in Saigon, started a new covert operation aimed at North Vietnam. The CIA recruited and trained Vietnamese to be commandos who could be dropped or inserted into North Vietnam to carry out missions involving sabotage, small unit action, and intelligence. After OPLAN 34A was approved in January 1964, the U.S. military's Special Operations Group, which became the Studies and Observation Group (SOG), took over the program and continued to drop Vietnamese commando teams into North Vietnam. By the time the program was terminated as a failure in 1968, hundreds of Vietnamese commandos had been inserted into North Vietnam. All had been killed or captured, usually within a short time of their arrival. The secret missions were no secret to the North Vietnamese because the operation had been penetrated and compromised from the beginning.

The surviving commandos were imprisoned for years. The Americans declared them all dead and removed them from the payroll. When the Paris Peace Accords were signed in 1973 and hundreds of POWs were returned, none of the Vietnamese commandos were released and no effort was made to secure their release. After they were finally freed, many spent additional time in reeducation camps. Some gradually came to America and tried to rebuild their lives.[78] Their plight came to the attention of John Mattes, a lawyer who had worked for the Senate Select Committee on POW-MIA Affairs as it dug through mounds of classified information en route to publishing its report in 1993.[79]

Mattes decided to file suit against the government and to seek back pay for the "Lost Commandos."[80] In 1995, 281 OPLAN 34 A commandos and representatives of the estates of dead commandos sued the United States in the Court of Federal Claims.[81] They claimed they had a contract with the United States during the Vietnam War, and they sought monthly wages and benefits due under the contract. The former commandos also alleged that their contract entitled them to continued payment of wages while imprisoned. In February 1996, the government filed papers seeking to dismiss case. Among other things, the government argued that it did not have a contract with the commandos; that the matter involved state secrets and classified information; that the court couldn't

hear the case because a post–Civil War Supreme Court case said secret agreements were unenforceable;[82] and that the commandos had waited too long to
bring the case.

Mattes succeeded in getting pay records for the covert operation declassified.
In 1996 the case received significant media coverage, including a story on *60
Minutes*[83] and articles in the *New York Times*[84] and *TIME Magazine.*[85] The Senate Select Committee on Intelligence had a hearing on the issue.[86] After Vietnam veterans in the Senate pushed though an amendment to the Defense authorization bill to provide compensation for the former commandos, the court put
the case on hold and the bill became law.[87] The Department of Defense established a Vietnamese Commando Compensation Commission to review claims,
determine who was eligible, and approve payments of about $2,000 per year for
each year of imprisonment. The commission approved 359 claims amounting
to $14.6 million and denied 838 claims before it ceased operations in 2001.[88]
Secrets and deception that had long outlived their usefulness were not allowed
to block a modest measure of justice, but the government did try.

*Demands for Prepublication Review of Scott Ritter's Book about
UN Weapons Inspections in Iraq*

Scott Ritter is a former marine intelligence officer and a Gulf War veteran who
worked for seven years as a United Nations weapons inspector implementing Security Council resolutions calling for the disarmament of Iraq. The UN inspection
team headed by Ritter identified Iraq's chemical and biological weapons; moni-
tored their destruction; and sought to verify that Iraq was not reconstituting its
prohibited weapons programs. Ritter was direct and aggressive with the Iraqis and
frustrated with what he considered reluctance to confront the Iraqis. In August
1998, he resigned and criticized the United States and the UN Security Council
for undermining the weapons inspectors. Iraqis denounced him as a spy.

In January 1999, the *New York Times* reported that government officials had
admitted that some intelligence officers had worked undercover on the weapons
inspection teams; that American intelligence agencies had provided information
and technology; and that they had received information in return.[89] Ritter was
not identified as one of the intelligence officers. In an interview, Ritter "raised
the question of whether the inspectors improperly aided United States intelligence in ways that threatened the inspectors' independence, or opened them
up to charges of spying for Washington."[90] Ritter's question was answered the
next day when the *Times* reported that an intelligence officer disguised as a
weapons inspector had provided a sophisticated electronic eavesdropping system that enabled selected weapons inspectors and American intelligence to monitor for ten months "the cell phones, walkie-talkies and other communications

instruments" used by key Iraqis.[91] Because he was considered a security risk, Ritter had not been one of the weapons inspectors involved with this operation.[92]

As these disclosures were emerging, Ritter was preparing to publish *Endgame*, a book he had written about his experiences as a UN weapons inspector. The Pentagon learned of Ritter's pending book and demanded he submit it for prepublication review. After the *New York Times* published an article in which Ritter's lawyer characterized the Pentagon's demand "as part of an administration-wide attempt to intimidate Ritter into silence," the Pentagon dropped the demand.[93] A month later, the Pentagon changed its mind again and renewed the demand that Ritter submit his book for prepublication review. Another *New York Times* article included Ritter's lawyer's reaction: "This is a last-minute effort to delay publication. I don't think they have a legal leg to stand on."[94] Ritter declined to comply with the Pentagon's demand. The Pentagon did not seek an injunction to block publication, and Ritter's book was published in 1999.

Ritter continued to be a critic of the government's policy toward Iraq. When the Bush administration began advocating military action against Iraq, Ritter opposed the drive toward war, but the government's relentless assertions about the need for "regime change," the threat from Iraq's weapons of mass destruction, and Iraqi links to Al-Qaeda continued and the invasion of Iraq went forward.

Veto of a Law Criminalizing the Unauthorized Disclosure of Classified Information

The United States has never had an Official Secrets Act, as do Great Britain and Canada. In May 2000, however, the Senate Select Committee on Intelligence reported out a bill making unauthorized disclosure of classified information to anyone not authorized access to it a crime punishable by a fine up to $10,000, by imprisonment for up to three years, or both. The bill did not make the publication of classified information by the media a crime. No public hearings were held on the new measure to criminalize leaks of secrets.

The Senate and the House approved their versions of the Intelligence Authorization Act in October 2000. The Conference Report, which reflected slight amendments to the language making unauthorized disclosure of classified information a crime, was subsequently approved and the legislation went to President Clinton for his signature. The press and civil liberties organizations urged the president to veto it.

On November 4, 2000, the president vetoed the Intelligence Authorization Act "because of one badly flawed provision that would have made a felony of unauthorized disclosures of classified information."[95] The president's statement, which said the provision was "overbroad and may unnecessarily chill legitimate activities that are at the heart of a democracy," included two quotations from the Supreme Court's decision in the Pentagon Papers case.[96] The president declared that the legislation did "not achieve the proper balance" between the obligation "to protect not only our Government's vital information from improper disclosure, but also to protect the rights of citizens to receive the information necessary for democracy to work."[97]

He saw a "serious risk that this legislation would tend to have a chilling effect" and the risk of criminal prosecution "might discourage Government officials from engaging even in appropriate public discussion, press briefings, or other legitimate official activities."[98] Similarly, the president was concerned that "the legislation may unduly restrain the ability of former Government officials to teach, write, or engage in any activity aimed at building public understanding of complex issues."[99]

Congress passed the Intelligence Authorization Act without the objectionable provision, but after the presidential election, it was reintroduced in the next session of Congress as the Classified Information Protection Act of 2001 and again inserted in the Intelligence Authorization Act. By August 2001, the Bush White House was still undecided about whether to support the bill to make leaks of classified information a felony. When the Senate Select Committee on Intelligence scheduled a September 5, 2001, hearing on the measure, four major media organizations requested that the committee delay the hearing. Then Attorney General John Ashcroft asked the committee not to have the hearing, and it was canceled.

Several days later, members of Al-Qaeda on a suicide mission hijacked four fuel-laden airliners filled with passengers, crashed three of them into the World Trade Center and the Pentagon, and killed approximately three thousand people. The fourth airliner, whose target was reportedly the Capitol in Washington, D.C., crashed in Pennsylvania, apparently after a struggle between hijackers and passengers.

The Legacy of the Pentagon Papers Case in the Wake of the War on Terrorism and the Invasion of Iraq

After the horrifying events of September 11, 2001, uncertainty and anxiety about more attacks soared. Concerns about national security and a military response were intense. On September 14, 2001, President Bush declared a national emergency. Congress passed a resolution authorizing the use of military force.[100] The president declared war on global-reach terrorism and ordered the military to invade Afghanistan and destroy Al-Qaeda.

An expansion of executive power and secrecy followed the events of September 11. In October 2001, the president signed a broad new antiterrorism law that gave police and intelligence agencies sweeping new powers.[101] The FBI detained hundreds and held them without charges for extended periods.[102] On October 12, 2001, a memo from the attorney general revised the policy on releasing documents under the Freedom of Information Act and urged agencies to pay more heed to "institutional, commercial, and personal privacy interests." In November 2001, the president issued a new executive order that imposed greater secrecy on presidential records and allowed him or a former president to veto release of the former president's records.[103] Later that month the president suddenly issued a broad executive order authorizing military tribunals to try terrorism suspects and impose the death penalty without judicial review by civilian courts.

In December 2001, Congress passed an Intelligence Authorization Act, which called for "a comprehensive review of protections against the unauthorized disclosure of classified information."[104] The creation of a new Department of Homeland Security and a new domestic military antiterrorism command, the Northern Command, followed. In September 2002, the president announced a new National Security Strategy, which emphasized military supremacy and spoke of "the option of preemptive actions."[105] The following month an anxious Congress, about to face a midterm election, passed a resolution authorizing the use of military force against Iraq.[106]

Later that same month, the attorney general completed his "comprehensive review of protections against the unauthorized disclosure of classified information." He reported to Congress that "there is no comprehensive statute that provides criminal penalties for the unauthorized disclosure of classified information irrespective of the type of information or recipient involved." The attorney general, however, did not recommend that Congress enact such a law. Instead, he said: "Given the nature of unauthorized disclosures of classified information that have occurred, . . . I conclude that current statutes provide a legal basis to prosecute those who engage in unauthorized disclosures, if they can be identified."

The attorney general did not describe "the nature of unauthorized disclosures," but a perusal of major newspapers during the previous year would show that some of the unauthorized disclosures included a congressional leak of certain NSA intercepts the day before September 11, 2001;[107] several articles about the Pentagon's secret battle plans for the invasion of Iraq;[108] and a leak about covert assistance to Iraq during the Iran-Iraq War.[109] Reading forward, one would encounter an article about "Secret, Scary Plans" to strike North Korea"[110] and another about the Pentagon's secret twenty- to thirty-year antiterror plan.[111]

The attorney general's report assured Congress that those who "disclose classified information without authority to do so will face severe consequences under the law." Leaks of classified information continued after the attorney general's report. In March 2003, about a week after he ordered the invasion of Iraq, the president issued a new executive order on classified information.[112] The new executive order allows a three-year delay in the otherwise automatic twenty-five-year declassification of millions of pages of records and expands the government's power to reclassify information. Other changes reflect a framework for greater secrecy. This, however, may be difficult to attain given the recent unprecedented volume of leaks of secrets from the Pentagon and the intelligence agencies as the guerrilla war in Iraq intensifies; no weapons of mass destruction have yet been found in Iraq, and critical questions about the quality and distortion of prewar intelligence are being raised.

Over three decades have passed since the Supreme Court decided the Pentagon Papers case while the nation was at war. The nation is again at war and another president is being questioned about the intelligence, assumptions, and assertions related to the latest war. Elsewhere in the world, the CIA and Special Operations forces are busy with a multitude of covert operations related to the global war on terrorism.

The cult of secrecy still exists and still persists. The Pentagon Papers case does not guarantee that the First Amendment will always prevail. Lower court developments in that case and in *The Progressive*'s H-bomb article case demonstrate that it is possible for the government to rush into court with exaggerated claims of damage to the national security and to persuade a judge to impose a prior restraint on the publication of allegedly secret information the government doesn't want the public to know. The government's use of injunctions to restrain the press from publishing secrets, however, has been, and is likely to be, rare because the government usually doesn't know in advance that classified information will be published. More common than injunctions are the various forms of prior restraint used with individuals. These include secrecy agreements that require prepublication review and that can be and have been enforced through the courts; security clearances that can be revoked with resultant loss of employment as a sanction for unauthorized disclosure of classified information; and plain, old-fashioned persuasion or intimidation. Self-restraint is the most effective form of prior restraint.

Some classified information is legitimately classified and should remain so for an appropriate period of time. The year before the Supreme Court's decision in the Pentagon Papers case, however, the Report of the Defense Science Board Task Force on Secrecy found that "the amount of scientific and technical information which is classified could profitably be decreased perhaps as much as 90 percent by limiting the amount of information classified and the duration of its classification."[113] Massive overclassification and slow declassification remain a problem, but the new executive order on classified information and the current national security climate indicate that the problem will persist.

Excessive secrecy in the name of national security can undermine constitutional rights and civil liberties. Secret arrests, denial of access to a lawyer, indefinite detention, monitoring conversations between a lawyer and a client, and secret evidence in secret trials[114] are repulsive to the Constitution. There is a balance to be struck between the right of the public to be informed and the need for national security. That balance cannot be struck exclusively on the Executive's terms. As the perpetual war on terrorism unfolds, the public must be vigilant in safeguarding its rights and liberties, particularly when claims of national security are asserted to justify their erosion.

Notes

INTRODUCTION

1 It is worth noting that the language in the executive orders that permits officials to keep documents secret requires them to be able to demonstrate "identifiable" damage to U.S. national security that would flow from release of the material.

CHAPTER 1: CREATING THE PENTAGON PAPERS

1 Robert S. McNamara with Brian VanDeMark, *In Retrospect: The Tragedy and Lessons of Vietnam* (New York: Times Books, 1995), p. 256.
2 Ernest R. May, interview, Washington D.C., June 7, 2003.
3 Robert S. McNamara, telephone interview, June 2, 2003.
4 Lieutenant General Robert G. Gard, interview, June 4, 2003.
5 Harrison E. Salisbury, *Without Fear or Favor: An Uncompromising Look at the New York Times* (New York: Times Books, 1980), p. 59.
6 McNamara, interview.
7 Leslie H. Gelb, "Misreading the Pentagon Papers," *New York Times*, June 29, 2001. Note, however, that Gelb had previously written: "No instructions were given to me about what topics to select for monographs." Leslie H. Gelb, "The Pentagon Papers and the Vantage Point," *Foreign Policy* 6 (spring 1972): 27.
8 Henry Kissinger, *Ending the Vietnam War: A History of America's Involvement in and Extrication from the Vietnam War* (New York: Simon & Schuster, 2003).
9 May, interview.
10 From an Ullman article in *Foreign Policy* magazine, quoted by Sanford G. Ungar, *The Papers and the Papers: An Account of the Legal and Political Battle over the Pentagon Papers* (New York: E. P. Dutton, 1972), quoted p. 26.
11 McNamara and VanDeMark, *In Retrospect*, p. 282.
12 Gelb, "The Pentagon Papers and the Vantage Point," pp. 28–29.
13 Gelb, "The Pentagon Papers and the Vantage Point," p. 26.
14 Leslie H. Gelb, "Memorandum for the Secretary of Defense: Final Report, OSD Vietnam Task Force," January 15, 1969. Printed in the Pentagon Papers.
15 Leslie H. Gelb, "Today's Lessons from the Pentagon Papers," *Life*, September 23, 1971, p. 34.
16 Gelb, "Today's Lessons from the Pentagon Papers," p. 34.
17 William Simons, interview, June 19, 2003.
18 Gard, interview.
19 Hedrick Smith, "Vast Review of War Took a Year," *New York Times*, June 13, 1971.

20 Gelb, "The Pentagon Papers and the Vantage Point," p. 27.

21 Gelb, "The Pentagon Papers and the Vantage Point," p. 29.

22 Ibid.

23 Ungar, *The Papers and the Papers,* p. 39.

24 Leslie H. Gelb and Richard K. Betts, *The Irony of Vietnam: The System Worked* (Washington, D.C.: Brookings Institution, 1979).

25 Gelb, "Today's Lessons from the Pentagon Papers," pp. 35–36.

26 Daniel Ellsberg, *Papers on the War* (New York: Simon & Schuster, 1972).

CHAPTER 2: PUBLISHING THE PAPERS

1 Daniel Ellsberg, *Secrets: A Memoir of Vietnam and the Pentagon Papers* (New York: Viking, 2002), quoted p. 347.

2 Ralph Stavins, Richard J. Barnett, and Marcus Raskin, *Washington Plans an Aggressive War* (New York: W. W. Norton, 1972).

3 Salisbury, *Without Fear or Favor,* p. 80.

4 Salisbury, *Without Fear or Favor,* p. 122.

5 Ibid., quoted p. 194.

6 However, note the following from Sanford Ungar, who has written a full study of how the press handled the Pentagon Papers: "Contrary to Daniel Ellsberg's later private claims, the *Times* officials had no notion they were under obligation, as a condition of obtaining the Pentagon Papers, to use them in a particular way" (*The Papers and the Papers,* p. 100).

7 Ben Bradlee, *A Good Life: Newspapering and Other Adventures* (New York: Simon & Schuster, 1995), p. 311.

8 Evan Thomas, *The Man to See: Edward Bennett Williams Ultimate Insider; Legendary Trial Lawyer* (New York: Simon & Schuster, 1991), quoted p. 266.

9 Katharine Graham, *Personal History* (New York: Vintage Books, 1998), quoted p. 450.

10 *The Pentagon Papers: The Defense Department History of United States Decisionmaking on Vietnam,* Gravel ed., 5 vols. (Boston: Beacon Press, 1971, 1972).

11 *The Senator Gravel Edition: The Pentagon Papers: Critical Essays* (Boston: Beacon Press, 1972), pp. 320–41.

12 Noam Chomsky and Howard Zinn, eds., *The Pentagon Papers,* vol. 5: *Critical Essays* (Boston: Beacon Press, 1972).

13 U.S. Congress, House Armed Services Committee, *United States–Vietnam Relations, 1945–1967: Study Prepared by the Department of Defense,* 12 vols. (Washington, D.C.: Government Printing Office, 1971).

14 George C. Herring, *The Secret Diplomacy of the Vietnam War: The Negotiating Volumes of the Pentagon Papers* (Austin: University of Texas Press, 1983).

15 National Security Archive, *U.S. Policy in the Vietnam War,* vol. 2, *1969–1975,* ed. John Prados (Alexandria, Va.: Chadwyck-Healey, 2003).

CHAPTER 3: NIXON INTERVENES

1 David Rudenstine, *The Day the Presses Stopped: A History of the Pentagon Papers Case* (Berkeley: University of California Press, 1996).

2   Ibid., quoted p. 71.

3   Ibid.

4   Rudenstine, *The Day the Presses Stopped,* p. 72.

5   Alexander M. Haig Jr., *Inner Circles: How America Changed the World: A Memoir* (New York: Warner Books, 1992).

6   Henry Kissinger, *The White House Years* (Boston: Little, Brown, 1978), p. 729.

7   Ibid.

8   Ibid., pp. 729–30.

9   Kissinger, *Ending the Vietnam War.*

10 Kissinger, *White House Years,* p. 730.

11 H. R. Haldeman with Joseph DiMona, *The Ends of Power* (New York: Dell Books, 1978), p. 154.

12 Ibid., p. 155. A number of the Ehrlichman notes, plus memoranda as well, were given to the House Judiciary Committee during its consideration of impeachment proceedings against President Richard Nixon and were eventually published in Appendix III (Supplementary Documents) of its record. Several more complete versions of the same memoranda were declassified later by request of Morton H. Halperin under FOIA.

13 H. R. Haldeman, *The Haldeman Diaries: Inside the Nixon White House* (New York: G. P. Putnam's Sons, 1994), p. 299.

14 Ibid.

15 Salisbury, *Without Fear or Favor,* p. 210.

16 Charles W. Colson, *Born Again: What Really Happened to the White House Hatchet Man* (Old Tappan, N.J.: Chosen Books, 1976), p. 57.

17 Ibid., quoted pp. 57, 58.

18 Ibid., p. 58. One may well speculate as to the reasons Kissinger was so vehement on the Pentagon Papers. This may have had to do with the prevalence of leaks, many of which Nixon attributed to "liberals" on Kissinger's NSC staff. Colson recalls an evening aboard the presidential yacht *Sequoia* just a few weeks before (May 20), when Nixon raised that very issue, in that way he had of pretending to tease when he was dead serious. Colson recalls Henry "launched into an impassioned defense" of his staff (Colson, p. 44). In the Pentagon Papers case, Kissinger could have seen himself as making a preemptive defense, or as demonstrating loyalty (see also the discussion of the views of Ehrlichman and Haldeman later in this text).

19 John Dean, *The Rehnquist Choice* (New York: Simon & Schuster, 2001), p. 267.

20 Rudenstine, *The Day the Presses Stopped,* pp. 77–95. In fact, Rehnquist prepared a memorandum at John Dean's request that was completed on June 16. The Rehnquist memo skipped over First Amendment and policy questions, "treating them as non-issues," and asserted that "the only reason there was no precedent for prosecuting reporters or news organizations under the available laws was the result of (unspecified) earlier policy decisions (Dean, *The Rehnquist Choice,* p. 267).

21 Richard Nixon–H. R. Haldeman Meeting, June 15, 1971, 9:56 A.M. (Nixon Library Materials Project, Oval Office Tape 520–3). Notes by John Prados.

22 Salisbury, *Without Fear or Favor,* pp. 262–63.

23 *Department of State Bulletin* 65, no. 1671 (July 5, 1971): 3–4.

24 Haldeman, *The Haldeman Diaries,* p. 301.

25 Ibid., p. 302.

26 Salisbury, *Without Fear or Favor,* p. 263 n.

27 Colson, *Born Again,* p. 59. Colson subsequently leaked damaging material from FBI files regarding Ellsberg's attorney, and later tried to use friendly congressional staff to initiate a public investigation of Dr. Ellsberg.

28 Salisbury, *Without Fear or Favor,* p. 266. The previous quotes from Ehrlichman's meeting notes appear there and on pp. 267 and 269.

29 Ibid.

30 William Safire, *Before the Fall: An Inside View of the Pre-Watergate White House* (New York: Belmont Tower Books, 1975), p. 357.

31 For this and the following quotes: John Ehrlichman, *Witness to Power* (New York: Pocket Books, 1982), pp. 275–76.

32 For this and the following: Haldeman and DiMona, *The Ends of Power,* p. 155.

33 Salisbury, *Without Fear or Favor,* quoted p. 274.

34 *Department of State Bulletin* 65, no. 1673 (July 15, 1971): 78–79.

35 Ehrlichman, *Witness to Power,* p. 143.

36 *The Watergate Hearings: Break-in and Coverup: Proceedings of the Senate Select Committee on Presidential Campaign Activities as edited by the Staff of the New York Times* (New York: Bantam Books, 1973), p. 777.

37 Anthony Russo, Dr. Ellsberg's RAND Corporation colleague who had assisted in the original photocopying of the Pentagon Papers and arranged for the machine the men used for this purpose, would be indicted along with Ellsberg in the eventual criminal prosecution.

38 John Kincaid, "Secrecy and Democracy: The Unresolved Legacy of the Pentagon Papers," in *Watergate and Afterward: The Legacy of Richard Nixon,* ed. Leon Friedman and William F. Levantrosser (Westport, Conn.: Greenwood Press, 1992), p. 155.

39 Anthony J. Russo, telephone interview, March 31, 2001.

40 The best account of the Ellsberg-Russo trial is in Peter Schrag, *Test of Loyalty: Daniel Ellsberg and the Rituals of Secret Government* (New York: Simon & Schuster, 1974).

41 The West German leader, visiting Washington, was to be honored that evening with a state dinner at the White House.

CHAPTER 4: FIRST AMENDMENT RIGHTS

1 Floyd Abrams, "The First Amendment: 1991," *Prologue* 24, no. 1 (spring 1992): 53.

2 Rudenstine, *The Day the Presses Stopped.*

3 "Stop the Presses," *New York Times,* June 23, 1996, p. E5 reprints this telegram.

4 McNamara and VanDeMark, *In Retrospect,* p. 281. McNamara is silent on how he felt about giving advice on legal issues arising from the study project he had ordered. Incidentally the other account of this dinner, by *Times*man Harrison Salisbury (*Without Fear or Favor,* p. 239), has this dinner coming about because McNamara begged Reston and wife Sally to keep him company as his own wife, Margery, was in the hospital. McNamara's memoir makes clear that Margery was hostess at their dinner that night.

5 In addition, the final chapter will describe the applicable law and subsequent developments.

6 Joel M. Gora, "The Pentagon Papers Case and the Path Not Taken: A Personal Memoir on the First Amendment and the Separation of Powers," *Cardozo Law Review* 19,

no. 4 (1998): 1316. In passing we should note here that, in addition to the frontline legal battle between the newspapers and the government over the Pentagon Papers, there were a host of other participants, not least the American Civil Liberties Union. There were other advocacy groups, ad hoc coalitions of congressmen, businessmen, and others. Indeed, by far more pages of the legal briefs filed with the Supreme Court in the Pentagon Papers case came from these friends of the court than from either the newspapers defending themselves or the government seeking its prior restraint order.

7   Floyd Abrams, "The Pentagon Papers a Decade Later," *New York Times Magazine,* November 8, 1981, quoted p. 25. Interviewed by Abrams for this article in 1981, Admiral Blouin said, "Looking at them today, I don't think there was any great loss in substance" (ibid.).

8   Rudenstine, *The Day the Presses Stopped,* p. 154.

9   Ibid., p. 156. Note from the telephone transcripts in the last chapter that President Nixon, Henry Kissinger, Alexander Haig, and other senior officials were all alert to the view the papers were a historical record as much as was the *New York Times* and that they in fact schemed to make this historical record yield political benefits to the administration.

10 Interviewed by Floyd Abrams in 1981, Macomber's reflection was, "I think that, even though I've been a diplomat all my life and nothing is more important to me than the security of the United States, the First Amendment is, in another way, the security of the United States. You can't save something and take the heart out of it" (Abrams, "The Pentagon Papers a Decade Later," quoted p. 72).

11 Ibid., quoted p. 25.

12 Rudenstine, *The Day the Presses Stopped,* p. 218.

13 William R. Glendon, "The Pentagon Papers: Victory for a Free Press," *Cardozo Law Review* 19, no. 4 (March 1998): 1299.

14 William Glendon, "The Pentagon Papers: Victory for a Free Press," pp. 1302–3.

15 William R. Simons, telephone interview, June 2003.

16 Abrams, "The First Amendment: 1991," p. 51.

CHAPTER 5: WHAT WAS SO SECRET?

1   Erwin N. Griswold, "Secrets Not Worth Keeping," *Washington Post,* February 15, 1989, p. A25.

2   Rudenstine, *The Day the Presses Stopped.*

3   Whitney North Seymour Jr., "At Last the Truth Is Out," *Cardozo Law Review* 19, no. 4 (March 1998): 1359.

4   David Rudenstine, "The Book in Retrospect," *Cardozo Law Review* 19, no. 4 (March 1998): 1283–94.

5   Abrams, "The First Amendment: 1991," pp. 48–54.

6   Rudenstine, *The Day the Presses Stopped,* p. 9. The "three books" in the quote is a reference to the three versions of the Pentagon Papers: that published by the *New York Times,* the Senator Gravel edition, and the government version published under the auspices of the House Armed Services Committee.

7   Ibid., p. 327.

8 Rudenstine, "The Book in Retrospect," p. 1283.
9 Readers may judge for themselves. The passages are in *The Day the Presses Stopped,*
   pp. 84–87, 195–201, 218–24, and 267–72.
10 In other passages not nominated, such as those describing the evidence in the *Washington Post* case, the procedure is identical.
11 Rudenstine, *The Day the Presses Stopped,* pp. 386–87, nn. 8–11.
12 Griswold, "Secrets Not Worth Keeping," p. A25, for this and all preceding material from
   Solicitor General Griswold's work on the sealed brief.
13 Schrag, *Test of Loyalty,* pp. 260–73. In connection with the Nixon administration's sudden antipathy for the sensitivity analysis that Gerhard had made of the Pentagon
   Papers, it is relevant to note that the National Security Agency *subsequently* chose Gerhard to be the lead author of its official history study of the 1967 Israeli attack on the
   USS *Liberty.* See William D. Gerhard and Henry W. Millington, *United States Cryp-
   tologic History: Special Series Crisis Collection.* Vol. 1, *Attack on a Sigint Collector, the
   U.S.S. Liberty* (National Security Agency, 1981, declassified July 2, 2003).
14 A more extensive version of this commentary, which actually reproduces the portions
   of the text of the Pentagon Papers associated with each of the government claims in
   the solicitor general's sealed brief and in the "Special Appendix," is available in the
   National Security Archive microfiche collection *United States Policy in the Vietnam
   War, II: 1969–1975* (Alexandria, Va.: Proquest, 2003). That set is available for research
   in paper form at the National Security Archive at George Washington University.
15 Griswold, "Secrets Not Worth Keeping."

CHAPTER 6: THE IMPACT OF THE PENTAGON PAPERS

1 Kissinger, *White House Years,* p. 1021.
2 Abrams, "The Pentagon Papers a Decade Later," quoted p. 76.

CHAPTER 7: LEGAL AND CONSTITUTIONAL ISSUES

1 283 U.S. 697, 712.
2 283 U.S. at 716.
3 283 U.S. at 716.
4 Id. *Near* also observed that "on similar grounds, the primary requirements of decency
   may be enforced against obscene publications [and] [t]he security of the community
   life may be protected against incitements to acts of violence and the overthrow by force
   of orderly government" (283 U.S. at 716).
5 The case involved alleged government negligence in an airplane crash that killed several people. The information withheld on national security grounds was an accident
   investigation report which the government claimed included information about secret
   electronic equipment. The trial court held that the government's withholding of the
   secret information meant that the issue of negligence had to be decided in the plaintiffs' favor. The Supreme Court overturned this ruling and held that the government
   could invoke a "state secrets" privilege without having the trial court rule against the

government because of the withheld information. When the case was retried after the Supreme Court's ruling, plaintiffs lost. In 2000, the accident report and related documents were declassified. The plaintiffs' families saw that the accident report did not appear to contain secrets and did include information suggesting that the government had been at fault. The plaintiffs' families petitioned the Supreme Court for further review, but the Supreme Court denied the petition in 2003.

6 403 U.S. 713.

7 Id. at 714. As the second paragraph of the short per curiam decision stated: "Any system of prior restraints of expression comes to this Court bearing a heavy presumption against its constitutional validity." *Bantam Books, Inc. v. Sullivan,* 372 U.S. 58, 70 (1963); see also *Near v. Minnesota,* 283 U.S. 697 (1931). The government "thus carries a heavy burden of showing justification for the imposition of such a restraint." *Organization for a Better Austin v. Keefe,* 402 U.S. 415, 419 (1971). The District Court for the Southern District of New York in the *New York Times* case and the District Court for the District of Columbia and the Court of Appeals for the District of Columbia Circuit in the *Washington Post* case held that the government had not met that burden. We agree.

8 Bradlee, *A Good Life,* pp. 320–22. Bradlee, then the managing editor of the *Washington Post,* initially declined to report this little anecdote, but a *Post* reporter mentioned it in a column after the Supreme Court decision. Bradlee's memoirs recount his reaction when asked if the *Post* should carry the story: "What story?" I shouted. "Just because the Chief Justice of the United States Supreme Court comes to the door of his house in the dead of night in his jammies, waving a gun at two *Washington Post* reporters in the middle of a vital legal case involving the *Washington Post,* you guys think that's a story?" (p. 321). "I wanted to avoid pissing him off a few days before he took our fate in his hands," Bradlee later recalled (p. 322).

9 403 U.S. 713, 715.

10 403 U.S. at 719. Less than a year after the Pentagon Papers decision, the Supreme Court rejected the Nixon administration's claim that the president had inherent power "to authorize electronic surveillance in internal security matters without prior judicial approval." *United States v. United States District Court,* 407 U.S. 297 (1972). The government had argued that "the special circumstances applicable to domestic security surveillances necessitate a further exception to the warrant requirement"; that "the requirement of prior judicial review would obstruct the President in the discharge of his constitutional duty to protect domestic security"; that the surveillance was "directed primarily to the collecting and maintaining of intelligence with respect to subversive forces"; that "courts . . . have neither the knowledge nor the techniques necessary to determine whether there was probable cause to believe that surveillance was necessary to protect national security"; that these security problems were "beyond the competence of courts to evaluate"; and that "'[s]ecrecy is the essential ingredient in intelligence gathering'" and "requiring prior judicial authorization would create a greater 'danger of leaks.'" 407 U.S. 297, 318–19. In rejecting these arguments, the Court held that the Fourth Amendment requires prior judicial approval for the type of domestic security surveillance involved in the case. Id. at pp. 314–21; 323–24.

11 Id. at 720.

12 18 U.S.C. § 793.

13 Id. at 721–23.

14 Id. at 724.

15 Id. at 725.

16 Id. at 727.

17 Id.

18 Id. at 730.

19 In a subsequent Supreme Court decision, Chief Justice Burger asserted that, in the Pentagon Papers decision, "every member of the Court, tacitly or explicitly, accepted the *Near* and *Keefe* condemnation of prior restraint as presumptively unconstitutional." *Nebraska Press Assn. v. Stuart,* 427 U.S. 539, 559 (1976), citing *Pittsburgh Press Co. v. Human Rel. Comm'n,* 413 U.S. 376, 396 (1973) (Burger, C. J., dissenting). In *Nebraska Press Assn. v. Stuart,* 427 U.S. 539, the Court unanimously held that a judicial "gag" order, which barred the press from publishing information about a criminal defendant's confession or "other facts strongly implicative of the accused," was an impermissible prior restraint that violated the First Amendment.

20 Given the state of the law then, the outcome of such prosecutions was uncertain. See Harold Edgar and Benno C. Schmidt Jr., "The Espionage Statutes and Publication of Defense Information," *Columbia Law Review* 73, no. 5 (May 1973): 930.

21 As a general matter, any party seeking an injunction must, in part, establish that there will be "irreparable injury" or "irreparable harm" unless the court grants the injunction. The many cases involving injunctions in a wide variety of factual settings indicate that courts do not always agree on what constitutes "irreparable injury" or "irreparable harm."

22 Art. 1, sec. 6, cl. 1 of the Constitution provides:

The Senators and Representatives shall receive a Compensation for their Services, to be ascertained by Law, and paid out of the Treasury of the United States. They shall in all Cases, except Treason, Felony and Breach of the Peace, be privileged from Arrest during their Attendance at the Session of their respective Houses, and in going to and returning from the same; and for any Speech or Debate in either House, they shall not be questioned in any other Place.

23 As Senator Gravel said years later: "The papers were turned over to me by Ben Bagdikian of the *Washington Post.* . . . I met him at midnight under the marquee of the Mayflower Hotel in the heart of Washington. His car was parked and I pulled up abreast of it. He opened the trunk, tossed the papers in my trunk, and I sped away. He had suggested we do it in the dark in some suburb, but I had once been a counterintelligence officer, and I said the hell with that — that's just inviting someone to frag you." "A Courageous Press Confronts a Deceptive Government," *UU World* 15, no. 4 (September/October 2001): 64. www.uua.org/world/2001/04/lookingback.html.

24 The call from Nixon came before Beacon Press had made a final decision to publish the Pentagon Papers, but the Nixon call convinced Beacon Press that it should publish. As Gobin Stair remembers the event:

One day at home, I got a phone call at home from Richard Nixon. I recognized his voice, and he said, "Gobin, we have been investigating you around Boston, and we know you are apparently a pretty nice and smart guy . . ." and he said, "I hear you are going to do that set of papers by that guy Gravel, the guy who collected the Pentagon Papers."

And it was obvious he was going to ask me not to publish it. And I didn't want to give him an idea whether we would or wouldn't. But it was obvious that he was putting pressure on me to turn it down. He knew it and I knew it. The result was that as the guy in charge at Beacon, I was in real trouble. Before we decided yes or no, we were told not to do it. We were publishing books we like and that we think we can sell, and to be told by Nixon . . . not to do it, convinced me before I had [completely] decided, that it was a book to do. ("Gobin Stair and Rev. Robert West Recount UUA/Beacon Press Publication of 'The Pentagon Papers,'" UUs & the News: National Focus [2002]. www.uua.org/news/2002/civil/pentagon.html).

25 Id.

26 18 U.S.C. § 793.

27 Rudenstine, *The Day the Presses Stopped,* p. 342.

28 *Gravel v. United States,* 408 U.S. 606 (1972).

29 Id., at 625–26.

30 "Pentagon Papers Charges Are Dismissed; Judge Byrne Frees Ellsberg and Russo, Assails 'Improper Government Conduct,'" *New York Times,* May 12, 1973, p. 1. A poll of the jurors the day the charges were dismissed "showed that at least half of them would have voted to acquit the defendants." When Ellsberg was asked if he would disclose the Pentagon Papers again, he answered, "I would do it tomorrow, if I could do it."

31 Id.

32 Rudenstine, *The Day the Presses Stopped,* p. 342.

33 The three versions, none of which was complete, are: (1) *The Pentagon Papers* (New York: Bantam Books, 1971), 677 pp. (the *New York Times* version); (2) *The Pentagon Papers: The Defense Department History of United States Decisionmaking on Vietnam,* 5 vols. (Boston: Beacon Press, 1971, 1972) (the Gravel edition); and (3) U.S. Congress, House Committee on Armed Services, *United States–Vietnam Relations, 1945–1967: A Study Prepared by the Department of Defense,* 12 vols. (Washington, D.C.: Government Printing Office, 1971).

34 Griswold, "Secrets Not Worth Keeping," p. A25.

35 H. R. Haldeman to President Nixon, Monday, June 14, 1971, 3:09 P.M. meeting. www.gwu.edu/~nsarchiv/NSAEBB/NSAEBB48.

36 *Report of the Commission on Protecting and Reducing Government Secrecy,* 103d Cong., 1st sess., S. Doc. 105–2 (Washington, D.C.: Government Printing Office, 1997). The commission was created under Title IX of the Foreign Relations Authorization Act for Fiscal Years 1994 and 1995 (P.L. 103–236) to conduct "an investigation into all matters in any way related to any legislation, executive order, regulation, practice, or procedure relating to classified information or granting security clearances" and to submit a final report containing recommendations covering these areas.

37 Id.

38 5 U.S.C. § 552 (b)(1) exempts from disclosure under FOIA matters that are "specifically authorized under criteria established by an Executive order to be kept secret in the interest of national defense or foreign policy and . . . are in fact properly classified pursuant to such Executive order."

39 *EPA v. Mink,* 410 U.S. 73 (1973).

40 U.S. Department of Justice's online FOIA Guide (May 2002) contains extensive citations to cases involving FOIA's national security exemption. www.usdoj.gov/oip/exemption1.htm.

41 *United States v. Marchetti,* 466 F.2d 1309 (4th Cir.), *cert. denied,* 409 U.S. 1063 (1972).

42 As the Court of Appeals explained:

Marchetti by accepting employment with the CIA and by signing a secrecy agreement did not surrender his First Amendment right of free speech. The agreement is enforceable only because it is not a violation of those rights. We would decline enforcement of the secrecy oath signed when he left the employment of the CIA to the extent that it purports to prevent disclosure of unclassified information, for, to that extent, the oath would be in contravention of his First Amendment rights. Thus Marchetti retains the right to speak and write about the CIA and its operations, and to criticize it as any other citizen may, but he may not disclose classified information obtained by him during the course of his employment which is not already in the public domain. (*United States v. Marchetti*, 466 F.2d 1309, 1317)

43 *Alfred A. Knopf, Inc. v. Colby*, 509 F.2d 1362, 1371 (4th Cir. 1975). As the Court of Appeals ruled:

We decline to modify our previous holding that the First Amendment is no bar against an injunction forbidding the disclosure of classifiable information within the guidelines of the Executive Orders when (1) the classified information was acquired, during the course of his employment, by an employee of a United States agency or department in which such information is handled and (2) its disclosure would violate a solemn agreement made by the employee at the commencement of his employment.

44 *Haig v. Agee*, 453 U.S. 280 (1981).

45 453 U.S. 280, 283, n. 1.

46 The government's demand for Agee's profits followed a recent Supreme Court decision requiring another former CIA employee to pay the government profits from a book published without prepublication review by the CIA. *Snepp v. United States*, 444 U.S. 507 (1980).

47 *Agee v. Central Intelligence Agency*, 500 F. Supp. 506 (D.D.C. 1980).

48 500 F. Supp. 506, 509 (footnote omitted).

49 *Haig v. Agee*, 453 U.S. 280.

50 50 U.S.C. § 421. In 2003 a White House staff member leaked the name of an undercover CIA operative to a reporter who included the name of the CIA operative in an article. The FBI is currently investigating the White House in an attempt to determine who leaked classified information (the name of the CIA operative) to the reporter.

51 *United States v. Progressive, Inc.*, 467 F. Supp. 990 (W.D. Wis. 1979), dismissed voluntarily, 610 F.2d 819 (7th Cir. 1979).

52 Although the district court's decision does not describe the H-bomb secret, the three concepts underlying radiation implosion are: separate stages, compression, and radiation coupling. Morland's original H-bomb article for *The Progressive*, however, incorrectly described the third concept of radiation coupling. Howard Morland, "The Holocaust Bomb: A Question of Time." Washington, D.C.: Federation of American Scientists, November 15, 1999 (revised February 5, 2003). www.fas.org/sgp/eprint/morland.html.

53 42 U.S.C. § 2014 defined "restricted data" as "all data concerning 1) design, manufacture, or utilization of atomic weapons; 2) the production of special nuclear material; or 3) the use of special nuclear material in the production of energy, but shall not include data declassified or removed from the Restricted Data category pursuant to section 2162 of this title."

54 42 U.S.C. §§ 2274 (b) and 2280. The judge was convinced that "the defendants had reason to believe that the data in the article, if published, would injure the United

States or give an advantage to a foreign nation." *United States v. Progressive, Inc.*, 467 F. Supp. 990.

55 467 F. Supp. 990. The district court's facile characterization of the government's national security claims in the Pentagon Papers case is highly misleading. The origins of the "no cogent reasons" characterization lie in Judge Gurfein's district court decision denying the government's request for a preliminary injunction against the *New York Times*. This decision preceded the government's attempts to develop better arguments and better evidence about the alleged damage to national security in Courts of Appeals and in the Supreme Court. The district court's attempt in the H-bomb article case to distinguish the Pentagon Papers case on this basis was flawed and unpersuasive.

56 Id.

57 Id.

58 Id.

59 Id.

60 As Howard Morland later explained in "The Holocaust Bomb: A Question of Time":

> Other journalists and researchers were duplicating the story from scratch, and underground copies of *The Progressive* manuscript were popping up in places like Australia and Honolulu. An author named Chuck Hansen in California gave the case its coup de grace with a long letter to Senator Charles Percy, which was widely circulated, declared classified, and then published in defiance of court orders by the Madison Press Connection, a short-lived newspaper operated by striking reporters.

61 *Snepp v. United States*, 444 U.S. 507, 508 (1980) (per curiam).

62 444 U.S. 507, 508, n. 1.

63 In legal terms, the court imposed a "constructive trust" on Snepp's profits from the book.

64 *Snepp v. United States*, 595 F.2d 926, 935–36 (4th Cir. 1979).

65 444 U.S. at 510.

66 Id. at 512.

67 Frank Snepp, *Irreparable Harm: A Firsthand Account of How One Agent Took on the CIA in an Epic Battle over Free Speech* (New York: Random House, 1999), p. 357. Paperback edition published by University Press of Kansas in 2001.

68 444 U.S. at 516–17.

69 Id. at 521.

70 Id. at 517.

71 Id. at 526.

72 For years after he was crushed by the Supreme Court, Snepp wondered what had happened inside the Court with his case and why he had not been allowed to file a brief and argue his case. The Court's internal deliberations are normally secret unless and until the private papers of deceased or retired Justices become available to researchers. In 1997, Snepp was able to review Justice Marshall's private papers, which he left to the Library of Congress. Retired Justice Brennan also allowed Snepp to review his private records of the case. From the Marshall-Brennan papers Snepp learned (1) that the Court had initially decided not to take his case, but that Justice Powell had asked that the Court reconsider taking the case and (2) that Justice Powell wrote the per curiam opinion and was the force behind the Court's unusual decision to decide his case adversely without waiting for briefs or oral argument. *Irreparable Harm*, pp. 347–54.

73 718 F.2d 1137, 1141 (D.C. Cir. 1983) (citations omitted).

74 Id. at 1141, n. 9.

75 *Irreparable Harm* at 356.

76 *Morison v. United States,* 844 F.2d 1057 (4th Cir. 1988); *cert. denied,* 488 U.S. 908 (1988).

77 "Clinton Ignored CIA in Pardoning Intelligence Analyst," *Washington Post,* February 17, 2001.

78 "Senate Bill Aims to Curb News Leaks: Revealing Classified Data Would Be Felony," *Washington Post,* June 14, 2000.

79 "U.S. Falsely Wrote Off Vietnamese Secret Agents As Dead," *Toronto Globe & Mail* (*New York Times* News Service), June 10, 1991. www.ipsystems.com/powmia/documents/Scorpion.html.

80 Senate Select Committee on POW/MIA Affairs, *POW/MIA's Report,* 103d Cong., 1st sess., January 13, 1993, S. Rept. 103–1 (Washington, D.C.: Government Printing Office, 1993).

81 Sedgwick D. Tourison Jr., *Secret Army, Secret War: Washington's Tragic Spy Operation in Vietnam* (Annapolis: Naval Institute Press, 1995).

82 *Au Duong Quy, et al./ Lost Army Commandos v. United States,* No. 95–309C (Fed. Cl., filed April 24, 1995). Several years before this case, the courts had rejected a claim for compensation from a former OPLAN 34A commando. *Vu Doc Guong v. United States,* 860 F.2d 1063, 1065–66 (Fed. Cir. 1988), *cert. denied,* 490 U.S. 1023 (1989).

83 *Totten, Administrator v. United States,* 92 U.S. 105 (1875).

84 *60 Minutes: Lost Commandos* (CBS television broadcast, May 5, 1996).

85 "U.S. Lied about Vietnamese Commandos' Fate, *Times* Says," CNN, June 9, 1996. www.cnn.com/US/9606/09/vietnam.agents/index.html.

86 "Victims of Vietnam Lies," *TIME Magazine,* June 24, 1996. www.ipsystems.com/powmia/documents/unlies.html.

87 *Vietnamese Commandos: Hearings Before the Senate Select Committee on Intelligence,* 104th Cong., 2d sess., 1996.

88 National Defense Authorization Act for Fiscal Year 1997, Public Law 104–201, § 657(a)(1) (1996).

89 www.hqda.army.mil/dusa_ia_vccc/frequent.htm#Stats.

90 "U.S. Spied on Iraq under UN Cover, Officials Now Say," *New York Times,* January 7, 1999.

91 Id.

92 "U.S. Aides Say U.N. Team Helped to Install Spy Device in Iraq," *New York Times,* January 8, 1999.

93 Id.

94 "Pentagon Backs Down over Ritter's New Book," CNN, January 18, 1999. www.cnn.com/books/news/9901/18/ritter.

95 "Pentagon Revives Move to Halt Book on Iraqi Arms," *New York Times,* February 21, 1999.

96 Statement by the President to the House of Representatives, White House, November 4, 2000. www.fas.org/sgp/news/2000/11/wh110400.html.

97 Id.

98 Id.

99 Id.

100 Id.

101 Congress passed the Uniting and Strengthening America by Providing Appropriate Tools Required to Intercept and Obstruct Terrorism (USA PATRIOT) Act by overwhelming majorities of 98 to 1 in the Senate and 357 to 66 in the House.

102 In June 2003, a report by the Justice Department's Inspector General documented government abuses in the treatment of more than seven hundred detainees. Two weeks later a federal appeals court allowed the government to withhold names and other information about hundreds of detainees rounded up after September 11. *Center for National Security Studies v. Department of Justice,* 331 F.3d 918 (D.C. Cir. 2003).

103 "A Veto over Presidential Papers: Order Lets Sitting or Former President Block Release," *Washington Post,* November 2, 2001, p. A01.

104 Section 310 of the Intelligence Authorization Act for Fiscal Year 2002 (Public Law 107–108, December 28, 2001) provides: "The Attorney General shall, in consultation with the Secretary of Defense, Secretary of State, Secretary of Energy, Director of Central Intelligence, and heads of such other departments, agencies, and entities of the United States Government as the Attorney General considers appropriate, carry out a comprehensive review of current protections against the unauthorized disclosure of classified information." When the president signed this act, he said he reserved the right to withhold from Congress "information the disclosure of which could impair foreign relations, the national security, the deliberative processes of the Executive, or the performance of the Executive's constitutional duties." Statement by the President on the Intelligence Authorization Act for FY 2002, Washington: White House (December 28, 2001). www.fas.org/irp/news/2001/12/wh122801.html.

105 National Security Strategy of the United States of America, Washington: White House (September 2002). www.whitehouse.gov/nsc/nssall.html.

106 Congress approved the Iraq Resolution with a vote of 77 to 23 in the Senate and 296 to 133 in the House.

107 "Cheney Blames Leaks on Congress," *Washington Post,* June 21, 2002, p. A12.

108 "U.S. Plan for Iraq Is Said to Include Attack on Three Sides," *New York Times,* July 5, 2002, p. 1; "Battle Plans for Iraq," *New York Times,* July 6, 2002, p. 12; "U.S. Exploring Baghdad Strike as Option," *New York Times,* July 29, 2002, p. 1; "The World: War Games; For Each Audience, Another Secret Plan to Attack Iraq," *New York Times,* August 11, 2002, p. 1.

109 "Officers Say U.S. Aided Iraq in Iran-Iraq War Despite Use of Gas," *New York Times,* August 18, 2002, p. 1.

110 *New York Times,* February 28, 2003, p. 25.

111 "Pentagon Draws Up a Twenty- to Thirty-Year Antiterror Plan," *New York Times,* January 17, 2003, p. 10.

112 Executive Order 13292 (March 25, 2003).

113 Report of the Defense Science Board Task Force on Secrecy, Office of the Director of Defense Research and Engineering (July 1, 1970), p. 1.

114 In May 2003, the Supreme Court declined to review an appellate decision that upheld the constitutionality of secret deportation hearings for hundreds of detainees rounded up after September 11. "High Court Stays Out of Secrecy Fray," *Washington Post,* May 28, 2003, p. A04.

Bibliography

Abrams, Floyd. "The First Amendment: 1991," *Prologue* 24, no. 1 (spring 1992).
_____. "The Pentagon Papers a Decade Later." *New York Times Magazine* (November 8, 1981).
Bamford, James. *Body of Secrets.* New York: Doubleday, 2001.
Berman, Larry. *No Peace, No Honor: Nixon, Kissinger, and Betrayal in Vietnam.* New York: Free Press, 2001.
_____. *Planning a Tragedy: The Americanization of the Vietnam War.* New York, 1982.
Bradlee, Ben. *A Good Life: Newspapering and Other Adventures.* New York: Simon & Schuster, 1995.
Bray, Howard. *The Pillars of The Post: The Making of a News Empire in Washington.* New York: W. W. Norton, 1980.
Chomsky, Noam, and Howard Zinn, eds. *The Pentagon Papers.* Vol. 5: *Critical Essays.* Boston: Beacon Press, 1972.
Colson, Charles W. *Born Again: What Really Happened to the White House Hatchet Man.* New Jersey: Chosen Books, 1976.
Cooper, Chester. *Lost Crusade: America in Vietnam.* Rev. ed. New York: Dodd, Mead, 1973.
Dean, John. *The Rehnquist Choice.* New York: Simon & Schuster, 2001.
Diamond, Edwin. *Behind the Times: Inside the New York Times.* Chicago: University of Chicago Press, 1993.
Ehrlichman, John. *Witness to Power: The Nixon Years.* New York: Pocket Books, 1982.
Ellsberg, Daniel. *Papers on the War.* New York: Simon & Schuster, 1972.
_____. *Secrets: A Memoir of Vietnam and the Pentagon Papers.* New York: Viking Books, 2002.
Frankel, Max. *The Times of My Life: And My Life with the Times.* New York: Random House, 1999.
Frantz, Douglas, and David Mckean. *Friends in High Places: The Rise and Fall of Clark Clifford.* New York: Little, Brown, 1995.
Gelb, Leslie H. "Memorandum for the Secretary of Defense: Final Report, OSD Vietnam Task Force." *The Pentagon Papers,* January 15, 1969.
_____. "Misreading the Pentagon Papers." *New York Times,* June 29, 2001.
_____. "The Pentagon Papers and the Vantage Point." *Foreign Policy* 6 (spring 1972).
_____. "Today's Lessons from the Pentagon Papers," *Life,* September 23, 1971.
Gelb, Leslie H., and Richard K. Betts. *The Irony of Vietnam: The System Worked.* Washington, D.C.: Brookings Institution, 1979.
Glendon, William R. "Fifteen Days in June that Shook the First Amendment: A First Person Account of the Pentagon Papers Case." *New York State Bar Journal* (November 1993).

_____. "The Pentagon Papers: Victory for a Free Press." *Cardozo Law Review* 19, no. 4 (March 1998).

Gora, Joel M. "The Pentagon Papers Case and the Path Not Taken: A Personal Memoir on the First Amendment and the Separation of Powers." *Cardozo Law Review* 19, no. 4 (March 1998).

Graham, Katharine. *Personal History.* New York: Vintage Books, 1998.

Griswold, Erwin N. "Secrets Not Worth Keeping." *Washington Post,* February 15, 1989.

Haig, Alexander M., Jr. *Inner Circles: How America Changed the World: A Memoir.* New York: Warner Books, 1992.

Haldeman, Harry R. *The Haldeman Diaries: Inside the Nixon White House.* New York: G. P. Putnam's Sons, 1994.

Haldeman, Harry R., and Joseph DiMona. *The Ends of Power.* New York: Dell Books, 1978.

Herring, George C. ed. *The Secret Diplomacy of the Vietnam War: The Negotiating Volumes of the Pentagon Papers.* Austin: University of Texas Press, 1983.

Hersh, Seymour M. *The Price of Power: Kissinger in The Nixon White House.* New York: Simon & Schuster, 1983.

Indochina Information Project. *A Pentagon Papers Digest.* New York: Indochina Information Project, n.d.

Isaacson, Walter. *Kissinger: A Biography.* New York: Simon & Schuster, 1992.

Kincaid, John. "Secrecy and Democracy: The Unresolved Legacy of the Pentagon Papers." In *Watergate and Afterward: The Legacy of Richard Nixon.* Edited by Leon Friedman and William F. Levantrosser. Westport, Conn.: Greenwood Press, 1992.

Kissinger, Henry. *Ending the Vietnam War: A History of America's Involvement in and Extrication from the Vietnam War.* New York: Simon & Schuster, 2003.

_____. *The White House Years.* Boston: Little, Brown, 1978.

Kraslow, David, and Stuart H. *Loory: The Secret Secret for Peace in Vietnam.* New York: Random House, 1968.

McNamara, Robert S., and Brian VanDeMark. *In Retrospect: The Tragedy and Lessons of Vietnam.* New York: Random House, 1995.

Mitford, Jessica. *The Trial of Dr. Spock.* New York: Alfred A. Knopf, 1969.

National Defense Authorization Act for Fiscal Year 1997. Public Law 104–201, § 657(a)(1). ____Cong., ____ sess., 1996.

National Security Archive. *U.S. Policy in the Vietnam War.* Vol. 2, *1969–1975,* ed. John Prados. Alexandria, Va.: Proquest, 2004.

The Pentagon Papers: The Defense Department History of United States Decisionmaking on Vietnam. Gravel edition. 5 vols. Boston: Beacon Press, 1971, 1972.

Reston, James. *Deadline: A Memoir.* New York: Random House, 1991.

Rudenstine, David. "The Book in Retrospect." *Cardozo Law Review* 19, no. 4 (March 1998).

_____. *The Day the Presses Stopped: A History of the Pentagon Papers Case.* Berkeley: University of California Press, 1996.

_____. "The Pentagon Papers Case: Recovering its Meaning Twenty Years Later." *Cardozo Law Review* 12 (1991).

Russo, Anthony. "Inside the RAND Corporation." *Ramparts,* April 1971.

Safire, William. *Before the Fall: An Inside View of the Pre-Watergate White House.* New York: Belmont Tower Books, 1975.

Salisbury, Harrison E. *Without Fear or Favor: An Uncompromising Look at the New York Times.* New York: Times Books, 1980.

Schrag, Peter. *Test of Loyalty: Daniel Ellsberg and the Rituals of Secret Government.* New York: Simon & Schuster, 1974.

Seymour, Whitney North, Jr. "At Last the Truth Is Out." *Cardozo Law Review* 19, no. 4 (March 1998).

Shapiro, Martin M. *The Pentagon Papers and the Courts: A Study in Foreign Policy-making and Freedom of the Press.* San Francisco: Chandler, 1972.

Sheehan, Neil, et al. *The Pentagon Papers.* New York: Bantam, 1971.

Shepard, Richard F. *The Paper's Papers: A Reporter's Journey through the Archives of the New York Times.* New York: Random House, 1996.

Smith, Hedrick. "Vast Review of War Took a Year." *New York Times,* June 13, 1971.

Snepp, Frank. *Irreparable Harm: A Firsthand Account of How One Agent Took on the CIA in an Epic Battle over Free Speech.* New York: Random House, 1999.

Stacks, John F. *Scotty: James B. Reston and the Rise and Fall of American Journalism.* New York: Little, Brown, 2003.

Stavins, Ralph, Richard J. Barnett, and Marcus Raskin. *Washington Plans an Aggressive War.* New York: W. W. Norton, 1972.

Summer, Anthony. *The Arrogance of Power: The Secret World of Richard Nixon.* New York: Viking Press, 2000.

The Senator Gravel Edition: The Pentagon Papers. Boston: Beacon Press, 1972.

The Senator Gravel Edition: The Pentagon Papers: Critical Essays. Boston: Beacon Press, 1972.

Thomas, Evan. *The Man to See: Edward Bennett Williams Ultimate Insider; Legendary Trial Lawyer.* New York: Simon & Schuster, 1991.

Tourison Sedgwick D., Jr. *Secret Army, Secret War: Washington's Tragic Spy Operation in Vietnam.* Annapolis: Naval Institute Press, 1995.

Ungar, Sanford J. *The Papers and the Papers: An Account of the Legal and Political Battle over the Pentagon Papers.* New York: E. P. Dutton, 1972.

_____. "The Pentagon Papers Trial." *Atlantic Monthly,* November 1972.

U.S. Congress. House. Armed Services Committee. *United States–Vietnam Relations, 1945–1967: A Study Prepared by the Department of Defense.* 12 vols. Washington, D.C.: Government Printing Office, 1971.

U.S. Congress. Senate. *Report of the Commission on Protecting and Reducing Government Secrecy.* 103d Cong., ___ sess. S. Doc. 105–2. Washington, D.C.: Government Printing Office, 1997.

U.S. Congress. Senate. Select Committee on POW/MIA Affairs. *POW/MIA's Report.* 103d Cong., 1st sess., January 13, 1993. S. Rept. 103–1. Washington, D.C.: Government Printing Office, 1993.

The Watergate Hearings: Break-in and Coverup: Proceedings of the Senate Select Committee on Presidential Campaign Activities as edited by the Staff of the New York Times. New York: Bantam Books, 1973.

Wells, Tom. *Wild Man: The Life and Times of Daniel Ellsberg.* New York: Palgrave, 2001.

Wicker, Tom. *On Press: A Top Reporter's Life in, and Reflections on, American Journalism.* New York: Viking Press, 1978.

Woodward, Bob, and Carl Bernstein. *The Final Days.* New York: Simon & Schuster, 1987.

Contributors

WILLIAM F. CRANDELL: Vietnam veteran and member of Vietnam Veterans of America. Ph.D. from Ohio State University; Ohio state coordinator of Vietnam Veterans Against the War.

DANIEL ELLSBERG: Worked on the Pentagon Papers and leaked them to the *New York Times*. The Nixon administration's attempt to prosecute Ellsberg was thrown out of court for governmental misconduct after it was revealed that the White House Plumbers had broken into the office of Ellsberg's psychiatrist. Nixon had discussed with the judge in Ellsberg's case the potential for the judge becoming the director of the FBI. Ellsberg had been overheard on wiretaps. Ellsberg is the author of *Papers on the War* (1972).

MICHAEL J. GAFFNEY: A partner at Gaffney & Schember, P.C., Washington, D.C., and a Vietnam veteran, Gaffney is the general counsel of Vietnam Veterans of America.

WILLIAM R. GLENDON: As an attorney for the firm of Royall, Koegel, and Wells (now Rogers and Wells), Glendon represented the *Washington Post* in the U.S. District Court for the District of Columbia, the U.S. Court of Appeals for the District of Columbia Circuit, and the U.S. Supreme Court (*New York Times Co. v. United States*).

JAMES C. GOODALE: General counsel of the *New York Times* when the *Times* published the papers, now with the law firm of Debevois & Plimpton in New York City. The author of "The First Amendment and Freedom of the Press" in *Issues of Democracy,* U.S. Information Service.

SENATOR MIKE GRAVEL: Former U.S. senator (D-Alaska, 1969–1981). The evening before the Supreme Court's June 30, 1971, decision in the Pentagon Papers case, Senator Gravel, as chairman of the Subcommittee on Buildings and Grounds of the Senate Public Works Committee, convened a meeting of the subcommittee where he read aloud extensively from a copy of the Pentagon Papers. He then placed the available volumes of the study in the public record. He subsequently arranged for the papers to be published by Beacon Press. After the subcommittee meeting, a grand jury, convened to investigate whether federal law had been violated, subpoenaed an aide to the senator. Senator Gravel intervened and moved to squash the subpoena, contending that it would violate the Speech and Debate Clause to compel the aide to testify. That case also ended up before the Supreme Court.

MEL GURTOV: A Pentagon consultant and RAND Corporation analyst, Gurtov had studied the Geneva Conference of 1954 and the Dien Bien Phu crisis in graduate school and privately before coming back to the same topic in his work on the Pentagon Papers.

HOWARD MARGOLIS: One of the authors of the Pentagon Papers, Margolis is a professor in the Graduate School of Public Policy Studies at the University of Chicago. He has taught at the University of California-Irvine and has held research positions at the Institute of

Advanced Study, the Russell Sage Foundation, and the Massachusetts Institute of Technology. Prior to his academic career, Margolis worked in Washington, D.C., as a journalist and consultant.

DON OBERDORFER: A *Washington Post* war correspondent in Vietnam, Oberdorfer wrote the well-received book *Tet* (1971) and worked on the Pentagon Papers at the *Post*. He is the distinguished journalist in residence at the School of Advanced International Studies at Johns Hopkins University in Washington, D.C.

MARGARET PRATT PORTER: Director of communications and publications for Vietnam Veterans of America and editor of the *VVA Veteran*.

THOMAS POWERS: Author of *The Man Who Kept the Secrets: Richard Helms and the CIA* (1979), widely regarded as the best book on former director Richard Helms and the Vietnam-era CIA. A Pulitzer Prize recipient, he is one of the four founding partners of Steerforth Press, the small book publishing company that published former CIA analyst Sam Adams's *War of Numbers* (1994), which concerned the controversial Order of Battle dispute about the accuracy of military intelligence in Vietnam.

JOHN PRADOS: Historian who has written widely about the war for the *VVA Veteran*. His books include *The Blood Road: The Ho Chi Minh Trail and the Vietnam War* (1999); *The Hidden History of the Vietnam War* (1995); *The President's Secret Wars: CIA and Pentagon Covert Operations from World War II through the Persian Gulf* (1996); *Keepers of the Keys: A History of the National Security Council from Truman to Bush* (1991); and *Valley of Decision: The Siege of Khe Sanh* (1991) (with Ray W. Stubbe). Currently director of a project on declassified Vietnam War documents at the National Security Archive at George Washington University. His most recent books are *The Lost Crusader: The Secret Wars of CIA Director William Colby* and *White House Tapes*.

MARCUS RASKIN: Director for the Institute for Policy Studies to whom Ellsberg also leaked a copy of the Pentagon Papers. Raskin and coauthors Ralph Stavins and Richard Barnett used the papers to write *Washington Plans an Aggressive War* (1971).

DAVID RUDENSTINE: Constitutional law professor at Cardozo School of Law in New York City. He wrote *The Day the Presses Stopped* (1996), a comprehensive history of the legal fight about the Pentagon Papers.

ANTHONY RUSSO JR.: Former RAND Corporation analyst in Vietnam who was heavily involved with RAND's Vietcong motivation study. Russo and Ellsberg copied and leaked the Pentagon Papers.

COLONEL HERBERT SCHANDLER: Wrote part of the Pentagon Papers concerning events in early 1968. Later wrote *Lyndon Johnson and Vietnam: The Unmaking of a President* (1977) and coauthored *Argument without End: In Search of Answers to the Vietnam Tragedy* (1999).

HEDRICK SMITH: *New York Times* reporter with extensive experience in Vietnam who worked on the Pentagon Papers at the *Times* with Neil Sheehan and wrote one of the first *Times* articles, published on June 13, 1971. A Pulitzer Prize–winning former correspondent and author of several best-selling books, he has also created and served as correspondent for several PBS prime-time documentaries.

SANFORD UNGAR: Former director of the Voice of America. As a *Washington Post* reporter, Ungar covered the government's legal fight to block the *Post* from publishing the Pentagon Papers. He wrote *The Papers and the Papers* (1972), which won the George Polk Award in 1973, and several other books. Previously dean of the School of Communications at American University in Washington, D.C., he is currently president of Goucher College.

Index

diplomatic volumes, 48, 49, 61, 65, 82, 124, 149, 170, 176
distribution, 36
document study, 6, 15, 49
documents omitted, 37
editions, 61
and espionage law, 119–120, 121, 127
FOIA request for, 10, 61
Gravel edition, 47, 60–61, 72, 170, 179, 200, 223(n6)
impact of, 26, 183–196, 201–202
leak as principled act of moral decision, 191
leaked by Daniel Ellsberg, 3–8, 11, 23, 29, 44, 50, 53–57, 170, 185
leak investigation, 87
and media impact, 183–184, 191–192, 194, 195
on microfiche, 61
and military operations, 177–182
and national security, 9, 62, 65, 67–68, 118, 119, 121, 122, 126, 129, 147, 148–151, 157, 164–169, 170–176, 201, 229(n55)
negotiation volumes, 61
and Nixon (*see under* Nixon, Richard M.)
origin of, 13–22
period covered (post–World War II–1968), 147
and presidential cooperation, 22, 27, 38–39
publication as book, 60, 76
publication by newspapers, 56, 58, 59, 64, 68–71, 121, 124, 140, 191
publication injunctions, 9, 58, 59, 82, 87, 122, 128, 131, 134
publication press run (*NY Times*), 56
in public record (Congress), 60
read in Senate by Gravel, 73, 200
secret brief (*see under* Griswold, Erwin N.)
secrets in (*see* Pentagon Papers, and national security)
secret volumes and versions of, 9, 10, 11, 61, 147

suppression attempts, 80, 119, 124, 201, 126–127
and Supreme Court, 87, 126–127, 135–136, 150, 197–200
telephone transcripts, 9
top-secret documents, 37 133, 134, 143, 156, 175–176
trial, 89, 122–127, 150 (*see also under* Ellsberg, Daniel; Russo, Anthony)
and truth, 192–193
versions, 201, 223(n6), 227(n33)
volumes, 17, 18, 21–22, 23–50, 61, 151, 152, 156
See also Vietnam Study Task Force; *under* First Amendment
Pentagon Papers, The. Vol. 5. Critical Essays (Chomsky & Zinn), 61
Pentagon Papers, The: The Defense Department History of United States Decisionmaking on Vietnam (Gravel), 60–61, 200
Phelps, Robert, 53
Plagiarism, 122
Planning a Tragedy: The Americanization of the Vietnam War (Berman), 37
"Plumbers," 87–88, 201
Powell, Lewis, 208, 229(n72)
Powers, Thomas, 184, 191–193
Prados, John, 11, 41, 44, 50, 61, 89, 170, 184, 193–195
Presidency, 160
Presidential Power (Neustadt), 13
Price, Don K., 12
Primary and substantive powers (Congress), 122
Progressive (magazine), 195, 205, 206, 216
Pueblo (U.S. Navy spy ship), 180
Pursley, Robert E., 13, 14, 17, 82, 119

RAND Corporation, 3, 4, 5, 6, 7, 19, 20, 23, 33, 36, 42, 49, 87, 185
Randel, Jonathan, 210
Random House (publisher), 190
Raskin, Marcus, 8, 52, 57, 188–190, 195
Reagan, Ronald, 19, 194–195
Rebozo, Bebe, 76

Stockwell, John, 210
Studies and Observation Group (SOG), 211
Sulzberger, Arthur Ochs (Punch), 53, 54, 55, 56, 67, 120, 130
Supreme Court, 87, 197, 207–209, 210, 217
(*see also under* Pentagon Papers)

Taylor, Maxwell, 29, 30, 47
Terrorism, war on, 216
Tet Offensive (1968), 5, 6, 16, 18, 33, 35, 44
Thailand, 164–165, 171, 173, 194
Theft of government property statute, 210
Thompson, Llewellyn, 163, 169, 174
Tonkin. *See* Gulf of Tonkin; Gulf of Tonkin Resolution
Trend, Burke, 41
Truman, Harry S, 1, 48, 63

Ullman, Richard H., 16, 19–20, 22
Ungar, Sanford J., 137–141, 144
Unitarian Universalist Association (UUA), 200
United Nations, 49
U.S. Court of Appeals for the Second Circuit, 124, 126, 147
U.S. Policy in the Vietnam War, vol. 2, 1969–1975 (Prados) (microfiche set), 61
"United States—Vietnam Relations—1945–1967" (OSD), 156
United States v. Reynolds (1953), 198, 224–225(n5)
United States v. United States District Court (1972), 225(n10)
Uniting and Strengthening America by Providing Appropriate Tools Required to Intercept and Obstruct Terrorism (USA Patriot). *See* Patriot Act
UUA. *See* Unitarian Universalist Association

Vance, Cyrus R., 13, 183
VanDeMark, Brian (McNamara coauthor), 50
Vietcong, 43, 44–45 187

Vietcong Motivation and Morale Project (RAND), 24, 185, 186
Vietminh, 46
Vietnamese authors, 186
Vietnamese Commando Compensation Commission (DoD), 212
Vietnamization, 1, 164, 165, 168, 181
Vietnam partition. *See* Geneva Accords
Vietnam Reader, The (Fall & Raskin), 189
Vietnam Study Task Force (1967), 17–22, 82, 152
    outline of studies, 153–155
    personnel, 18, 19, 20–21, 23–50
Vietnam veterans, 2, 8, 73
Vietnam Veterans Against the War, 73, 184
Vietnam Veterans of America (VVA), 8, 9, 11, 45, 184
Vietnam War (1964–1975)
    antiwar protests, 2, 12, 13, 87
    civilian and military lies, 15, 25, 26, 29
    covert operations, 211–212
    critique of, 52 (*see also* Pentagon Papers)
    documentary, 43
    drafts, 72
    military deployment, 167
    nuclear weapons use proposal, 5
    number killed in action, 15
    pacification programs, 4, 5, 15, 20, 59, 167, 175
    peace accords (1973), 194, 211
    peace feelers, 16, 157
    peace negotiations, 20, 35
    Pentagon top-secret study (1971), 1, 5–6 (*see also* Pentagon Papers)
    policy (*see* Pentagon Papers)
    prisoners of war, 176, 211–212
    as racist, 186
    selective service system, 59
    and U.S. airpower, 2, 193
    U.S. involvement in, 1–2, 4, 5, 16
    unlawful detention of protesters, 2
    war crimes, 184, 189, 190
    winnable possibility, 15, 38–39, 41, 48, 50, 193
    withdrawal plans, 47, 49, 158, 171
    as wrong, 183

VNQDD (Vietnamese anticommunist
   nationalist party), 46
VVA. *See* Vietnam Veterans of America

Warnke, Paul, 14, 16, 35, 87
Washington Plans an Aggressive War
   (Stavins, Barnett & Raskin), 8, 52,
   57, 189, 190
Washington Post, 6, 8, 46, 56–59, 69–71,
   121, 124–125, 126, 137, 156, 198
Washington Wages an Aggressive War
   (IPS) (unpublished), 190
Waskow, Arthur, 189
Watergate investigation (1974), 87, 89
Wells, Tom, 186
Wenner, Jann, 51
Westmoreland, William C., 33, 36, 43–44,
   63

Wheeler, Earl, 63
White, Byron R., 199
White House Years, The (Kissinger), 78
Wicker, Tom, 53
*Wild Man: The Life and Times of Daniel
   Ellsberg* (Wells), 186
Wilkie (judge), 135
Williams, Edward Bennett, 58
Wilson, George, 125, 135
Wilson, Jerry, 139
Winter Soldier Investigation, 184
Wiretapping, 64, 201
Wolf, Louis, 234
Woodward, Bob, 208
World War II reclassified document, 10

Ziegler, Ron, 84
Zinn, Howard, 61